THE POSTCARDS OF L. A. HUFFMAN

MONTANA FRONTIER PHOTOGRAPHER

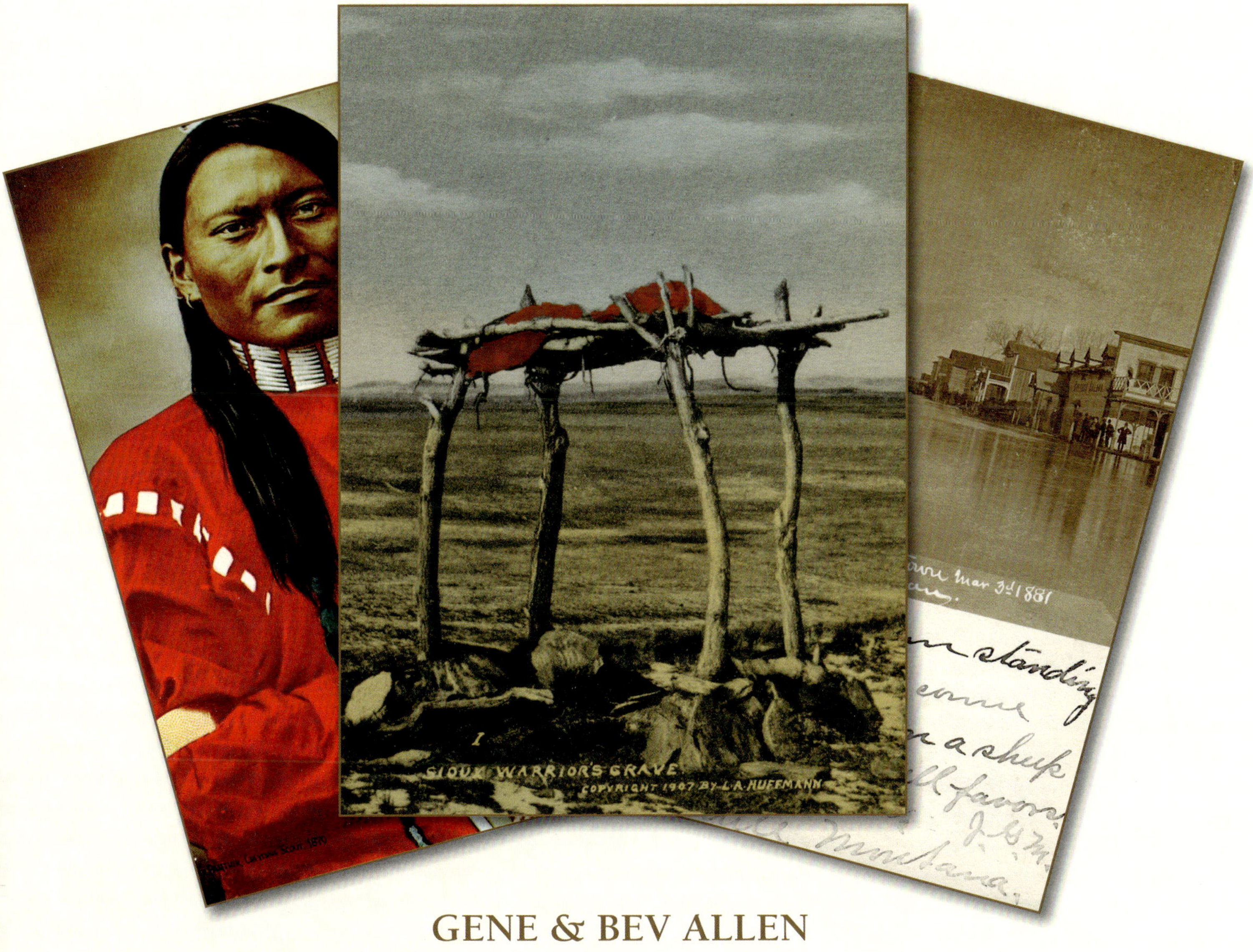

GENE & BEV ALLEN

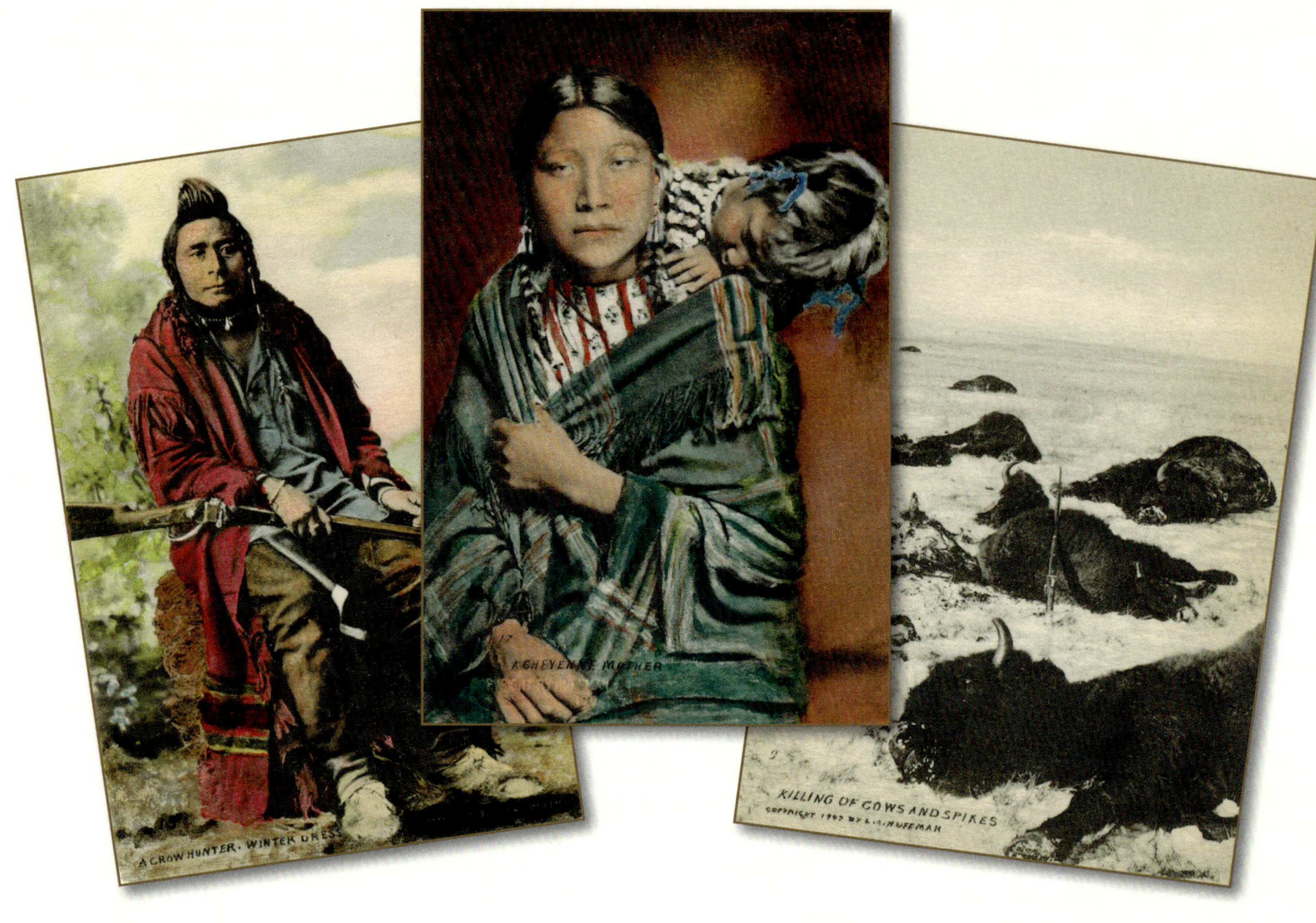

ISBN: 978-1-59152-212-6

Published by Gene and Bev Allen, Helena, Montana

© 2018 by Gene and Bev Allen

All rights reserved. This book may not be reproduced in whole or in part by any means
(with the exception of short quotes for the purpose of review) without the permission of the publisher.

For more information, contact Gene and Bev Allen; montbooks@icloud.com; Helena, Montana.

You may order extra copies of this book by calling Farcountry Press toll free
at (800) 821-3874.

sweetgrassbooks
a division of Farcountry Press

Produced by Sweetgrass Books.
PO Box 5630, Helena, MT 59604; (800) 821-3874; www.sweetgrassbooks.com.

The views expressed by the author/publisher in this book do not necessarily represent the views of,
nor should be attributed to Sweetgrass Books. Sweetgrass Books is not responsible for the content of the author/publisher's work.

Produced in the United States of America.
Printed in Canada.

22 21 20 19 18 1 2 3 4 5

Contents

10
SADDLEING A WILD HORSE
COPYRIGHT 1907 BY L.A. HUFFMAN

11
A WOLFER'S ROOST
COPYRIGHT 1907 BY L.A. HUFFMAN

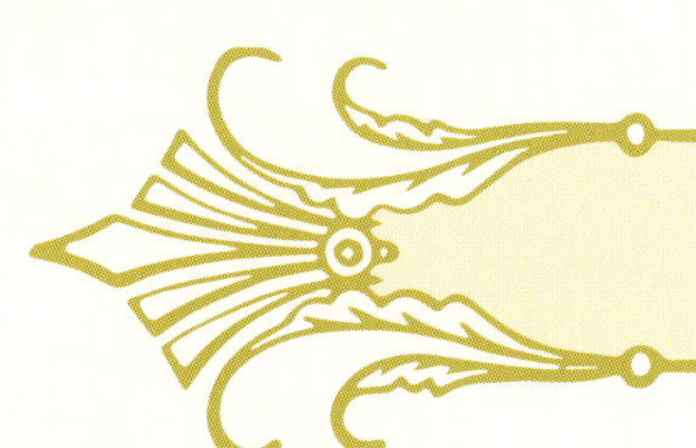

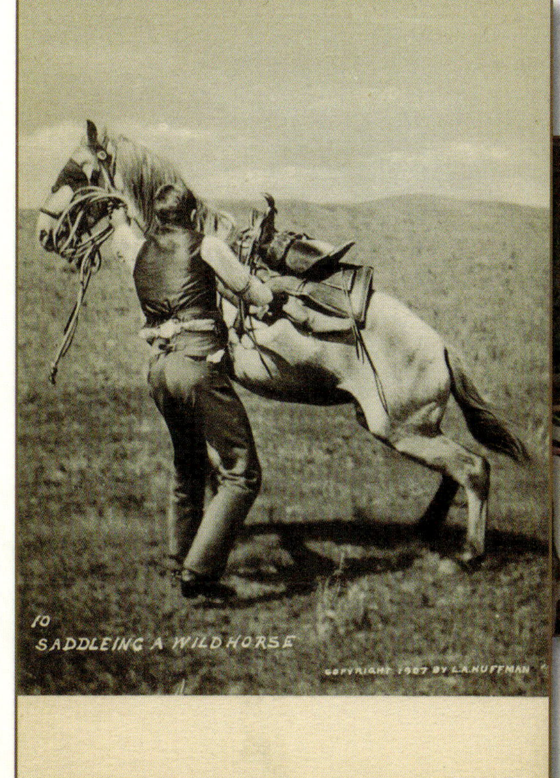

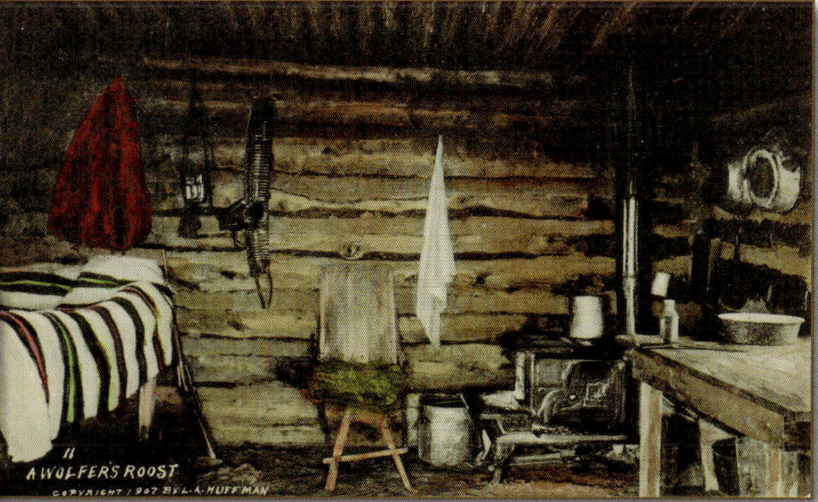

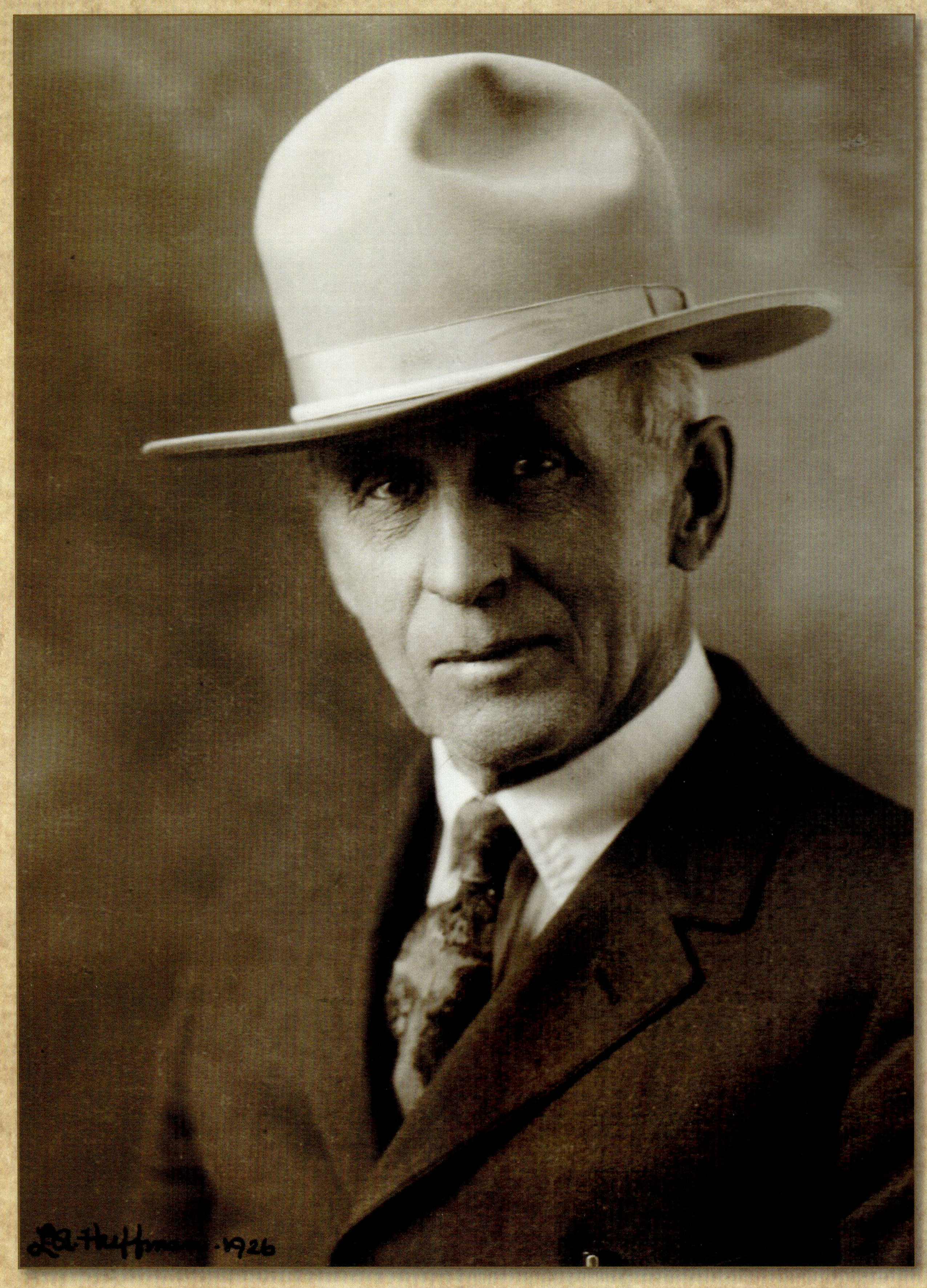
L.A. Huffman · 1926

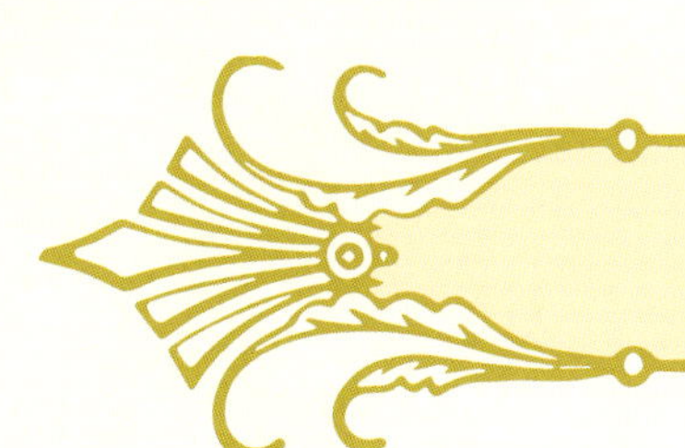

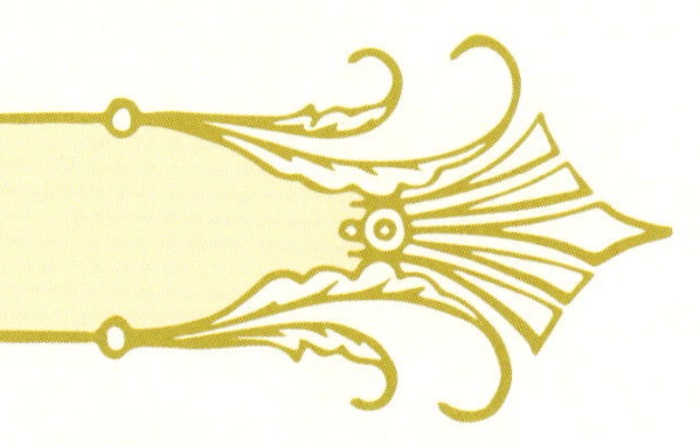

Preface

There are two basic types of postcards—printed and real photo. Printed cards are the result of a mechanical printing process while real photo cards are actual photographic prints. Printed cards are usually produced in relatively large quantities, often thousands; real photo cards during Huffman's day were made one at a time in a darkroom just like other photographic prints. A variety of images can be used on printed cards, including artwork, printed messages and greetings, advertisements, photography, etc. Images on real photo cards are always photographs.

During his career Huffman published four different groups of postcards—three sets of printed cards and an unknown but relatively few real photo cards. In 1907 he published his first set of printed cards—a series of 25 numbered cards. In 1926 he published a series of 15 numbered cards. His last involvement with postcards was in 1928 when the Northern Pacific Railroad published five colored cards. Most of his real photo cards were produced between 1906–1912. An additional group of printed color cards were produced by Miles City photographer Jack Coffrin during his tenure with the Huffman material during the 1960s–1970s (see biography). Most of Huffman's printed cards are relatively scarce, some more so than others. Assembling full sets of his 1907 and 1928 series would be challenging. All of his real photo cards must be considered rare. During his 52-year career in Montana, Huffman produced photographs using a variety of formats; a strong case can be made that his real photo postcard is the scarcest.

This book provides new information about a previously little known dimension of Huffman's work. In the following chapters, each of Huffman's postcard groups is discussed separately. Known production information is presented, followed by illustrations of all of the cards in that group. Each illustration in the 1907 and 1928 series is accompanied by Huffman's description. Additional information about any of the images will be found in "notes" following the illustrations. There is a brief chapter on postcard collecting that includes general value information for Huffman postcards. A complete checklist of all known Huffman postcards, by group, will be found at the end of the book. Unless otherwise noted, all resource material and images are from the authors' collection.

Misspellings and grammatical inconsistensies in photo titles and descriptions are courtesy of L. A. Huffman.

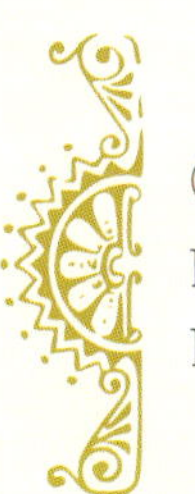

Gene and Bev Allen
Helena, Montana
March 2018

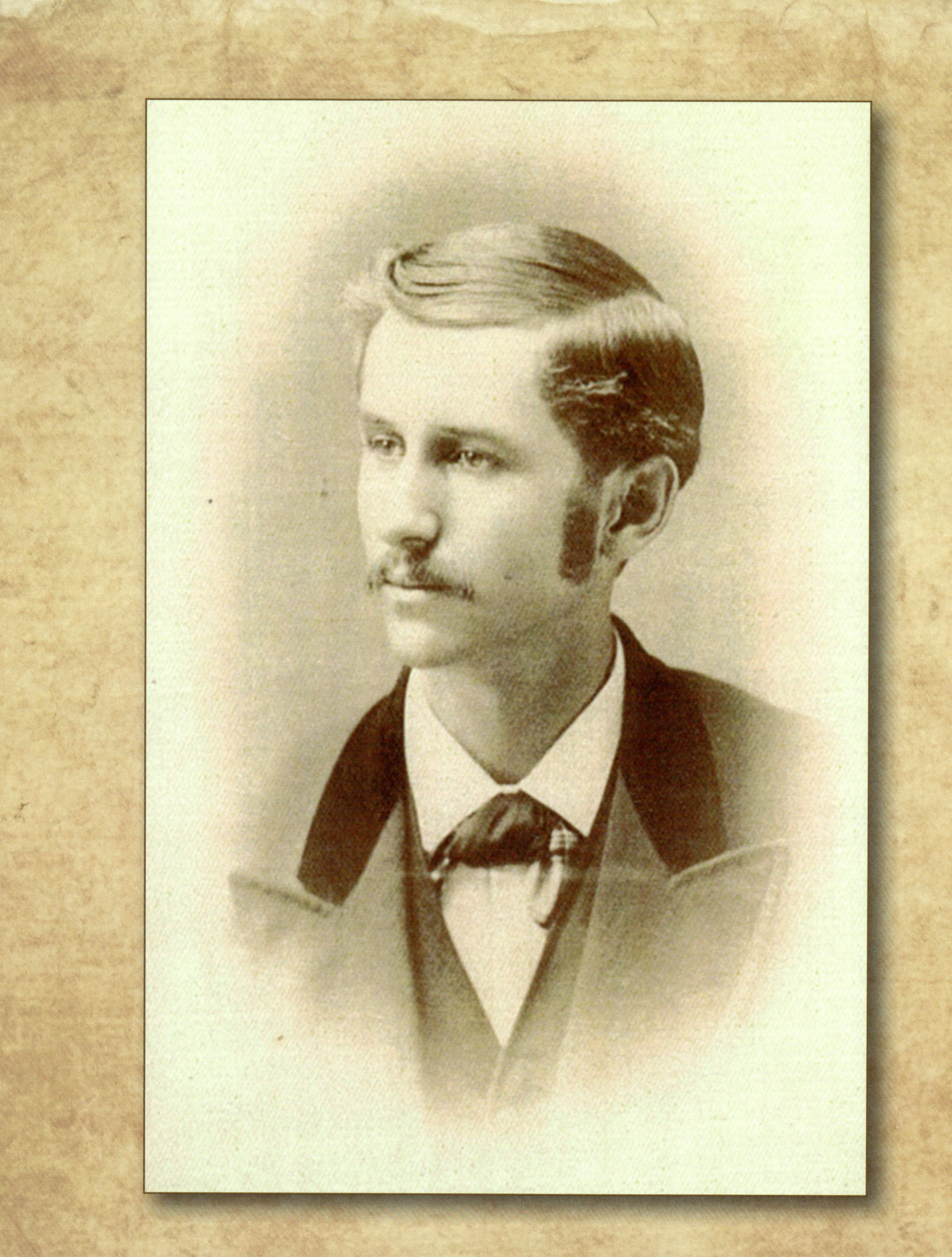

L. A. Huffman Biography

Huffman arrived in Montana at a rapidly changing time in its history. Hostilities between early settlers and Native Americans were drawing to a close and reservation life was beginning. The demise of the last great buffalo herd was near, clearing the way for large-scale cattle ranching. The railroad arrived in Miles City in the fall of 1881. Huffman called it a "fatal coming . . . there was no more West after that. It was a dream and a forgetting, a chapter forever closed." Later, farmers with their plows and fences would permanently alter the eastern Montana landscape. During all of these changes, Huffman was there taking photographs—landscapes, animals, early ranches, street scenes, and especially, people at work. He did this with relatively crude equipment and technology, yet produced hundreds of high quality, historically interesting images. He left us an unmatched visual record of early days in eastern Montana.

Laton Alton Huffman was born in 1854 to a farm family near Castalia, Iowa. His childhood was nurtured by early day tales told by his grandfathers, western books and daydreaming about what adventures lay beyond the horizon. As a teenager he left school and family and wandered for a time, working a variety of jobs wherever he could, getting as far north as Devils Lake, Dakota Territory. By the mid 1870s he returned to work with his father who then operated a photographic studio in Waukon, Iowa. After learning the trade, he opened his own studio in neighboring Postville. In 1878, following the abrupt ending of a three-year courtship of a local schoolteacher, he again went north and soon found employment with pioneer photographer F. Jay Haynes in Moorhead, Minnesota.

LEFT: Back of Huffman CDV card.

FACING PAGE: Young L. A. Huffman c. 1878 on front of card.

In fall of 1879, he learned of an opening for a post photographer at Fort Keogh, a military outpost in Montana Territory established shortly after the Battle of the Little Bighorn. With his few years of photographic experience, and total assets of $20 in his pocket, this time he went west. Huffman was 25 years old when he arrived in Miles City, Montana Territory, in December 1879. He was appointed post photographer, an unpaid position that provided a dirt floor log studio and an opportunity to make and sell photographs. For Huffman, becoming a part of the living frontier fulfilled a boyhood dream.

During Huffman's career, he used a variety of cameras and types of prints. For the first few years, he did his work with two cameras—a studio camera for portrait work and a stereoscopic camera for outdoor work. He most likely acquired his first cameras from his predecessor at Fort Keogh, Stanley J. Morrow, who was still in the area when Huffman arrived. Morrow's home base was Yankton, Dakota Territory, and he operated photo studios for a brief period at Fort Keogh and Fort Custer (on the Bighorn River) prior to Huffman's arrival. An announcement in a May 1880 issue of *The Yellowstone Journal* Huffman states he has "purchased the photographic gallery formerly owned by S. J. Morrow" and hopes to "merit the patronage of the people of Fort Keogh and Miles City." By October, he had opened a second studio on Park Street in Miles City. He kept his position as post photographer at Fort Keogh for about two years.

Until sometime in 1880, wet plates were the only film available to photographers. Huffman mentions wet plates and the associated process occasionally in his writings—it was not one of his fond memories. When preparing to take a photograph, a glass plate was coated with a solution, and then sensitized with silver nitrate in a second solution. It was then placed in a lightproof film carrier. For outdoor photos, all of this had to be done on site and in total darkness! The carrier was then placed in the camera (on a tripod). After a several second exposure, the plate had to be developed in yet another solution (again in total darkness) before the sensitized coating dried. Even in nice weather, taking an outdoor photo with a wet plate must have been a formidable challenge. Photographers everywhere probably welcomed the availability of dry plates in 1880–1881. Dry plates came presensitized, ready to place in the camera with the added convenience of being able to take the exposed negative back to the studio for developing. In spite of the challenges, several of Huffman's most popular and historically important images were made with wet plate negatives.

Huffman's first known photo list was produced in the fall of 1881. It includes photos known to have been taken in September 1881 and does not include others taken in January 1882. It is a small (3½ x 4⅞), five panel, folded list with 137 entries in five categories: "Tinted Indian Portraits, cabinet size" (25 cabinet cards), "Indian Views, Stereoscopic" (20), "30 Days Hunt in Big Horn Mountains, Sep 1881" (30), "Custer Battlefield" (13), and "General Views Miles City, Glendive, Fort Keogh, Badlands, etc, etc" (49). The photos taken on the "30 Days Hunt" were taken with dry plates. All of the cabinet cards, most of the Custer Battlefield, and many, if not most of the rest of them were taken using wet plates. Several photos on this list were used later on Huffman's postcards.

HUFFMAN'S

Northern Pacific Views

YELLOWSTONE, BADLAND

AND

BIG HORN SCENERY,

Tinted Indian Portraits,

ETC., ETC.

L. A. HUFFMAN,

PUBLISHER,

MILES CITY, - MONTANA.

RATES TO THE TRADE.

ABOVE: Huffman's first known photo list produced in the fall of 1881.

The first photo on his 1881 list is a portrait of Rain-in-the-Face. It is titled *Eta-ma-gozua,* or *Rain-in-the-Face.* Shown is a cabinet card on an original 1880 mount, before the title is part of the image and is hand-written on the back. This image was taken during the fall of 1880 and got Huffman in a bit of trouble with Fort Keogh post commander, Colonel Nelson Miles.

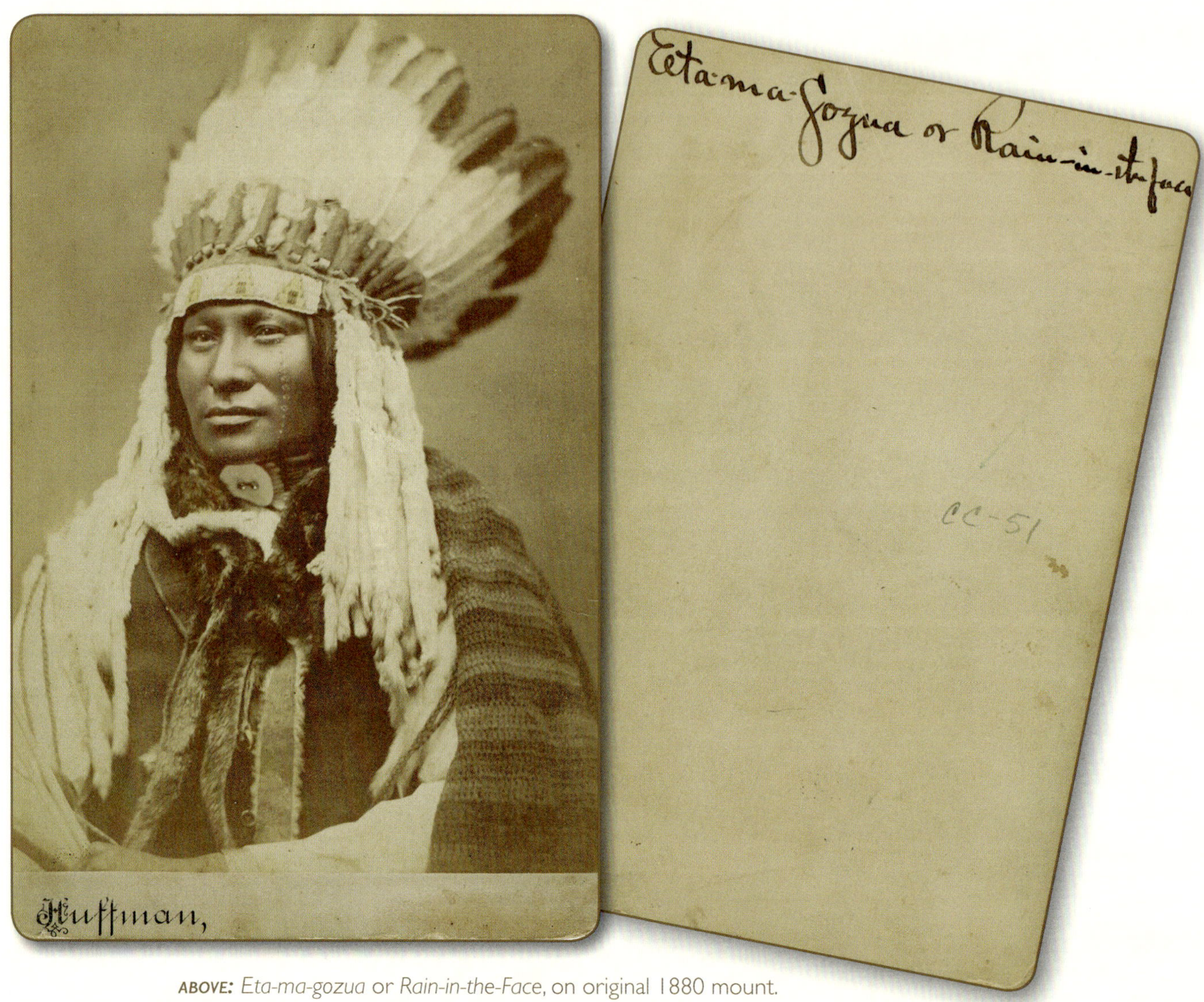

ABOVE: *Eta-ma-gozua* or *Rain-in-the-Face*, on original 1880 mount.

Early in the fall, most of the Sioux Indians that followed Sitting Bull when he retreated to Canada a few years before, decided to return to Montana. Rain-in-the-Face, Spotted Eagle, and other Sioux chiefs and their camps surrendered at Fort Keogh, more than 2,000 in all. They were encamped across the Tongue River from the small community of Miles City, near Fort Keogh. Although Miles states, "They remained peaceable, contented and industrious, fulfilling all requirements made of them," they were prisoners and were forbidden to leave their village and civilians from Miles City were forbidden to visit *(Personal Recollections of General Nelson A. Miles—1896).*

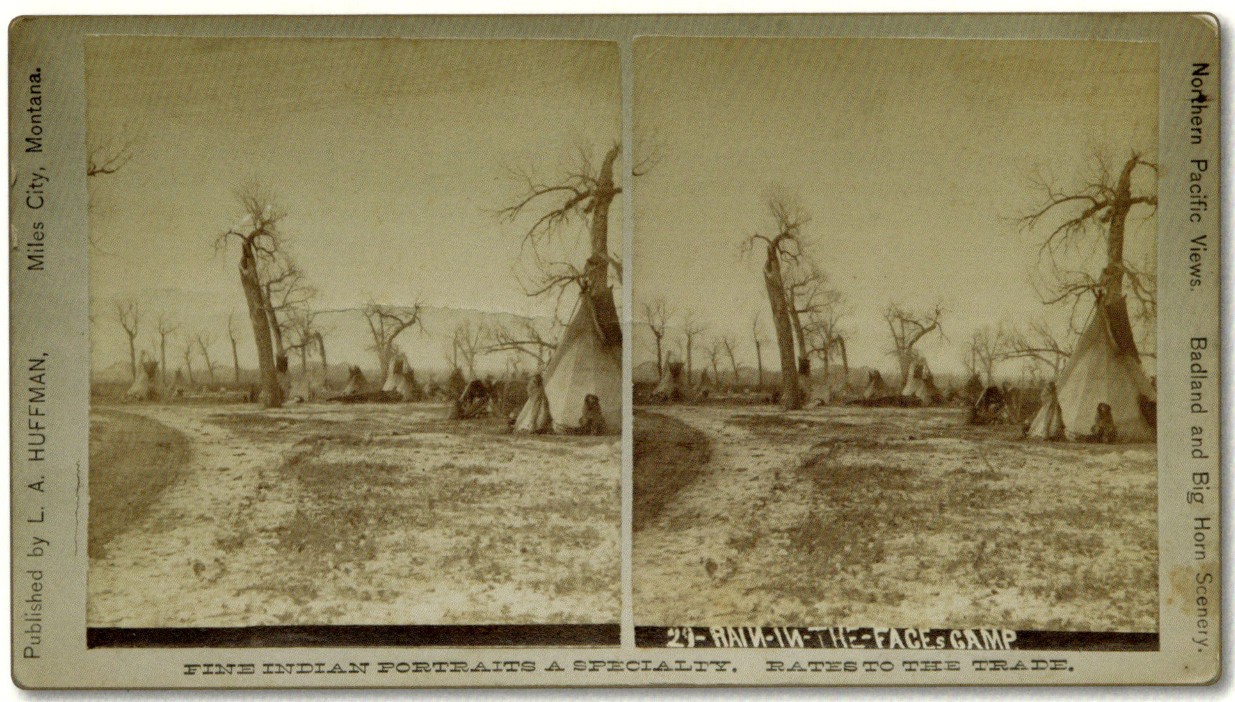

ABOVE: *Rain-in-the-Face's Camp*

Huffman was able to take a few photos of the camp and often referred to it as *Spotted Eagle's Hostile Village*.

He also wanted a photo of Rain-in-the-Face and enlisted the help of the driver of a delivery wagon who frequently visited the prisoner's camp. While they had no trouble taking the chief out of the camp, his several hour absence created concern among his followers. By the time they returned with the chief, the level of restlessness had reached Miles' office. Huffman was called on the carpet.

Miles said, "YOUNG MAN, IF YOU EVER TAKE ANOTHER PRISONER OUT OF CAMP WITHOUT THE PERMISSION OF THE ADJUTANT OR MYSELF, YOU WILL FIND YOURSELF IN VERY SERIOUS TROUBLE!" The Indians were held over winter until the next June when high water allowed steamboats to come up the Yellowstone River to Miles City; they were all transported down the Missouri River to the Sioux Reservation in Dakota Territory. Huffman photographed the event but the negatives (along with others) were destroyed in one of Miles City's early fires.

To supplement his income in the early years, Huffman did some guiding for eastern hunters and scientists. Two clients became lifelong friends and important men in Huffman's career. G. O. Shields was the editor of *American Field* magazine and the author of several books. He was the first to publish Huffman images in the December 1881 issue of *American Field*, and the first to publish Huffman images in a book in 1883 with his *Rustlings in the Rockies*. The "30 Days Hunt" category in Huffman's 1881 list refers to images taken on a September 1881 hunt with Shields that were used to illustrate the article in *American Field*. This may have been Huffman's first use of dry plates; they are specifically mentioned twice in the article.

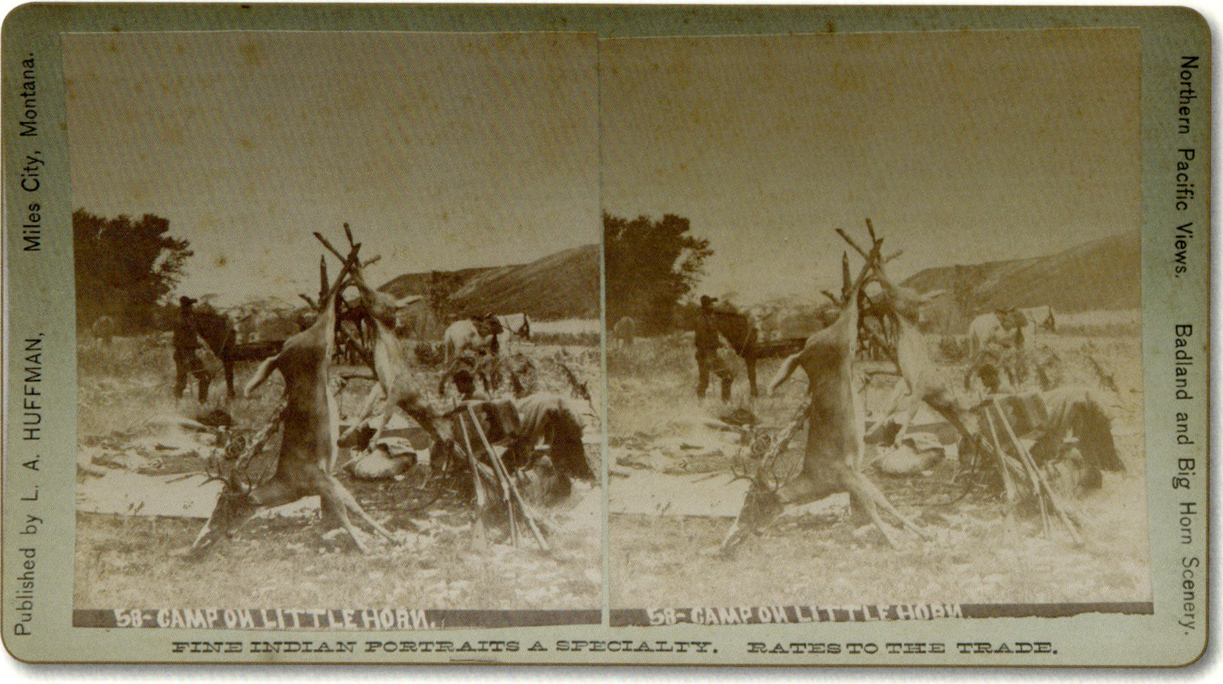

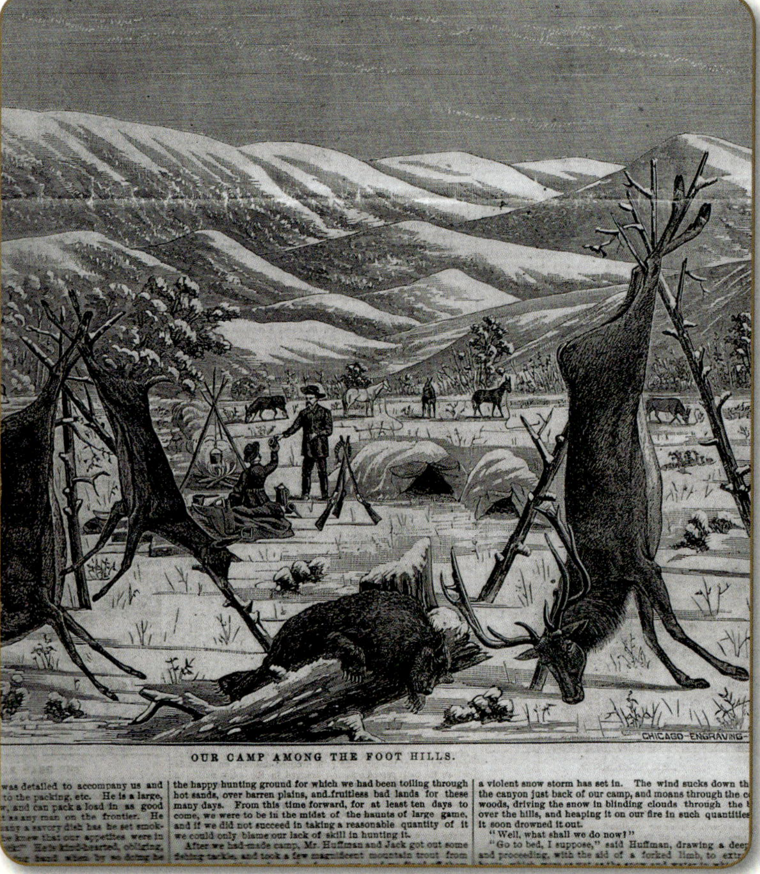

OUR CAMP AMONG THE FOOT HILLS.

was detailed to accompany us and to the packing, etc. He is a large, and can pack a load in as good as any man on the frontier. He many a savory dish has he set smok- he knew that our appetites were in He is kind-hearted, obliging,

the happy hunting ground for which we had been toiling through hot sands, over barren plains, and fruitless bad lands for these many days. From this time forward, for at least ten days to come, we were to be in the midst of the haunts of large game, and if we did not succeed in taking a reasonable quantity of it we could only blame our lack of skill in hunting it.

After we had made camp, Mr. Huffman and Jack got out some fishing tackle, and took a few magnificent mountain trout from

a violent snow storm has set in. The wind sucks down the canyon just back of our camp, and moans through the woods, driving the snow in blinding clouds through the over the hills, and heaping it on our fire in such quantities it soon drowned it out.

"Well, what shall we do now?"

"Go to bed, I suppose," said Huffman, drawing a deep and proceeding, with the aid of a forked limb, to ext

ABOVE: *Camp on Little Horn*, Huffman's first published image.

LEFT: Wood cut illustration based on Huffman's photo published in the December, 1881 issue of *American Field*.

FACING PAGE: *Where Custer Fell*, one of Stanley Morrow's original photos of the Custer Battlefield taken in 1879.

The other important client, William T. Hornaday, was director of the New York Zoological Society and hunted with Huffman on several occasions. One memorable hunt in 1901, in the Hell Creek area north of Jordan, Montana, led to the discovery of the fossilized remains of the world's first *Tyrannosaurus rex*.

Like many other early photographers, Huffman occasionally acquired negatives from other photographers. In a letter to his father in summer 1883, he states, "I must close and varnish up my new negatives bought four more nice lots last week making 10 some which have now increased to quite a handsome figure compared to their cost." Huffman put these negatives into his inventory and made prints under his name with no credit to the original photographer. This practice was not uncommon among early photographers; negatives were simply necessary business assets. They were trying to run businesses, often under the difficult circumstances of remote locations and scarcity of everything from photographic supplies to customers. Acquiring good negatives was just another way to help make the business profitable. We have several Huffman-produced photographs in our collection known to have been taken by other photographers.

Eight of the 13 "Custer Battlefield" views listed in Huffman's 1881 photo list were taken by his predecessor, Stanley Morrow. They were taken in spring 1879 when he accompanied an expedition from Fort Keogh, led by Captain George K. Sanderson, assigned to clean up the battlefield. One of those views is shown below.

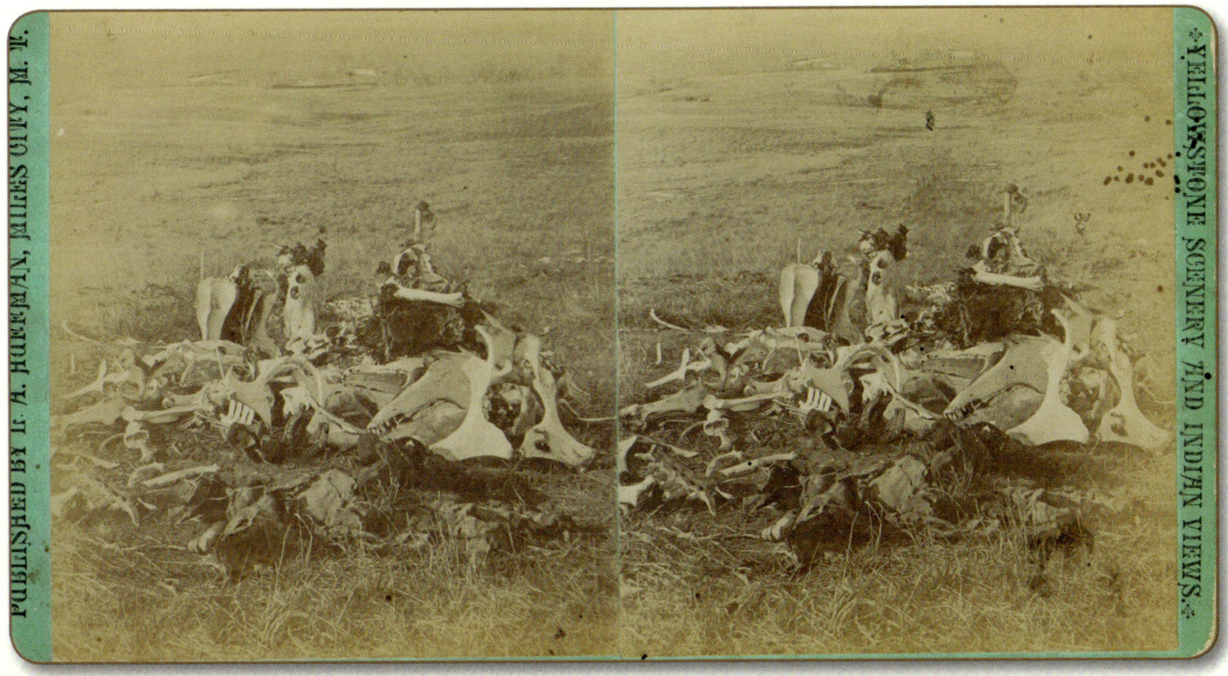

One can only assume Huffman acquired these negatives (and a few others) at the same time he acquired Morrow's gallery and equipment in the spring of 1880. One of Morrow's views was used on one of Huffman's postcards. The first photo of the battlefield was taken by John H. Fouch, the first post photographer at Fort Keogh. He was at Fort Keogh for only a brief time in 1877 and 1878. His rare photograph, *The Place Where Custer Fell,* taken in July 1877, "is now recognized as the earliest photograph of Custer's Battle Field" (*Where Custer Fell*, James S. Brust, et al—2005).

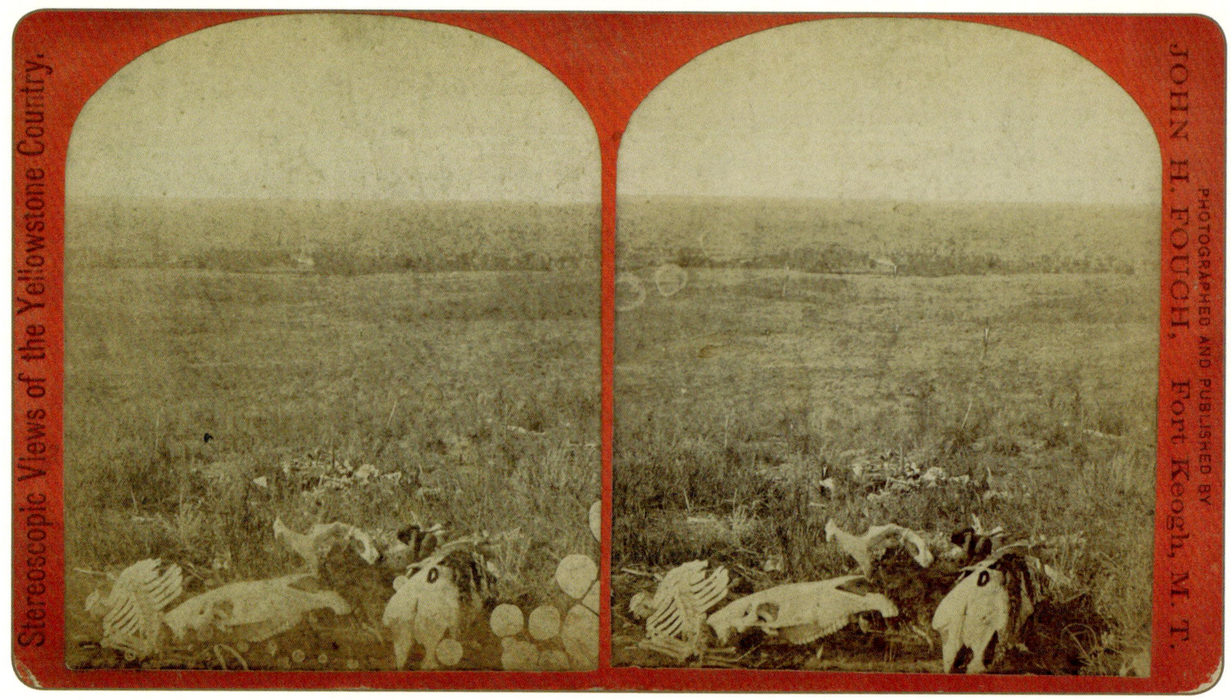

ABOVE: *The Place where Custer Fell,* the earliest photo of Custer's Battlefield taken by John Fouch, July 1877.

In spite of his busy schedule, Huffman apparently managed to do some socializing. On October 18, 1883, he married Eliza Ann Skinner (Lizzie), the daughter of a Miles City merchant and, by then, a next door neighbor. A daughter, Elizabeth (Bessie), was born in 1884 and another daughter, Ruth, was born in 1886. Ruth would play an important role in the future of The Huffman Pictures.

In 1883, Huffman published his next list (Huffman now calls it a catalogue); it includes 170 subjects in similar categories as 1881 with one major addition—Yellowstone National Park. That more than one-third of the list are views Huffman took during an 1882 summer visit to the National Park suggests a high interest in Yellowstone among travelers passing through Miles City.

The other significant change is in the "Hunting Scenes" category. Added are eight images taken in January 1882 during his participation in a buffalo hunt north of Miles City. The recent availability of dry plates allowed him to record the activities during that winter hunt. His few photographs of a hide hunter skinning a buffalo may be the only ones that exist and are among the most historically significant images of his career. Several of these images would be used on postcards. Huffman hunted again with G. O. Shields in the fall of 1882. In his 1883 list, he deleted 23 views from his 1881 hunt and added nine new ones from the 1882 hunt.

CATALOGUE

1883.

HUFFMAN'S

Latest Yellowstone National Park Views.

INDIAN PORTRAITS.

Miscellaneous Montana Views and the

ONLY CHOICE HUNTING SCENES PUBLISHED.

L. A. HUFFMAN, Photo and Publisher, MILES CITY, MONTANA.

INDIAN PORTRAITS, CABINET SIZES.

1. "Eta-ma-gozua," or "Rain-in-the-face."
2. "Scorched Lightning," Assinaboine Sioux.
3. Sioux Chieftain, "Spotted Eagle."
4. Young "Spotted Eagle."
5. Princess "Dull Knife," Cheyenne Maiden.
6. "Red Bead" Blackfoot Runner.
7. "Rain-in-the-face," Uncapappa Sioux who killed Custer.
8. Mrs. "Rain-in-the-face."
9. "Lone Wolf," Crow Scout.
10. "Pretty Eyes," Cheyenne Maiden.
11. "Two Moon's Children," Cheyennes.
12. "White Magpie," Teton Orator.
13. "Chief Joseph," Nez Perce.
14. "High Bear," Ogallalla.
15. Sioux Chief "Hump," and favorite wives.
16. "Man-on-the-hill" and wife.
17. Cheyenne Maid, "Medicine Walk."
18. Spotted Elk, Head Warrior, Minneconjoux Sioux.
19. Daughters of "Dull Knife," Cheyennes.
20. "Tall Bear," Minneconjoux Medicine Man.
39. Group of Cheyenne Girls.
21. "Wenopa," or Two Moon, Chief of Cheyennes.
36. Sioux Urchins.
22. "Wolf Voice," Gros Ventre warrior.
38. Sioux Woman and Pappoose.
370. "Big Bull," Crow Chief.
275. "Red Armed Panther," Cheyenne.
56. "White Bull," Sioux.
170. "Spotted Fawn," Cheyenne Maiden.
171. "Pretty Nose," Cheyenne Maiden.

INDIAN VIEWS, STEROSCOPIC.

177. Advance of Civilization, Wigwam and Locomotive
25. Sioux Village on the Yellowstone.
30. "Rain-in-the-face" at Home.
35. "Spotted Bear," Sioux Scout.
50. Sioux Scouts.
33. Sioux Camp Tongue River.
51. Young Teton Sioux.
24. Cheyenne Scouts.
28. Sioux Chief "Hump," and Head Warriors.
52. Yanktonais Camp, Tongue Valley, M. T.
194. "A Sioux Warrior's Grave," Buffalo Range, M. T.
29. "Rain-in-the-face's Camp."
34. Spotted Elk, Head Warrior, Minneconjoux Sioux.
55. Mother and Daughters, Sioux.
23. "Crow Maiden of Sixteen," Semi-nude.
26. "A Good Indian," Stiff.
37. Sweat Lodge, Sioux Village.

HUNTING SCENES.

196. A House of Buffalo Hides.
187. Camping on Northern Buffalo Range, winter.
195. Camp Emmett.
191. A Monster Buffalo Bull.
192. Taking the Monster's Robe.
193. After the Chase. Buffalo Bulls.
188. Five Minutes work, Nine Buffalo Cows.
189. Taking the Tongues.
71. A Mule Deer.

HUNTING SCENES—Continued.

58. Our Hunting Camp on Little Horn.
72. Our Outfit, Big Horn, 1881.
64. My First Bear.
69. His First Grizzly,
70. Skinning the Grizzly.
74. Our First Elk.
357. A Few Antelope.
358 Our Hunting Party, Clark's Fork Mountains.
350. "'Ow's These for 'Elk 'Orns."
347. Slain Monarch of the Mountains.
351. Elk Cow and Yearling.
356. "Here's Meat That'll Put Luther in Ye."
353. Successful After a Weary Climb.
354. Uncle Ed. Tells Me How He Got 'Em.
349. Glory Enough for a Day—Elk and Bears.
200. Mountain Sheep.

FORT KEOGH, M. T.

125. Bird's Eye View of Ft. Keogh.
114. Heart Arch, Bad Lands near Keogh.
123. Cheyenne Bluffs above Keogh.
129. Commanding Officers Res. Keogh.
127. Officers' Quarters, Keogh.
128. Barracks, Keogh.

MILES CITY.

161. East on Main Street, Miles City, M. T., 1881.
162. West " " " "
165. Freighting Outfit " "
105. Park Av. Looking North " 1882.
Miles City from Inter Ocean Hotel.
Inter Ocean Hotel.
167. West Main Street.
102. Main Street During March Flood, 1881.
Glendive and Vicinity.
145. Glendive from East.
148. " West.
118. Glendive in 1881.
363. Depot and Merrill House, Glendive.
147. Eagle Butte Cut.
152. Eagle Butte.
143. Bad Lands near Eagle Butte.
144. Toll Road " "
154. Old Government Trail, Bad Lands.
141. Eagle Butte Toll Road.
146. Cedar Bluff Side Cut.

CUSTER'S BATTLE FIELD.

91. Where Custer Fell.
Grave of Lieut. Sturgis.
93. " Col. Keogh.
" Lieut. Crittenden.
99. Monument on Custer's Hill.
Miscellaneous Views.
209. Terry's Landing.
217. Pompey's Pillar.
214. Guys Bluffs from West.
218. Coulson, M. T., from Bluffs.
221. Street View, Billings, 1882.
361. Testing Bismarck Bridge Oct. 21, 1882.
81. Black Canon, Big Horn,
82. Leaning Tower, Black Canon.

YELLOWSTONE NATIONAL PARK.

250. Liberty Cap Mammoth Hot Springs.
252. Specimen Falls " " "
254. Terraces at " " "
256. North from Terraces " "
258. "The Squash" " "
259. Toward Headquarters " "
261. Beautiful Terraces " "
262. Devils Thumb " " "
263. Canon of West Gardiner, near Mammoth Hot Springs.
264. Falls " " " "
266. Canon and Falls of Middle Gardiner.
267. Gibbon Boiling Spring.
268. Roadside Geyser.
269. North from Fountain Geyser, Lower Basin.
270. Fountain Geyser in Action.
271. Paint Pot, Lower Basin.
272. Firehole at Hell's Half Acre.
274. Phil. Sheridan in Action Three Miles Distant.
275. Gen. Sheridan and Party—Old Faithful in
277. Gen. Sheridan's Headquarters, Upper Basin.
278. " " Pack Train in Camp Upper Basin
279. Old Faithful in Action.
291. " " Getting Ready for Business.
293. Boiling Pool Banks of Firehole River.
294. Tower Castle Geyser from Bee Hive.
295. Giant Geyser Cone, Upper Basin.
296. Giant Geyser in Action.
297. Near View of Giant's Cone.
298. Crater of the Splendid.
299. Splendid from Grotto.
300. Grotto Geyser Cone, Upper Basin.
301. Beautiful Grotto " "
304. Castle Geyser Cone " "
306. Bee Hive Geyser Cone " "
307. Yellowstone Canon near Tower Falls.
309. Tower Falls.
310. " "
311. Jack Baronett's Bridge from South.
312. " " " " North.
313. General View of Upper Basin—Morning.
315. Grand Canon of the Yellowstone.
316. " " " "
317. " " " "
318. Down Grand Canon from Lower Falls.
322. Over the Bank of Lower Falls.
325. Lower Falls, 360 Feet High.
326. Lower Falls, Two Miles Distant.
329. A Glimpse of Lower Falls.
330. Canon and Falls from "Eagle Nest."
321. Upper Falls from Bridle Path.
333. Cascade near Lower Falls.
334. Camping Point Above the Falls.
335. Soda Butte.
336. Soda Butte and Soda Springs.
337. Soda Butte Valley.
338. Soda Butte Creek and Grand Mountain.
339. Soda Butte Creek near Cook City.
341. Soda Butte Creek and Specimen Mountain.
343. Antelope Camp, Bennett's Creek Clark's Fork.

Price per dozen, post paid .... $..........

Price per gross, post paid .... $..........

ABOVE: Huffman's 1883 catalogue with the additions of Yellowstone National Park and hunting scenes.

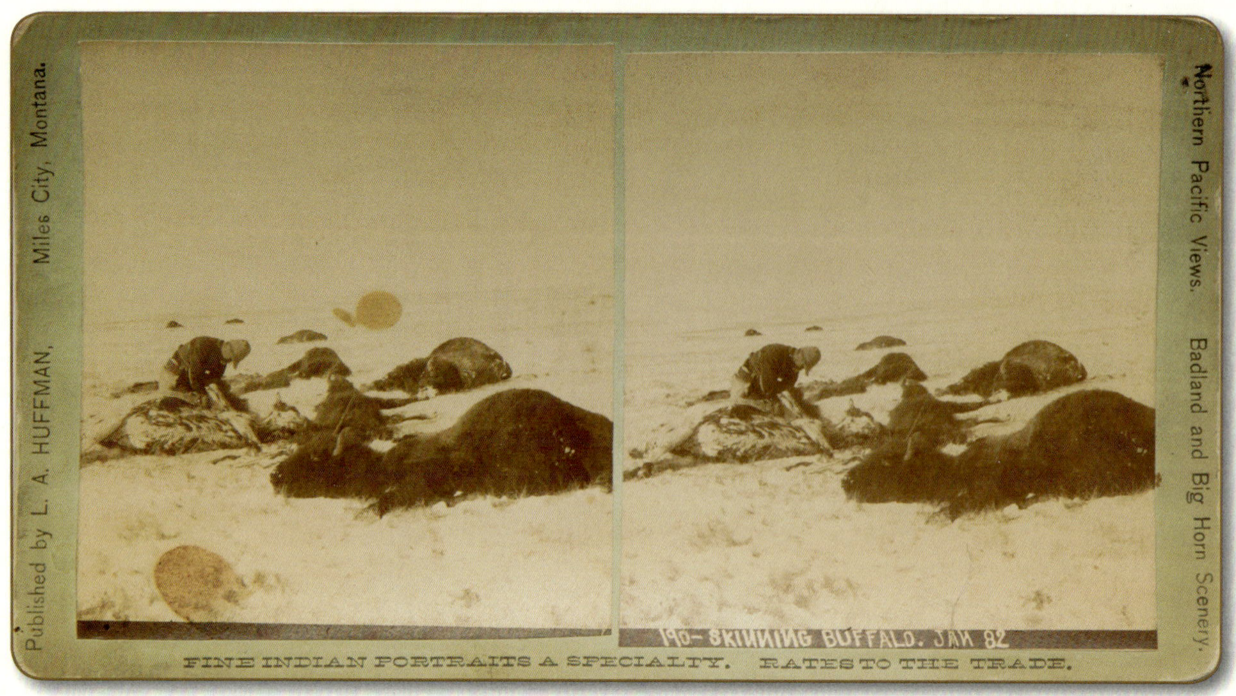

About this time Huffman refers to a homemade camera that used the new 6½ x 8½ inch dry plates. He said it weighed about 50 pounds, which sounds like a bit of an exaggeration. It became his new outdoor camera. In a letter to his father dated June 7, 1885, Huffman states, "I just returned a few days ago from a 12 days ride with the Powder River Roundup—I shall soon show you what can be done from the saddle without ground glass and tripod. Please notice when you get the specimens that they were made with the lens wide open and many of the best exposed when my horse was in motion." The specimens he was referring to was a series of 40 photographs he titled *The Spring Round-up.* He described them as "a series of instantaneous photographs, taken from the saddle, showing some Montana horse and cattle ranches and illustrating features of handling wild cattle and horses on the prairies." At least two images from this group were later used as postcards.

TOP: *Skinning Buffalo,* taken in January 1882 during Huffman's participation in a buffalo hunt north of Miles City—one of the most historically significant images of his career.

RIGHT: *Branding a Calf,* taken with his new homemade camera in June 1885, at the Powder River Roundup.

FACING PAGE: *Going to the Roundup.*

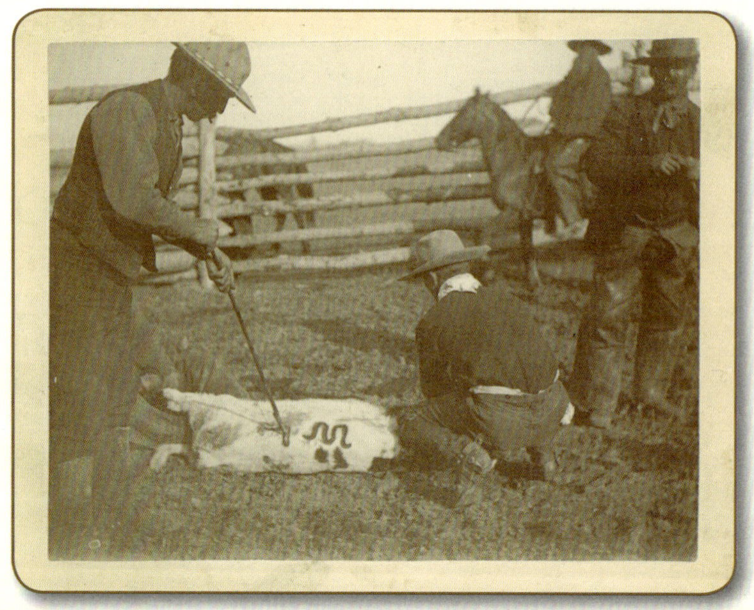

Although still crude by today's standards of high quality lenses and fast shutters, his new homemade camera, used with the new ready-made dry plates, was a big improvement. In spite of a large, heavy camera with a wide open lens and relatively slow shutter, astride a moving "4 legged tripod," he was able to produce some of the first action photos taken of roundup activities. That he did this with no apparent permanent damage to either equipment or self attests to both his ability as a photographer and his horsemanship.

For a brief period in the early 1880s, Huffman, with a partner, tried his hand at ranching. They owned the first ranch in the Rosebud Valley near present-day Lame Deer. He participated in roundups, helped with the activities and knew many of the area's ranchers and cowboys. Although his part-time ranching career was brief, his experiences helped him anticipate the action and to be in the right place at the right time. His early action-stopping photos, many taken from the saddle, are unequaled.

His most complete body of work relates to the cattle industry and associated activities. He photographed the beginning, heyday and end of the open-range days and, for that period, no one did it better. In an article in a 1955 issue of *The Shamrock* magazine, western historian J. Evetts Haley said, "For sheer versatility of significant and historic subject matter close to the range of the grass, [Huffman's collection] surpasses them all." In the autumn, 1975 issue of *Hoofprints* (Yellowstone Corral of the Westerners), Huffman historian Mark H. Brown said, "If there was any one quality that sets the Huffman collection apart, it is the intimate nature of the subject matter." Haley especially liked Huffman's roundup photo titled *Going to the Roundup*. Of that image he said, "This could be the finest range scene ever made."

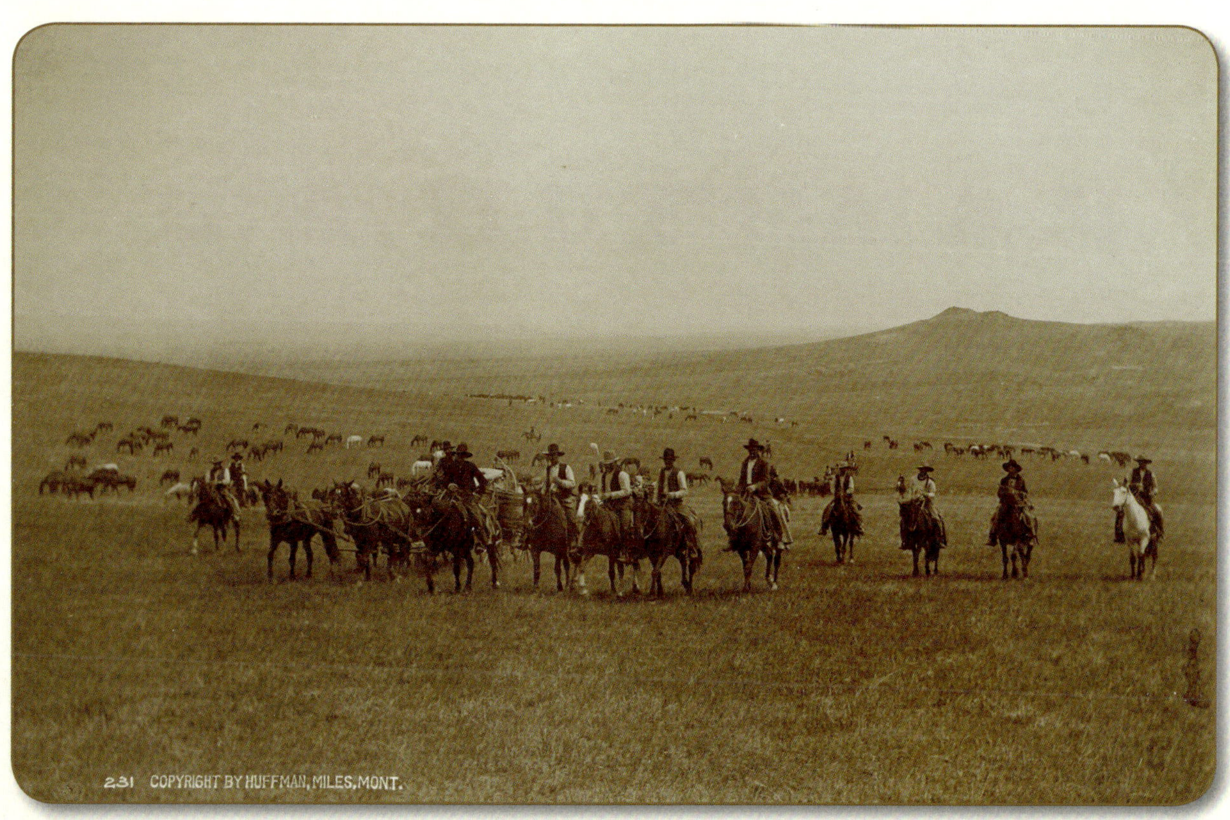

Erwin Smith (1886–1947), noted photographer of the Texas cattle range, liked it enough to order a 12 x 24 enlargement. In the April 1919 letter accompanying his $15 check, he says, "I think this is the greatest picture I ever saw showing an outfit on the move—chuck wagons, cowboys and remuda strung out in their natural way" (McCracken Research Library, Buffalo Bill Historical Center, Cody, Wyoming). Nothing beats a compliment from one of your peers!

The next Huffman photo catalogue we are aware of is dated 1898. It is a 20 page, stapled booklet with string tied covers and measures 6¼ x 4⅝. It contains 154 entries in eight categories—some the same as the 1883 list, and several new ones. The new categories—roundup views, sheep and Indian views—are all taken with his new 6 x 8 camera. More than half of the sheep and roundup views are accompanied by descriptive explanations of the action captured in the image. He offers the pictures mounted or unmounted, individual or as sets. His price of $20 for the complete collection of 154 is a substantial discount compared to the individual prices. Several of the images made with his 6 x 8 camera were used later as postcards.

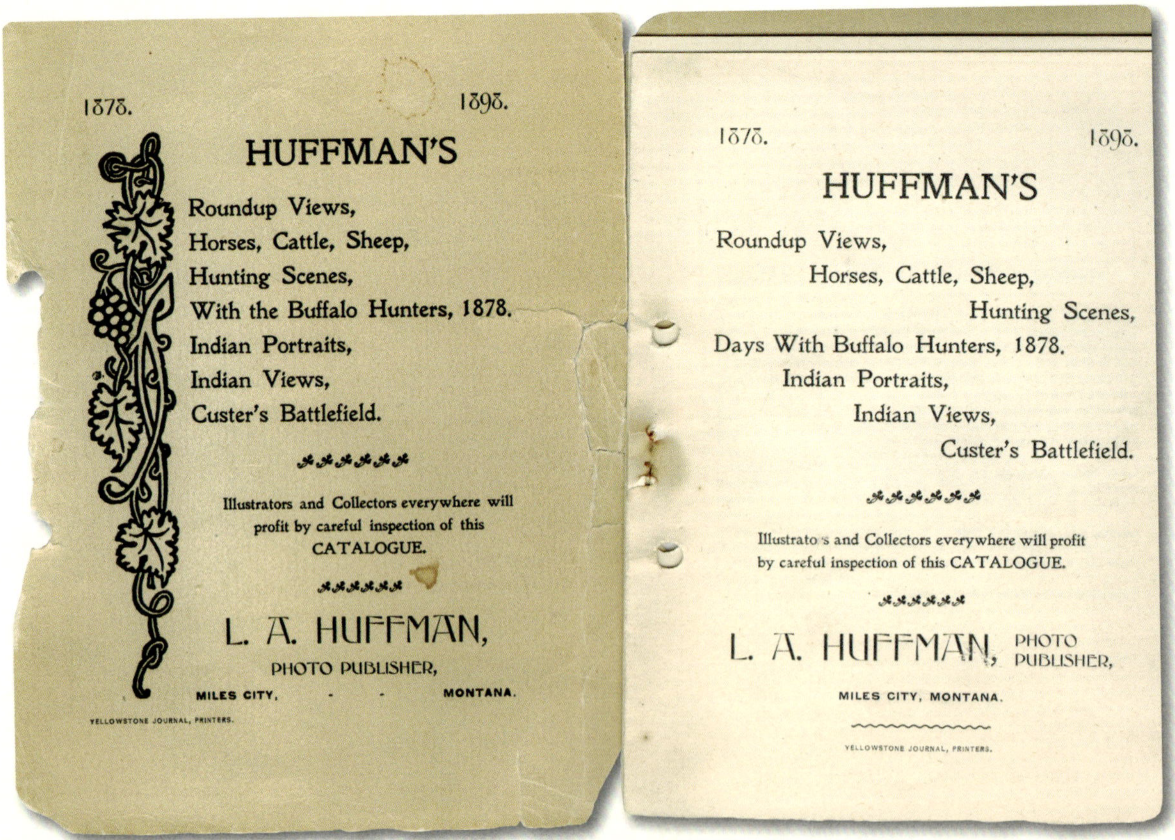

1878. 1898.

HUFFMAN'S

Roundup Views,
Horses, Cattle, Sheep,
Hunting Scenes,
With the Buffalo Hunters, 1878.
Indian Portraits,
Indian Views,
Custer's Battlefield.

Illustrators and Collectors everywhere will profit by careful inspection of this CATALOGUE.

L. A. HUFFMAN,
PHOTO PUBLISHER,
MILES CITY, - - MONTANA.

YELLOWSTONE JOURNAL, PRINTERS.

1878. 1898.

HUFFMAN'S

Roundup Views,
Horses, Cattle, Sheep,
Hunting Scenes,
Days With Buffalo Hunters, 1878.
Indian Portraits,
Indian Views,
Custer's Battlefield.

Illustrators and Collectors everywhere will profit by careful inspection of this CATALOGUE.

L. A. HUFFMAN, PHOTO PUBLISHER,
MILES CITY, MONTANA.

YELLOWSTONE JOURNAL, PRINTERS.

ABOVE: The cover and first page of Huffman's 1898 catalogue.

Noticeably absent from this catalogue are any views of Yellowstone National Park. While they dominated the 1883 list, in this one there are none. Demand for these views from the traveling public must have declined drastically during the 1890s to not merit the inclusion of at least a few. Coincidentally, and probably related, was the continued evolution of photography. Eastman's Kodak arrived in the

1880s, as did roll film. As technology improved, cameras became less expensive and easier to use. It set the stage for amateur photographers to take their own views when traveling to places like Yellowstone. We are not aware of any Yellowstone image used on one of his postcards.

Huffman issued his next catalogue in 1900. It is similar in format to 1898 but smaller in size (4¾ x 4) and with more pages (32). The only example we have seen is the mouse-chewed copy in our collection. Although he states there are 150 total images, the various lists appear to be the same as 1898 (154), plus he has added an additional 25 Indian images bringing the total to 179. They are still offered mounted or unmounted. A couple of small changes in the catalogue are the increase of the price for the collection from $20 to $25, and the addition of a New York City street address in addition to Miles City. We have no knowledge of his connection to that address.

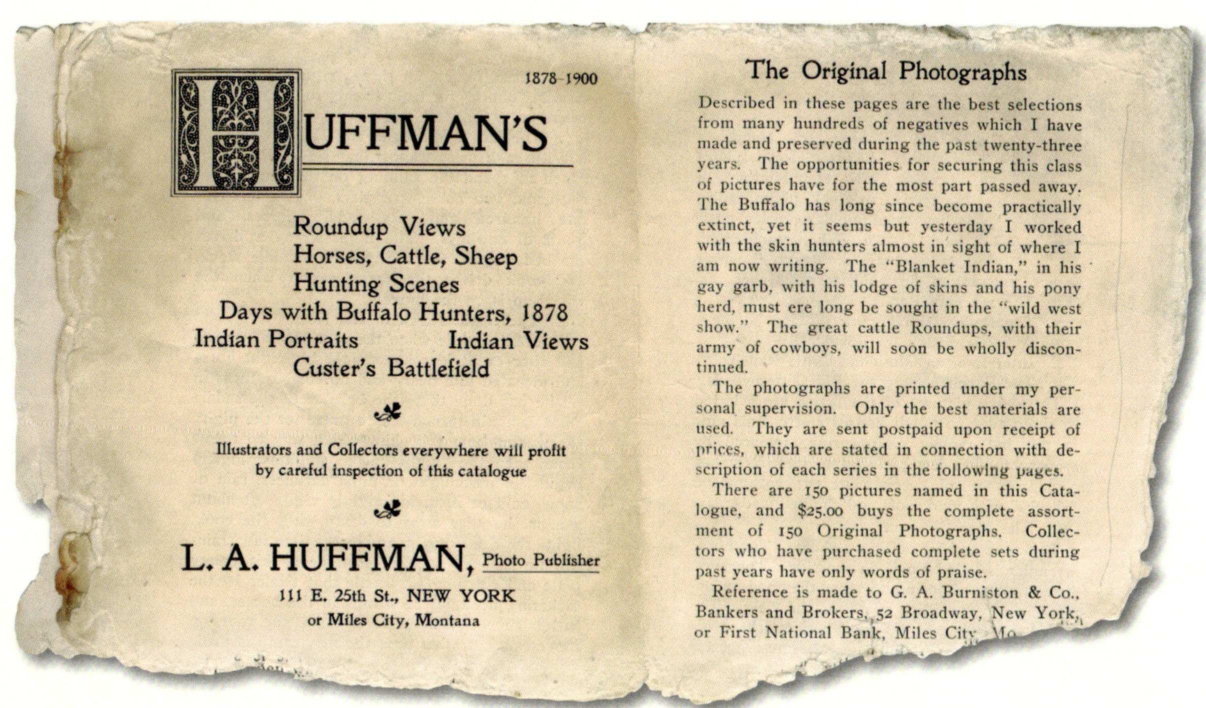

1878-1900

HUFFMAN'S

Roundup Views
Horses, Cattle, Sheep
Hunting Scenes
Days with Buffalo Hunters, 1878
Indian Portraits Indian Views
Custer's Battlefield

Illustrators and Collectors everywhere will profit by careful inspection of this catalogue

L. A. HUFFMAN, Photo Publisher
111 E. 25th St., NEW YORK
or Miles City, Montana

The Original Photographs

Described in these pages are the best selections from many hundreds of negatives which I have made and preserved during the past twenty-three years. The opportunities for securing this class of pictures have for the most part passed away. The Buffalo has long since become practically extinct, yet it seems but yesterday I worked with the skin hunters almost in sight of where I am now writing. The "Blanket Indian," in his gay garb, with his lodge of skins and his pony herd, must ere long be sought in the "wild west show." The great cattle Roundups, with their army of cowboys, will soon be wholly discontinued.

The photographs are printed under my personal supervision. Only the best materials are used. They are sent postpaid upon receipt of prices, which are stated in connection with description of each series in the following pages.

There are 150 pictures named in this Catalogue, and $25.00 buys the complete assortment of 150 Original Photographs. Collectors who have purchased complete sets during past years have only words of praise.

Reference is made to G. A. Burniston & Co., Bankers and Brokers, 52 Broadway, New York, or First National Bank, Miles City

ABOVE: The cover and first page of Huffman's 1900 catalogue.

For the first time, Huffman has assigned the letters A—H to his previous eight categories and now calls them a "series," as follows:

Series A—Roundup Views, new series (6 x 8, 36)

Series B—Roundup Views, from the saddle (from his 40 image 1885—*The Spring Roundup,* now 24)

Series C—Sheep (6 x 8, 10)

Series D—Hunting Scenes (mostly from his two Bighorn hunts, 12)

Series E—Hunting Scenes, Days with Buffalo Hunters, 1878 (8)

Series F—Custer's Battlefield, as it appeared in 1877 (the 6 views taken by S. V. Morrow in 1879)

Series G—Indian Cabinets (48)

Series H—Indian Pictures, Series 1898 (6 x 8, 10)

The 25 Indian views he added he calls Series M (with no title). It appears this series was an after thought, deciding to add it after the catalogue was printed. He printed an extra page and placed it following Series G, the other Indian images (and out of alphabetical order).

In a note at the end of the catalogue (following Series H) he offers, "oil colored platinoid enlargements . . . made to order, $8 to $25. They lead all Indian colored work." This is the first evidence we have seen that he is able to provide enlargements. It is not clear if Huffman is doing his own enlarging at this time or if they were being produced somewhere else. An April 1898 letter to Huffman from the Eastman Kodak Company in Rochester, New York indicates he had at least inquired about them making 14 x 20 size bromide prints from his negatives (McCracken Research Library). All previous catalogue offerings have been for contact prints (a print made by placing the sensitized paper in direct contact with the negative, producing a print the same size as the negative). He also states, "new edition of catalog, New Live Game Subjects, in preparation for 1901." If issued, we have not seen one.

By c. 1905, Huffman's offerings of contact prints has settled into its final form. He is now offering 10 series (he added Series K—Typical Montana) with a total of 141 images. They are sepia toned, sold only as unmounted sets and come in a manila envelope with an exterior label showing negative numbers and titles. We have seen no catalogue showing these lists.

Series.
A

HUFFMAN'S ROUNDUP VIEWS.

30 prints 6x8 unmounted sepia, $8 for the series.

154 At the Bow Gun Ranch.
149 The Ranch on Hanging Woman Creek.
187 Interior of an Old Time Ranch, Powder River.
231 Starting for the Roundup.
177 A Camp on the Roundup.
238 A Hot Noon Beside a Camp.
176 Breaking Camp.
239 The Roundup on the Move.
246 The Mess Wagon.
182 The Bow Gun Boys at Dinner.
180 Hat X Camp, Hungry Creek.
247 Roundup Cook and Pie Biter at Work.
240 Roping and Killing a Beef.
257 The Night Hawk in His Nest.
249 The Foreman Telling Off His Riders for the Circle.
253 Two Bow Gun Boys, Mounted.
250 A Typical Trio, Mounted.
259 Cowboy "Honey Cut" on White Star.
258 Cowboy "Tunis" on C Dot.
261 Saddling a Wild Horse.
203 Branding Calves in Corral.
179 Saddle Horses in Rope Corral.
237 Working Herd Among Old Buffalo Wallows.
206 The Branding Fire.
226 Herd Moving From Camp. Cache Creek.
234 Holding a Herd.
241 Throwing Cattle to the Roundup Ground.
229 Swimming a Herd—Powder River.
235 The Roundup, Cutting at Poker Jim Creek.
236 Working a Little Bunch in the Hills.

This Series A, with Series C, H, G, F, D and E, 101 prints in all, $20.00 prepaid. I should admire to see a collection of Original photographs their equal. L. A. HUFFMAN, Miles City, Montana.

Series.
B

HUFFMAN'S ROUNDUP VIEWS.

The 20 original sepia prints, $2.50.

1 A Typical Cattle Ranch. Bitter Creek.
2 Roundup Outfit in Camp. Big Dry.
3 The Mess Wagon, Dinner.
4 Cowboy and Broncho.
5 Range Cattle Grazing in the Badlands.
6 Snubbing a Wild Mare.
7 Putting on a Hackamore.
8 Picking a Brand to Determine Ownership.
9 Branding Calves in Corral.
10 The Branding Chute.
11 Working the Squeezer; Branding in a Chute.
12 Brands Enough for a Two-year-old.
13 Roping a Steer—Caught.
14 Roping a Steer—Heard Something Drop.
15 Roping a Steer—Wonders What it Was.
16 Roping a Steer—The Tail Holt.
17 Roping a Steer—Stretched.
18 Roping and ;Stretching—A Three-year-old Maverick
19 Conquering a Fighting Texan.
20 Cutting Out a Calf.

The twenty prints prepaid with Series K (eight 6x8 prints) and Series M, (12 Indian Cabinets) 40 prints in all, unmounted sepia, special for the 40 prepaid to you, $6.50. **Original prints every one, not reproductions.**

L. A. HUFFMAN,
Miles City, Montana.

Each print has a negative number and the credit "copyright by Huffman Miles, Mont." along the bottom (the Custer Battlefield photos have no numbers). Prints from earlier catalogues do not have the credit. He must have printed a significant number of each; after selling from this stock for the next 25 years, there was still an unsold supply of many of the images when he died in 1931. Except for real photo postcards, it is doubtful that he made any contact prints after 1905.

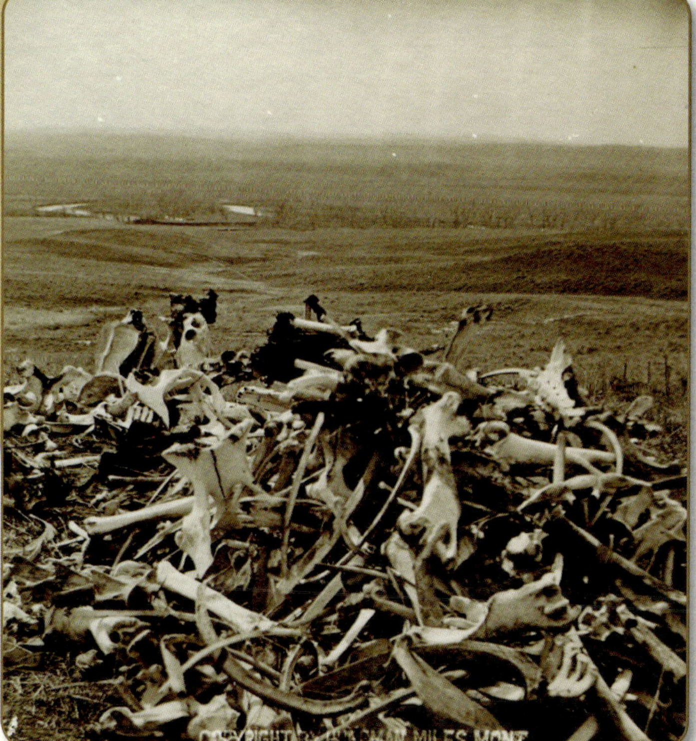

ABOVE: Manila envelope with exterior label showing contents.

RIGHT: Example of a 1905 print made on gold-toned matte collodian printing-out paper.

FACING PAGE: Envelope labels list negative numbers and titles.

The 1905 prints were made on gold-toned matte collodion printing-out paper (a print produced by exposure to daylight). Printing-out paper was in widespread use during the 1890s and early 1900s, but by 1905, was on the way out in favor of the improved developing-out paper (a print produced in chemicals). Developing-out paper provided the advantages of convenience, lower cost and faster production. The enlargements offered by Huffman in his 1900 catalogue were probably made with developing-out paper and 1900–1905 may have been his "transition period" from one to the other. It is only speculation, but Huffman may have used his 1905 Series prints as an opportunity to "use up" his remaining stock of printing-out paper.

The 1905 Series prints are of high quality and quite attractive. While they are all scarce, a few of the most popular images are rare and very desirable in the collector market. At the 2013 Coeur d'Alene Art Auction in Reno, an early Huffman photo album, containing all 141 images from the ten 1905 series, sold for $280,800!

Records and writings suggest that Huffman was on the financial edge much of his career. The early years saw enough demand for him to hire an assistant to help print an adequate inventory of cabinet cards and stereo views. Business was brisk and profits allowed him to acquire a modest amount of property. Some of the rental property helped carry him through the lean years, which lay ahead. By the mid 1880s the photography business was changing. In an August 1885 letter to his father he says, "business is fairly good . . . but the old line view business is about played out."

By 1890 he was discouraged enough to consider changing his line of work. In a March 2nd letter to his father he says, "After several weeks of hard work I have succeeded in closing up my affairs so as to make my going away for a few months possible. I shall go on the next train taking in all important railway points between here and Portland and possibly extend my journey to California for a short visit. I cannot tell where I shall fetch up for a new field of labor. What I shall follow for livelihood is somewhat undecided also—certain it is however I shall not long separate myself from my girls . . . we will see what we shall see." A May 6th letter to his family, written from the train on his return trip, indicates he visited California at least as far as Sacramento. He also spent some time in Chicago, probably with photographic firms. In 1895, he opened a second studio in Billings, Montana operated by an associate. In early 1897 he sold the Billings studio to his associate.

Throughout these uncertain and financially difficult years, Huffman continued to operate his Miles City studio, always looking for new opportunities. A studio letterhead, used in 1900, offers "Photo Supplies for Amateur and Professionals" and provides "Developing and Printing" services. His financial problems apparently continued to mount, and in 1905 he filed for bankruptcy (official notice appears in Dec. 18th issue of *The Yellowstone Journal*). It provided Huffman with an opportunity for a fresh start; it was time to make some changes.

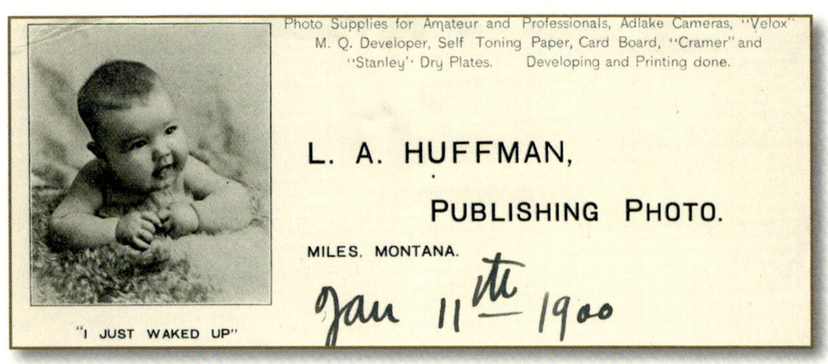
Photo Supplies for Amateur and Professionals, Adlake Cameras, "Velox" M. Q. Developer, Self Toning Paper, Card Board, "Cramer" and "Stanley" Dry Plates. Developing and Printing done.

L. A. HUFFMAN,

PUBLISHING PHOTO.

MILES, MONTANA.

Jan 11th 1900

"I JUST WAKED UP"

ABOVE: Huffman Studio 1900 letterhead offering supplies & services.

By 1906, Huffman had closed his downtown studio to casual business. While he continued to actively take photos, the emphasis for the rest of his career was the sale of contact and enlarged prints made from his early negatives, many of them hand-tinted. Like many other early photographers, Huffman also began producing photomechanical prints of several of his images. It was a way to drastically reduce the cost of making multiple copies of the same image. Huffman's prints were collotypes, a popular process at the time. A collotype is an ink print made from a photographically prepared glass plate used as a printing block. Eventually, he produced collotypes from more than 50 of his images. They are of high quality and proved to be popular; they accounted for a significant portion of his sales for the rest of his career. Our 2014 book, *The Collotypes of L. A. Huffman,* provides a detailed look at Huffman's collotypes.

Another change Huffman initiated in 1906 was precipitated by an act of Congress—postcards! Prior to 1898, all postcards were printed by the U.S. Postal Service. The USPS had been printing prestamped Postal Cards since 1873. They cost one cent and offered a large savings compared to the two-cent cost of mailing a letter. On May 19, 1898, Congress authorized the private production of cards that could be sent for one cent—they were called Private Mailing Cards. This is probably the single most important date in the history of postcard use in this country. Other important changes were coming.

RIGHT: Postal Card USPS courtesy Tom Mulvaney.

BELOW: Private Mailing Card courtesy Tom Mulvaney.

BOTTOM: Undivided back postcard.

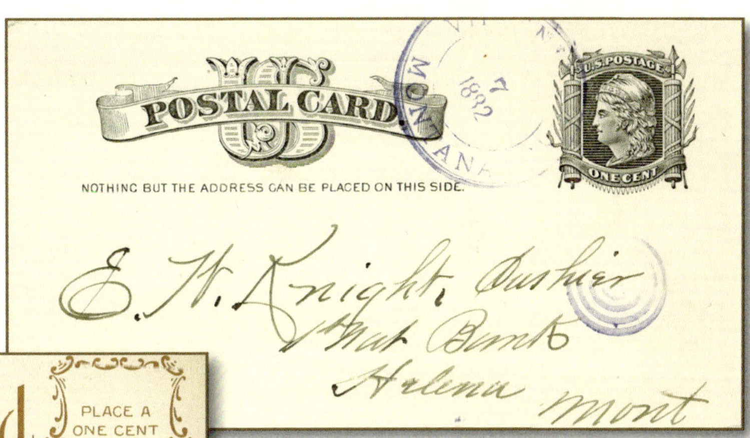

In 1901 the USPS authorized use of the word "postcard" on the privately printed cards instead of Private Mailing Card. At this time, only one side of the card could be used for personal use, i.e. messages, greetings, images, etc. The other side was reserved exclusively for the postage and mailing address. Postcard collectors call these "undivided backs." Postcards were an inexpensive and effective way to communicate and were becoming more and more popular. The use of both art and photography on images was also increasing. In 1903,

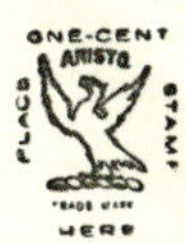

Kodak released its Folding Pocket Camera in 3¼ x 5½—postcard size. Other camera manufacturers soon followed. While real photo postcards first appeared in 1900, it was the availability of postcard-sized cameras that caused the most dramatic increase in the use of photographs on postcards, described in this book as "Real Photo Postcards."

March 1, 1907 is the next important date in the history of postcard use in America. Congress authorized that half of the postage/address side could now be used for a brief greeting or message. Postcard collectors call them "divided backs." It allowed the writing of a brief message without having to write it on the image side. England was the first country to allow divided backs in 1902, followed by France in 1904 and Germany in 1905. Divided backs ushered in what has been called the Golden Age of Postcards. During the period 1907–1915, collecting picture postcards became the world's number one collectible and billions of postcards were sold and used. U.S. Postal records for the fiscal year ending June 30, 1908, cite more than 667 million were mailed in this country alone! Early in the period, most cards were produced in Europe, the best ones from Germany. By the mid-teens the threat of and subsequent World War brought a rapid decline in the number of postcards imported from Europe, and an end to those coming from Germany. In spite of the ability of American card makers to fill in, the economic and political complications of the day ended the Golden Age of Postcards.

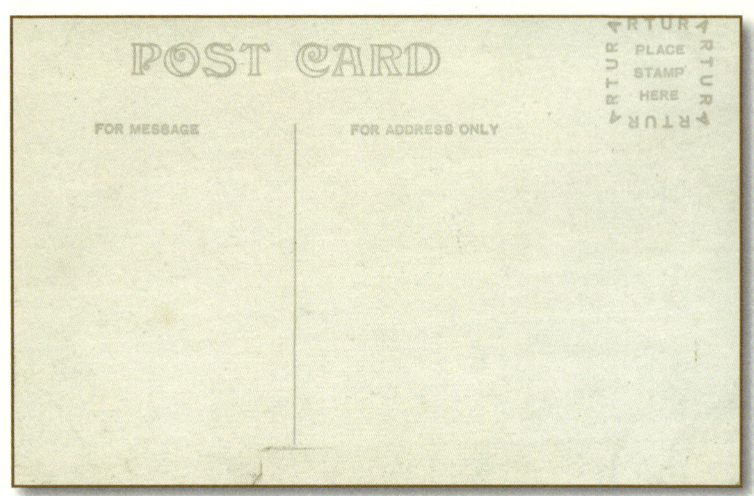

Bill Felton, Jr., Huffman's grandson, said that during his career, Huffman owned at least two Kodak Folding Pocket Cameras. One of them is in our collection. It is a No. 3-A, Model C and is postcard size; it was probably issued about 1910. Although it is well used, few of the photos taken with it were ever used as postcards. It came to us with Huffman's canvas shoulder carrying bag that he also probably used earlier when cameras were a bit larger. Following is a photo of Huffman with the carrying bag and camera, astride his "4 legged tripod."

Huffman's first known use of real photo postcards, which he produced himself, was with the undivided back variety in the fall of 1906. He was quick to take advantage of Congress's divided back postcard allowance the following year, issuing a set of 25 printed cards in divided back format. This was Huffman's first use of printed postcards. He also continued to produce his own real photo postcards over the next several years. His next venture into the realm of postcards was in 1926 with a 15 printed card set related to the Custer Battlefield. It was intended to coincide with the 50th anniversary of the battle. His last involvement with postcards was in 1928 with a five card colored set done in collaboration

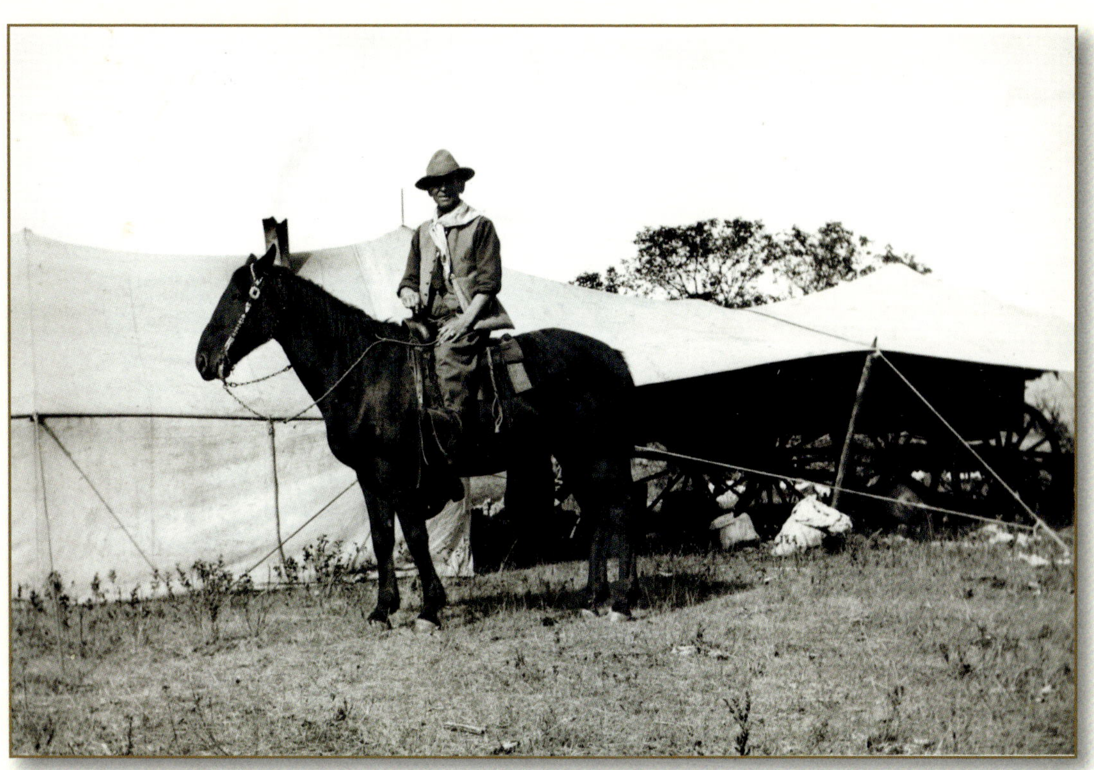

ABOVE: Huffman on his "4 legged tripod."

FACING PAGE: Divided back postcard.

with the Northern Pacific Railroad. While postcards are a relatively scarce and interesting aspect of Huffman's total body of work, it is doubtful they ever contributed much to his financial welfare.

By the late 1920s, Huffman was mostly selling enlarged, hand-colored prints of his earlier, most popular images. He sold these for $20. He also produced a small number of "heroic-sized photomurals," five to seven feet long. He sold these for as much as $250, nearly $3,500 in today's dollars! They are exceptionally rare today. Correspondence and sales records suggest that Huffman's best years were his last ones. In a November 12, 1930 letter to a client in New York City, he states, "1930 brought me double the orders of any previous year." It is remarkable, and a bit ironic, that Huffman had his best year as the country was slipping into the Great Depression.

Huffman died unexpectedly of a heart attack in December 1931. He and Mrs. Huffman were in Billings, Montana visiting their youngest daughter, Ruth, and son-in-law Verne Scott during the Christmas holidays. While his sudden death left much unfinished business, including a leftover inventory of photo prints, collotypes and postcards, it was not the end of The Huffman Pictures. The Scotts soon moved to Miles City to help care for Mrs. Huffman and to continue to run the business from the Huffman home and studio, something they would do for the next thirty plus years.

In the late 1940s, W. R. Felton, Huffman's other son-in-law, and Mark Brown were exploring the possibility of a book using Huffman's photos and stories. Felton lived in Sioux City, Iowa and ran the

Felton Seed Company, an agricultural supply store; Mark Brown was an area farmer, ex-military intelligence officer, a collector and historian. More important, they were friends and shared an interest in the Old West. Their collaboration was successful and resulted in *The Frontier Years* and *Before Barbed Wire* being published in 1955 and 1956.

In 1951 Brown and Felton stopped into a new photo studio in Miles City and asked Jack Coffrin if he could make quality prints from Huffman's old negatives that could be used in their books. It was the beginning of Coffrin's association with The Huffman Pictures that lasted 30 years. Felton would provide Ruth with a list of Huffman's negatives and she would deliver them to Coffrin for printing. During the next few years he produced several hundred prints for Brown and Felton. Eventually, 250 photos would be used in the two books. The books raised the awareness of Huffman and increased the demand for his work. Coffrin also provided prints for Ruth and Verne Scott as they continued to run the business through the 1950s and early 1960s.

With Verne Scott's death in 1964 and her own health failing, Ruth and Jack Coffrin entered into a business agreement. He could use the original negatives to make new prints to sell and was provided some original material including the remaining unsold inventory of collotypes and postcards. The Huffman Pictures soon dominated his business; he expanded his facility and it became "Coffrin's Old West Gallery."

He soon made a set of copy negatives so he wouldn't have to handle the fragile originals (he also added fluffy, white clouds to some of the images!). His gallery offered a wide variety of high quality prints, some of them beautifully hand colored. Several of the images were also reproduced as colored, lithographic prints. In 1968 he produced a series of printed color postcards. It is unknown how many postcards he made and sold during his tenure with the Huffman material, but they are quite common today. Coffrin retired in 1981. Huffman heirs recovered the negatives and other original material; they donated the original negatives to the Photo Archives section at the Montana Historical Society in Helena. Jack Coffrin died in 2006.

To people in Miles City, Huffman was more than just the local photographer. He was very sociable with a pleasant personality and had many friends and acquaintances. The Huffman home was often the scene of community social events. One of Mrs. Huffman's most dear friends was the wife of District Judge George Milburn, close neighbors. Milburn was elected to the Montana Supreme Court for the term commencing in January 1901. Within a week of the family's move to Helena, Mrs. Milburn died suddenly of pneumonia. Mrs. Huffman, with the two girls, moved to Helena and spent parts of the next two years caring for the Judge's young children, a son seven and a girl nine.

Huffman was active in his community and in the mid 1880s was elected to both the School Board and the County Commission. In 1893 he served as a Representative from Custer County in the Montana State Legislature. Although Huffman was an institution in Miles City, he never received widespread recognition during his lifetime. In 1927, the Montana Legislature had an opportunity to honor him for his life's work. A bill was introduced to appropriate $3,000 to purchase a representative sample of his photographs to permanently hang in the State Historical Library. The House of Representatives killed the bill. It wasn't until the mid-1950s and the publication of the two books, *The Frontier Years* and *Before Barbed Wire*, using Huffman photos and stories, that people again started taking notice of his work. His greatest recognition came in 1976 when he was inducted into the Hall of Great Westerners at the National Cowboy and Western Heritage Museum in Oklahoma City, Oklahoma. He was the first, and for many years, the only photographer so honored. An interesting side note, the person who wrote the nominating letter for Huffman's acceptance was Jack Milburn, son of Judge Milburn, whom Mrs. Huffman had helped care for as a seven year old 75 years before!

Huffman was 77 years old when he died in 1931. Although he struggled financially his entire career, he stayed with photography—for 52 years! That we are writing and reading books about him and his work more than 85 years later is a tribute to his legacy. We'll let Huffman have the last word—

"Kind fate had it I should be Post Photographer
with the Army during the Indian campaigns
close following the annihilation of Custer's command.
This Yellowstone-Big Horn country was then
unpenned of wire, and unspoiled by railway, dam or ditch.
Eastman had not yet made the Kodak,
but thanks be, there was the old wet plate,
the Collodion bottle and bath.
I made photographs.
With crude home-made cameras,
from saddle and in log shack,
I saved something."

—L. A. Huffman

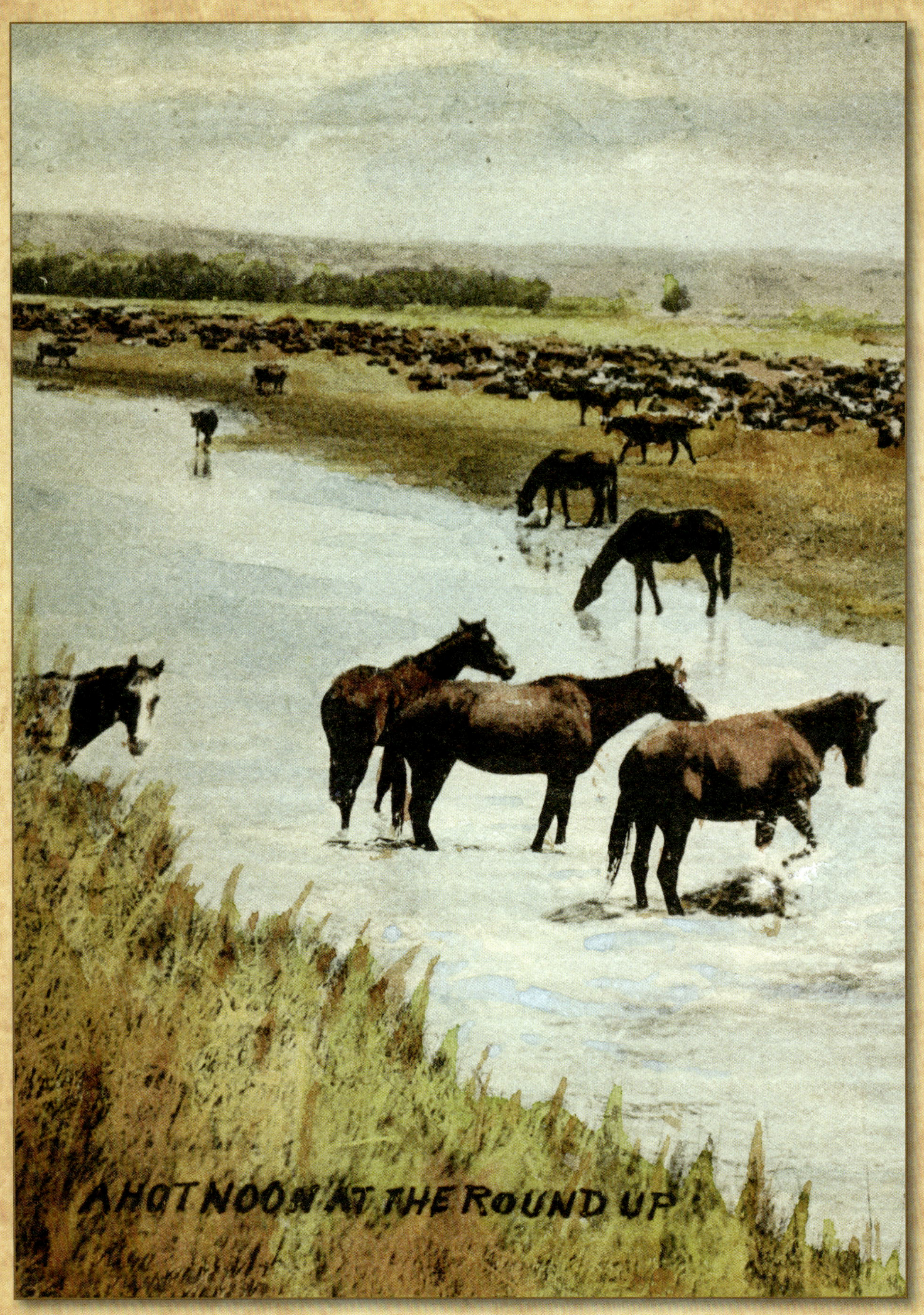
A HOT NOON AT THE ROUND UP

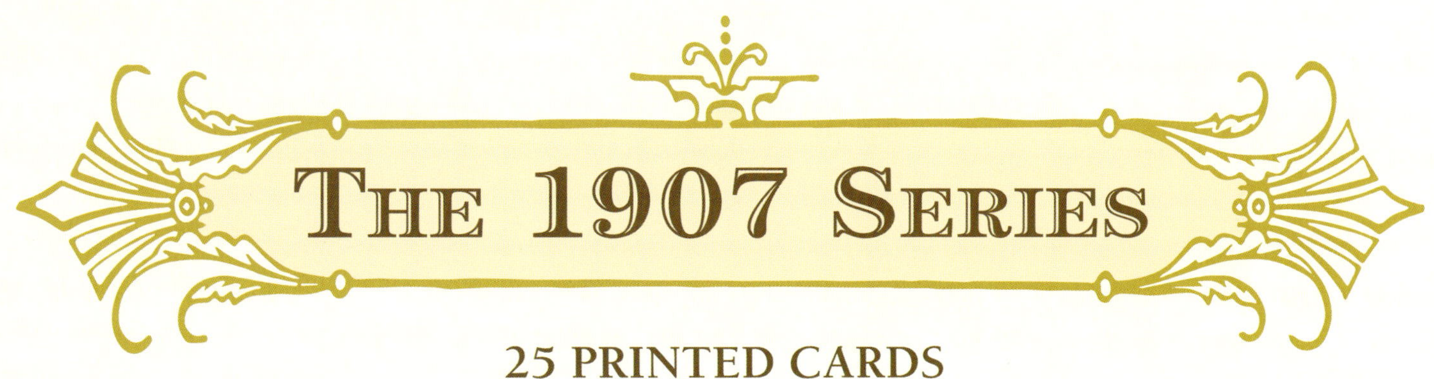

25 PRINTED CARDS

In a letter dated July 17, 1907, the Campbell Art Company of Elizabeth, New Jersey, responds to an earlier inquiry by Huffman regarding the printing of postcards (McCracken Research Library). It also includes a list of 27 images previously submitted to them by Huffman. The letter reveals they will print them 27 to a sheet, which explains the list of 27 different images previously sent by Huffman.

Huffman had apparently suggested a run of 5,000 sheets (135,000 cards). Because this is his first order, and they are "particularly anxious to have him successful in this matter and take as little risk as possible," they suggest a smaller run of 3,000 sheets (81,000 total cards) at the same cost of $5.50 per thousand cards that they had previously quoted him for the larger order of 5,000 sheets.

They also suggest he can "double up" an image by reducing the number of subjects, i.e. print 24 subjects and double the quantity of three, or 21 subjects and double the quantity of six, etc. To our knowledge, no one has seen a No. 2, *Typical Crow,* or No. 15, *Two Moon,* from Huffman's list; we believe he decided on 25 images and doubled the quantity of two of them. Because of the apparent greater abundance of No. 5, *A Killing of Cows and Spikes,* and No. 27, *A Hot Noon At the Roundup,* we believe these are the two cards that may have been printed in double quantity. If Huffman followed through with their suggestion of a smaller order, and we know of no evidence he didn't, a total of 81,000 cards were printed; 3,000 each of 23 subjects and 6,000 each of two subjects at a cost of slightly more than ½ cent each.

Most printed cards were the result of some type of halftone or lithographic process and reveal a dot pattern under magnification; these cards do not show a dot pattern. Rather, a series of dark, irregular blotches give the surface a salt and pepper appearance. The Campbell Art Company also produced some of Huffman's first collotypes, a photomechanical process commonly used at that time. Under magnification, the surface appearance of the postcards and collotypes is similar and the same process may have produced both of them.

The cards are printed on divided back stock. The images completely cover the front of the cards with no border. Along the bottom of each card, in the image, is a number (1 through 27), a title, and a dated (1907) copyright and credit. The numbers are not consistently placed and a few are difficult to spot; no number has been observed on card No. 4, *A Killing of Elk.* On the reverse side is a short paragraph of black, descriptive text in the space reserved for the message; the space for the address is blank. Shown is an example.

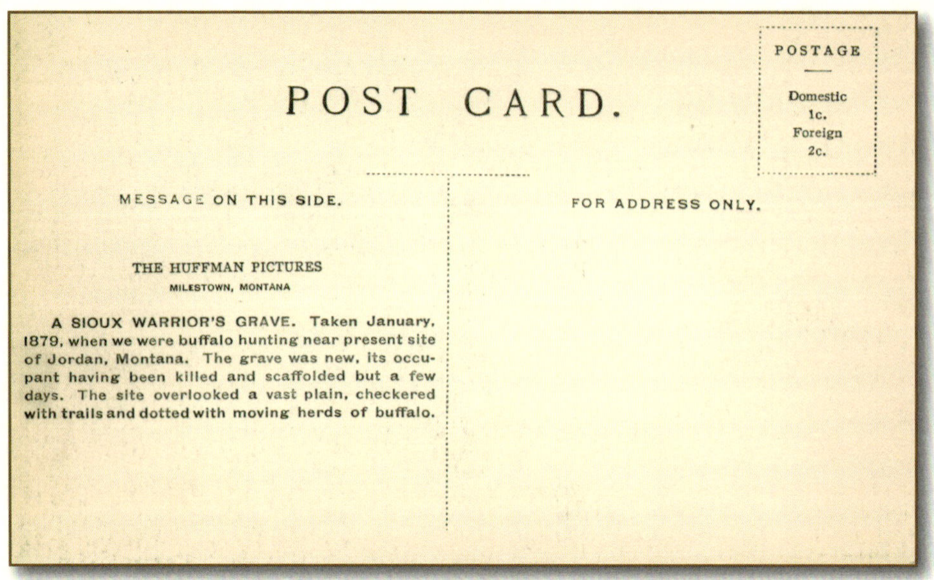

Sometime during the Coffrin Studio's tenure with the Huffman material (early 1960s–1981), Jack Coffrin used some of the original postcards to "overprint" an advertising message for his studio and The Huffman Pictures. The message is a 12-line paragraph, printed in red, in the space reserved for the address. The card was offered free and invites people to his studio "just east of the underpass" in Miles City to stop in and see the assortment of photos made from Huffman's old glass plate negatives. The distribution of these free postcards was probably limited to the Miles City area. While it is unknown how many cards carry this overprint, they are relatively common. We have seen several different images with this paragraph.

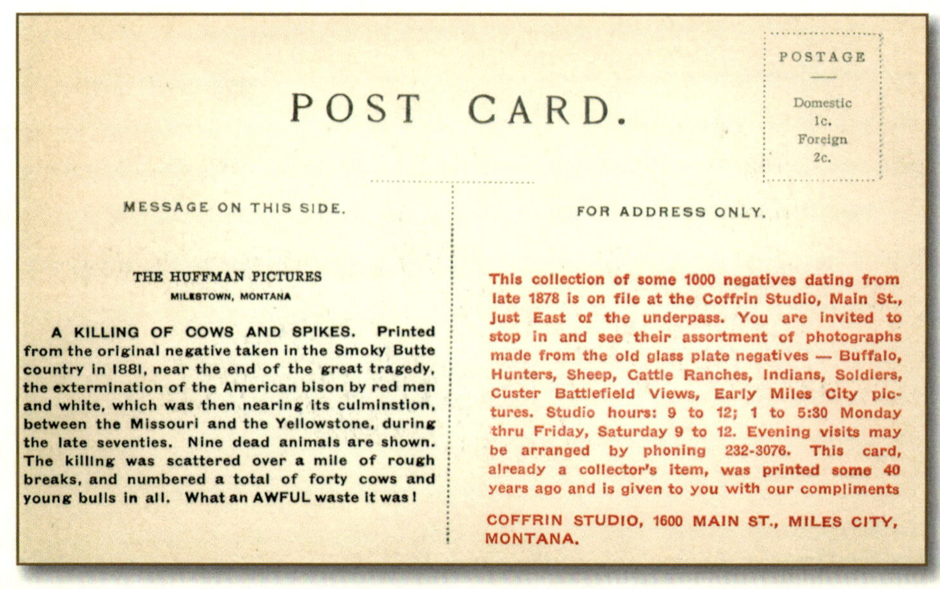

Huffman sometimes touched up or altered negatives, presumably because he thought it would improve the resulting print and make it more salable. The Campbell Art Company said "extra working of the negatives would be charged for, although we do not think this would amount to much except in the case of the 'Man Hunters' where the price of the suggested change would be $3.00." The change was made. Apparently Huffman thought the "Man Hunters" looked better in the out-of-doors than they did in the studio. Shown are both the postcard and the original photo for comparison.

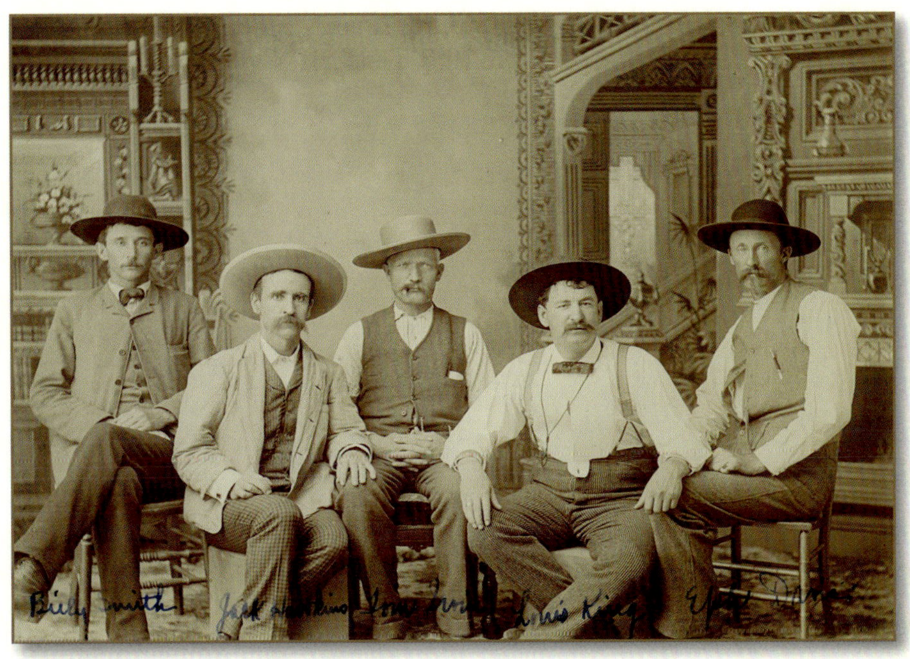

ABOVE: Original studio photo *Montana Manhunters of the Seventies.*

BELOW: *Montana Manhunters of the Seventies* postcard.

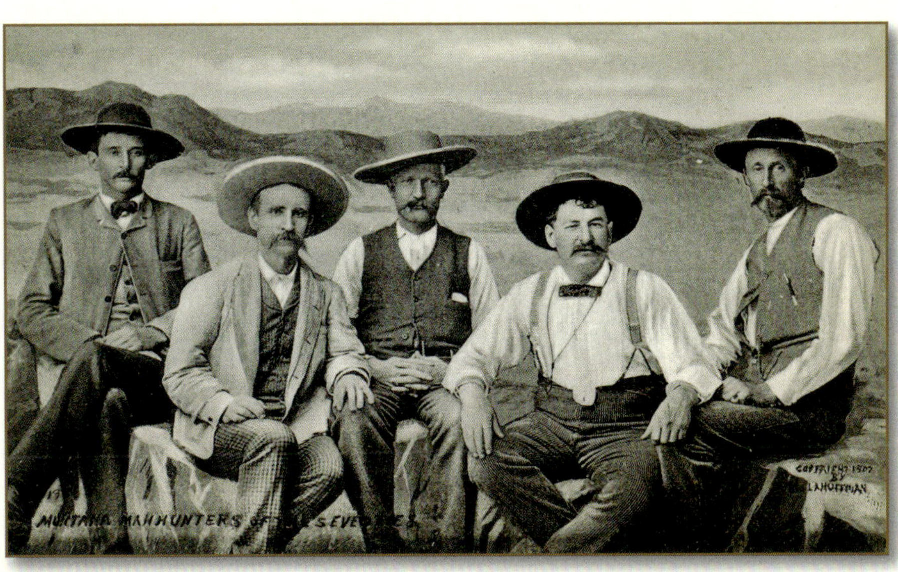

We have hand-colored examples of fourteen of the 25 images; a few of them are the only ones we have seen. All hand-colored Huffman postcards must be considered rare. While it is not possible to know for sure who colored them and when, we believe they were colored during Huffman's lifetime. We do know he was coloring collotypes as early as 1907.

The 25 images used in this series represent a good cross section of Huffman's early work. Except sheep! Not a single one. Native Americans (seven images), buffalo (six), cattle/horses/ranching (six), sheep (zip)! Domestic sheep arrived in the Miles City area before the first cattle drives and Huffman took many photos of them, some among his most artistically strong images. We can only speculate why none of them made it on his postcard list.

There is no way to know how many of these cards were sold; those actually used and postally cancelled are scarce. There was a substantial number still available during the Coffrin years and at the time of his retirement in 1981. While most of them remain moderately available, four of the buffalo images are very scarce to rare. Assembling a full set today presents a bit of a challenge.

The 1907 Postcards

Following are the 25 cards in the 1907 series.
Shown with each card is Huffman's description of the image as it appears on the back of the card. When available, a hand-colored example is also shown.

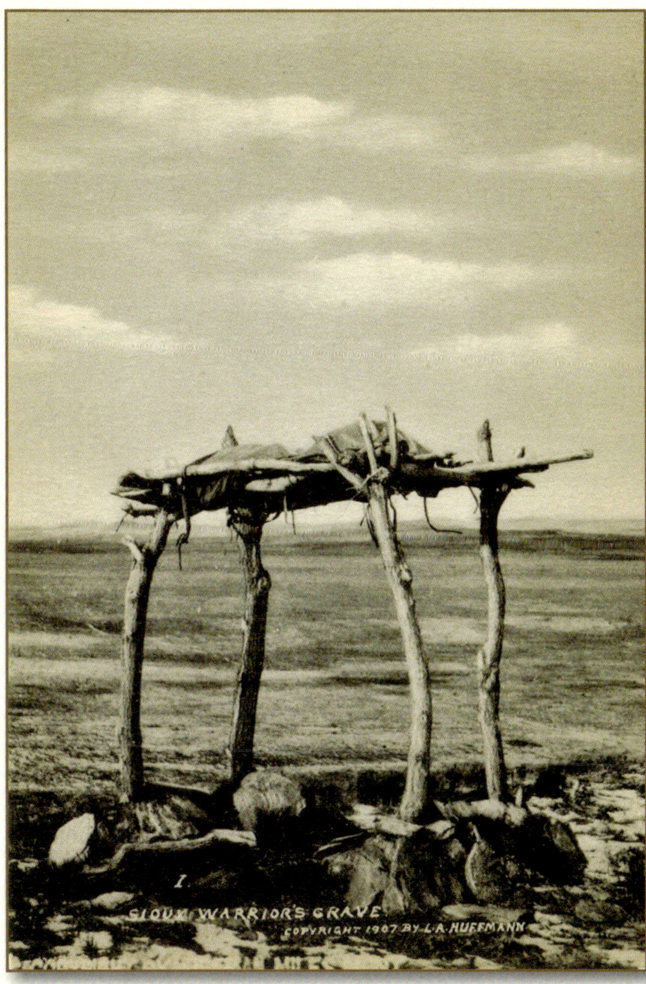

A SIOUX WARRIOR'S GRAVE. Taken January, 1879, when we were buffalo hunting near present site of Jordan, Montana. The grave was new, its occupant having been killed and scaffolded but a few days. The site overlooked a vast plain, checkered with trails and dotted with moving herds of buffalo.

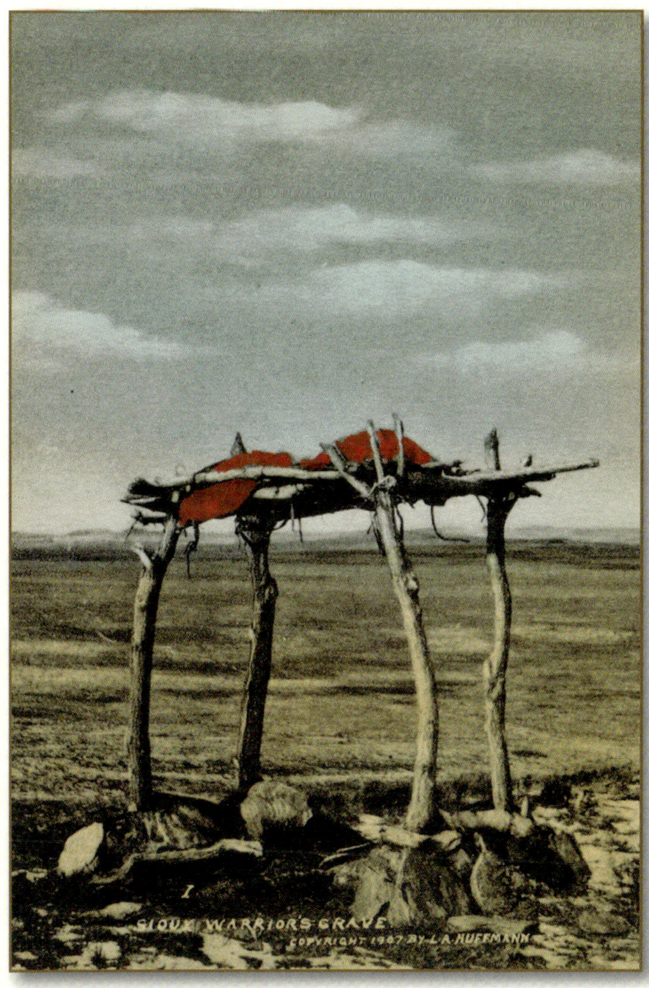

ABOVE: No. 1, *A Sioux Warrior's Grave*

RIGHT: No. 1, *A Sioux Warrior's Grave*—hand colored

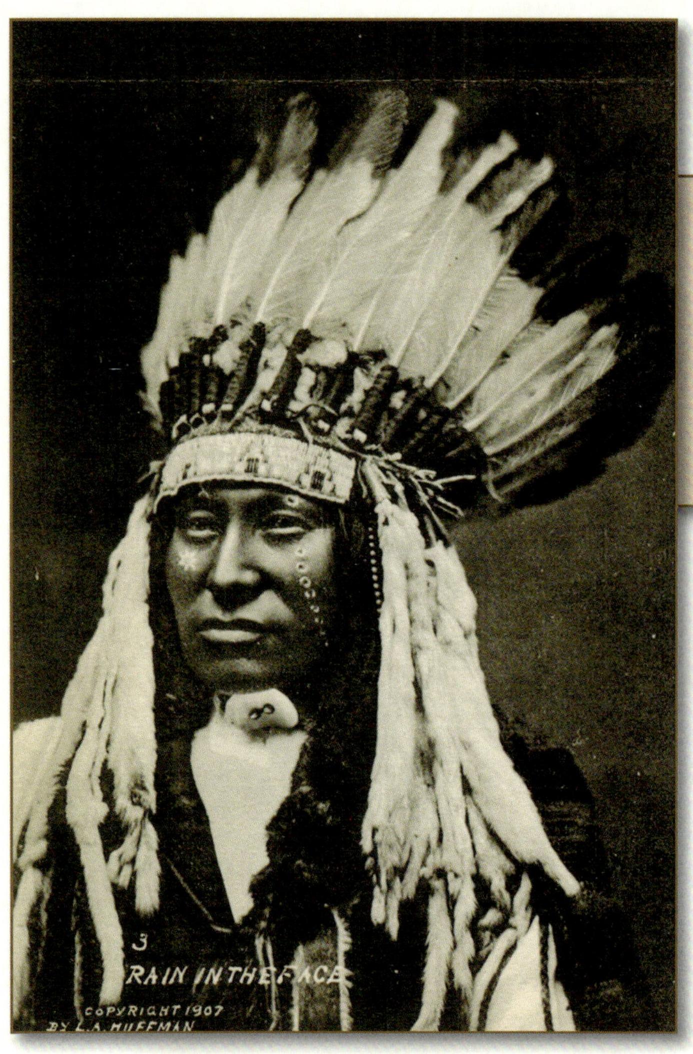

ETO-MO-GOZUA, (Rain-in-the-Face) the Uncappapa Sioux, who, Mrs. Custer in her book "Boots and Saddles" says, cut out Tom Custer's heart upon the Little Big Horn Battlefield in 1876. Rain-in-the-Face was wounded, lame and in sore distress in the winter of 1880. living in a tepee with the Spotted Eagle band, near Fort Keogh, Montana. I went in with an interpreter and brought him out and made this photograph, I think in the month of February of that year. The story of Rain-in-the-Face is well worth reading.

LEFT: No. 3, *Rain-in-the-Face*

BELOW: No. 4, *A Killing of Elk, 1875*

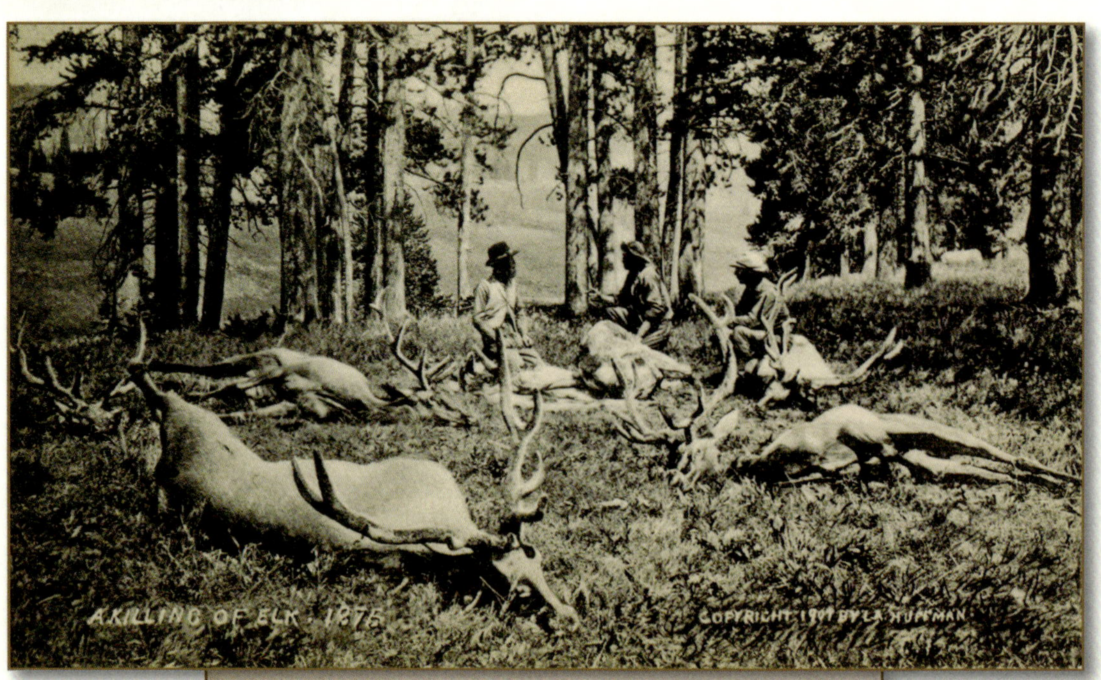

A KILLING OF ELK IN THE VELVET, 1875. There are still many thousands of elk in Montana, but they are no longer permitted to be slaughtered for their skins, as at the time this photograph was taken.

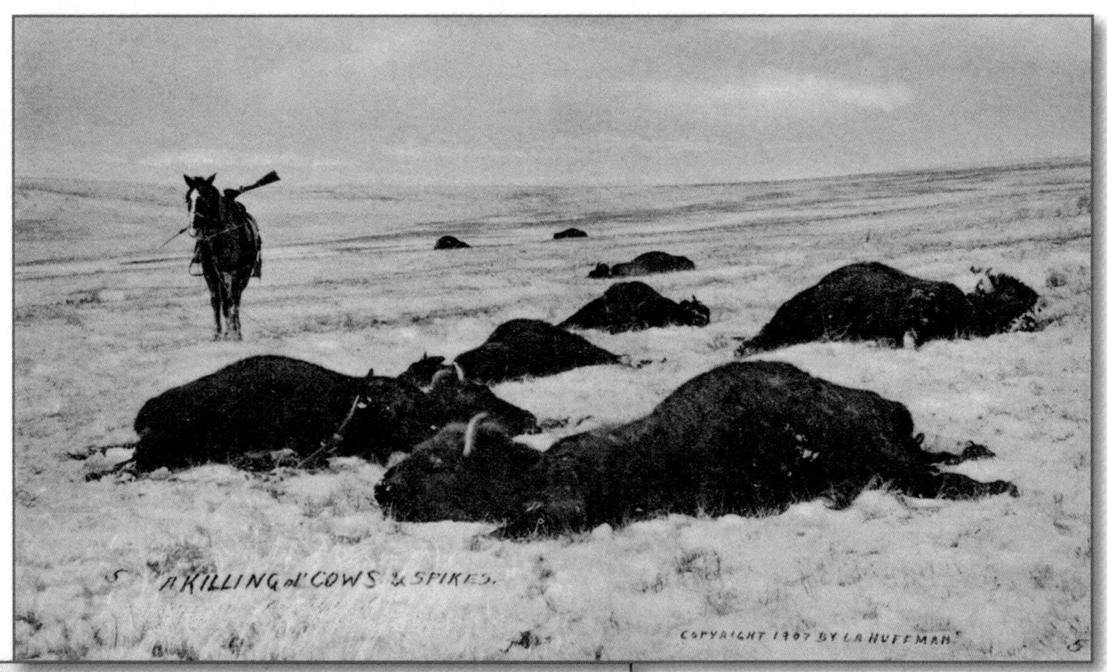

A KILLING OF COWS AND SPIKES. Printed from the original negative taken in the Smoky Butte country in 1881, near the end of the great tragedy, the extermination of the American bison by red men and white, which was then nearing its culmination, between the Missouri and the Yellowstone, during the late seventies. Nine dead animals are shown. The killing was scattered over a mile of rough breaks, and numbered a total of forty cows and young bulls in all. What an AWFUL waste it was!

ABOVE: No. 5, *A Killing of Cows and Spikes*
BELOW: No. 6, *A Cut Horse at Work*

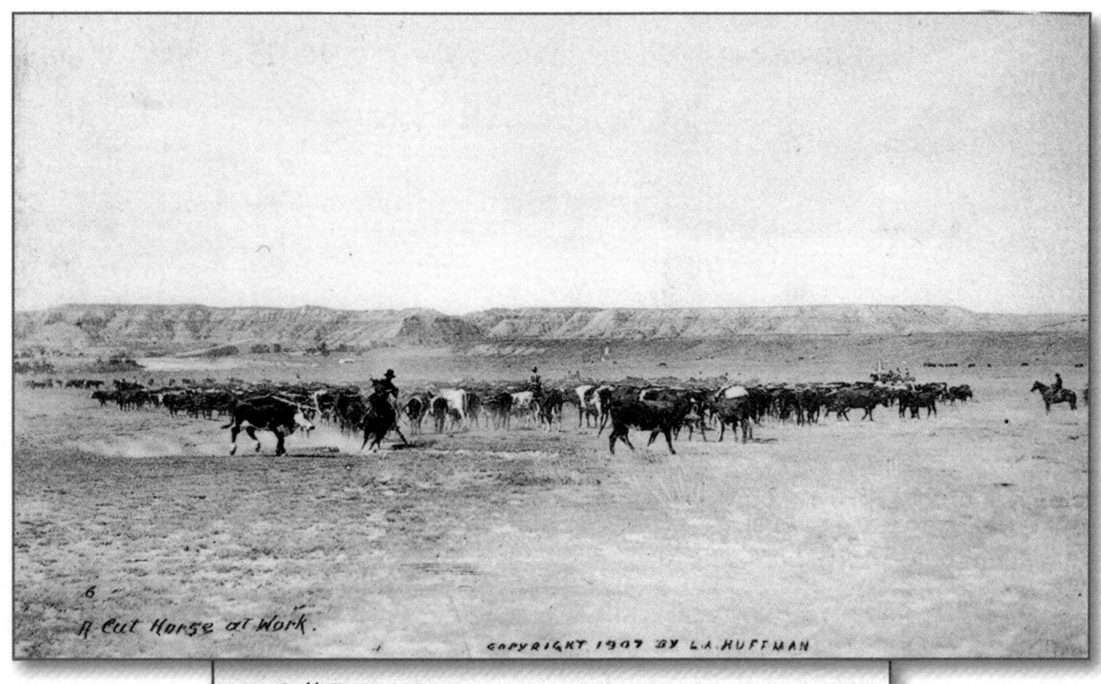

A "CUT HORSE" AT WORK. Every cowboy has six to ten saddle horses in his string. The little black is cutting the lop-horned steer from his family, in the round-up. Only a quick, wise, fresh horse can frustrate a fleet-footed wild steer's doubling and dodging.

THE OLD CATHOLIC MISSION, Tongue River, Montana, near Ashland, on Otter Creek. This is one of the old time Catholic missions, now rapidly falling to decay.

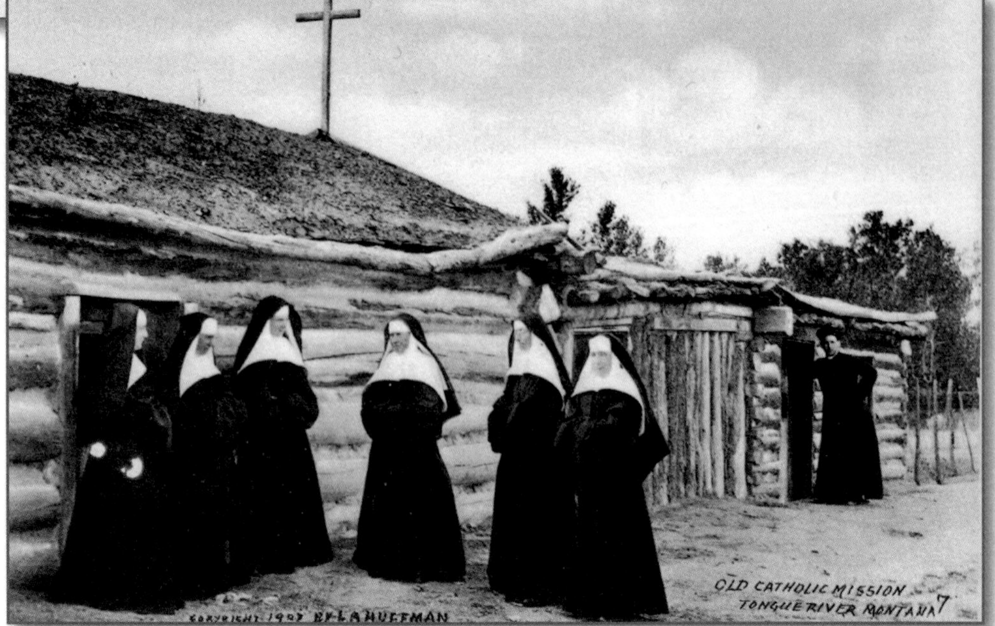

RIGHT: No. 7, *Old Catholic Mission, Tongue River Montana*

BELOW: No. 8, *After the Chase*

BELOW RIGHT: No. 9, *Killing of Cows and Spikes*

AFTER THE CHASE. Showing two old stump-horn bulls, the skinning wedge and our saddle ponies. I made this picture in the Smoky Butte country, between the Yellowstone and Missouri, in 1880 or 1881.

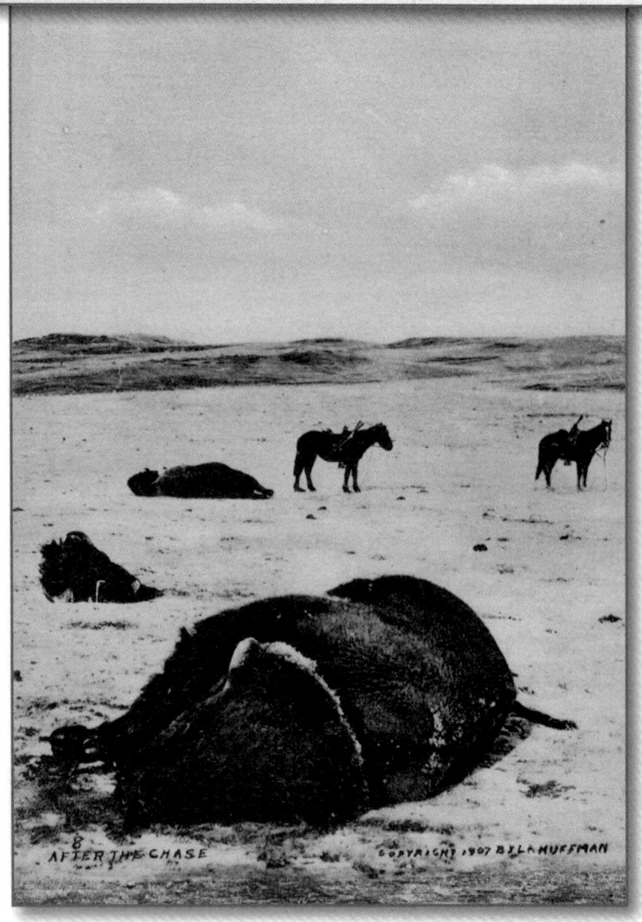

A KILLING OF COWS AND SPIKES IN THE SMOKY BUTTE COUNTRY, between the Missouri and the Yellowstone in 1881, while the skinners were at work taking the robes and tongues only. What an AWFUL waste it was, of life and man-energy!

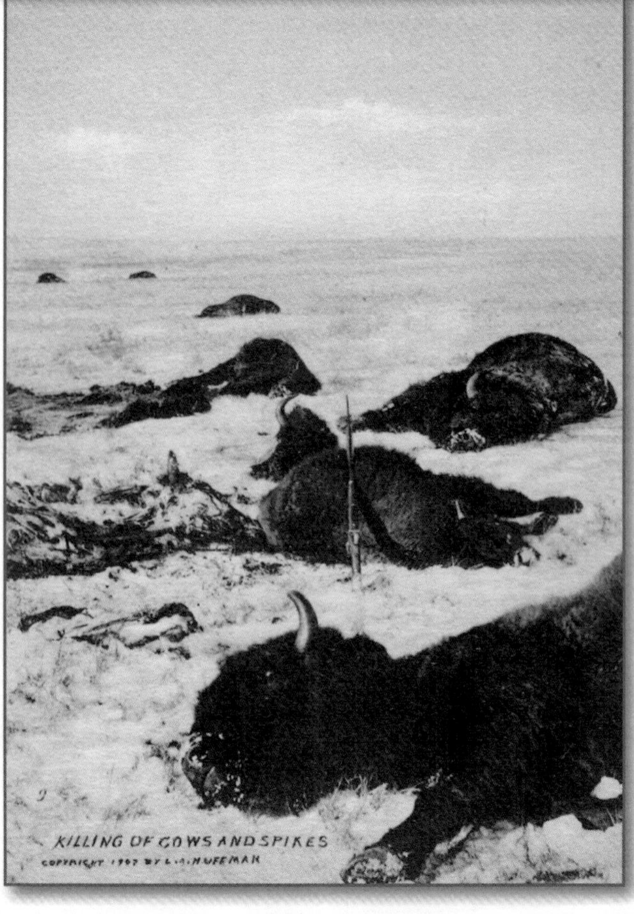

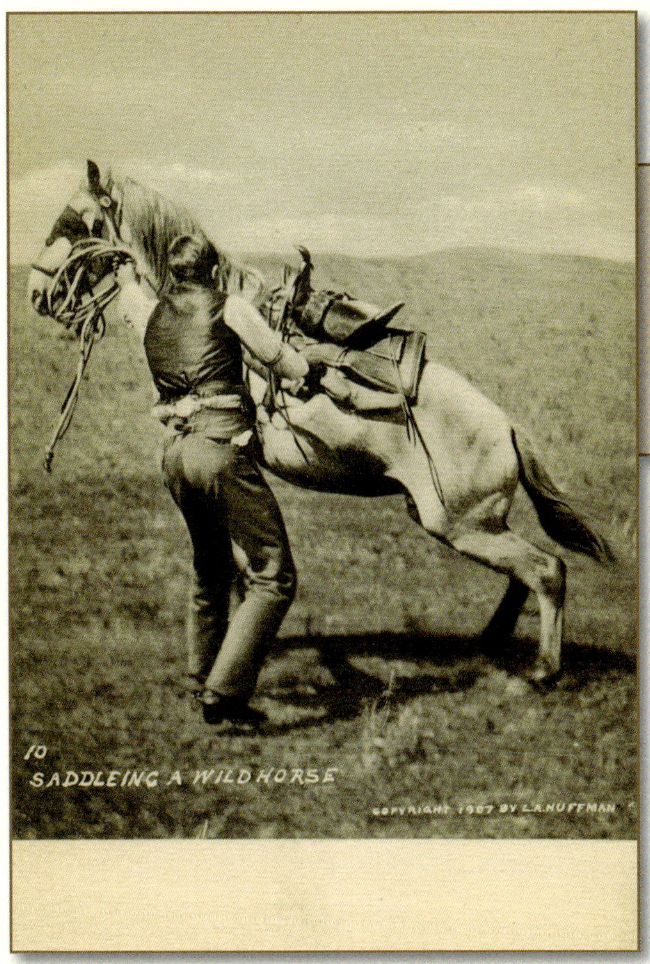

SADDLING A WILD HORSE. There are many ways of accomplishing this feat. The cowboy in this picture, a professional broncho-buster, proceeded to rope, blindfold and bridle the gray horse, then took him outside the corral at my request, and flung on the saddle, holding the horse by the bridle and hackamore. The picture I made just at the instant when he gave the first pull at the latigo, cinching the saddle.

ABOVE: No. 10, *Saddleing a Wild Horse*

RIGHT: No. 10, *Saddleing a Wild Horse*—hand colored

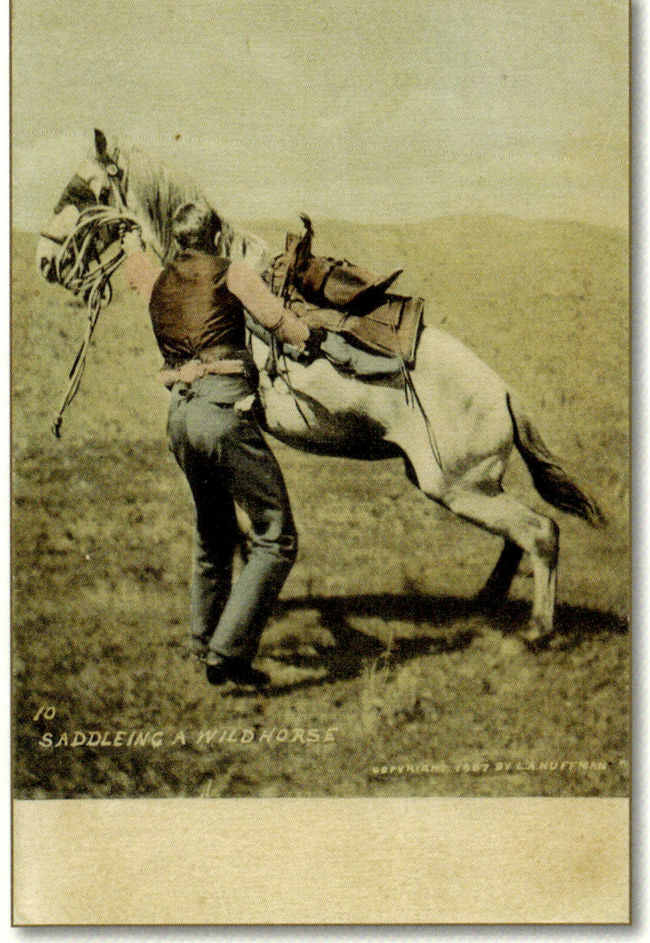

A PROFESSIONAL WOLFER'S "ROOST" IN THE HELL CREEK BREAKS OF NORTHERN MONTANA. Wolfers live a lonely life. Some of them are educated men and tidy house-keepers. A wolfer destroys wolves for the bounty paid by the state, the pelts sold to fur dealers, and ofttimes for an additional fee from nearby cattle men.

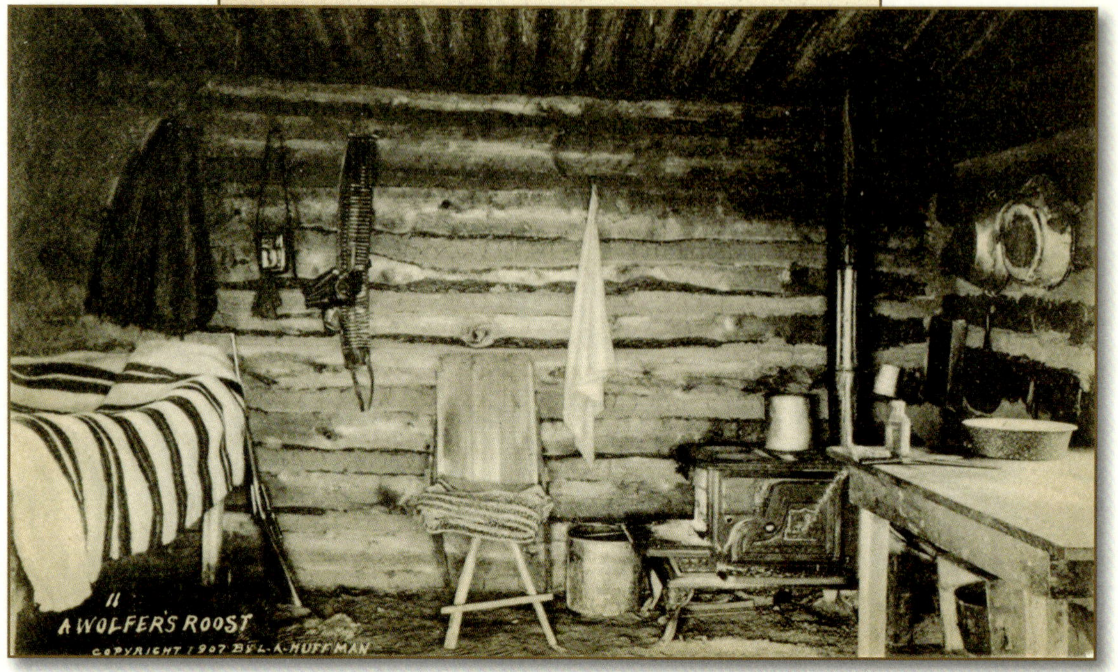

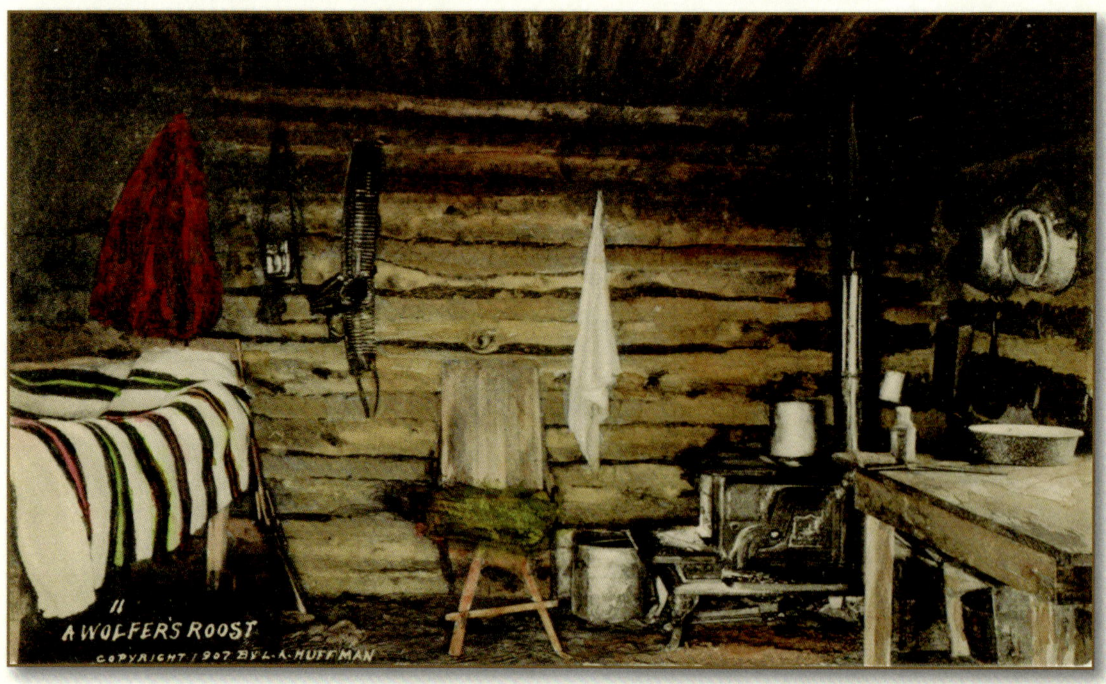

ABOVE: No. 11, *A Wolfer's Roost*—hand colored

TOP: No. 11, *A Wolfer's Roost*

THE DESERTED CAMP. A relic of the buffalo days. This old camp I knew when it was built, in the late seventies. The hill at the back of it was the hunter's lookout, from which he located the migrating herds of buffalo and planned his day's work. The spring had failed years before. Thrifty young pines and cedars grew in the path the hide hunters had made so long ago.

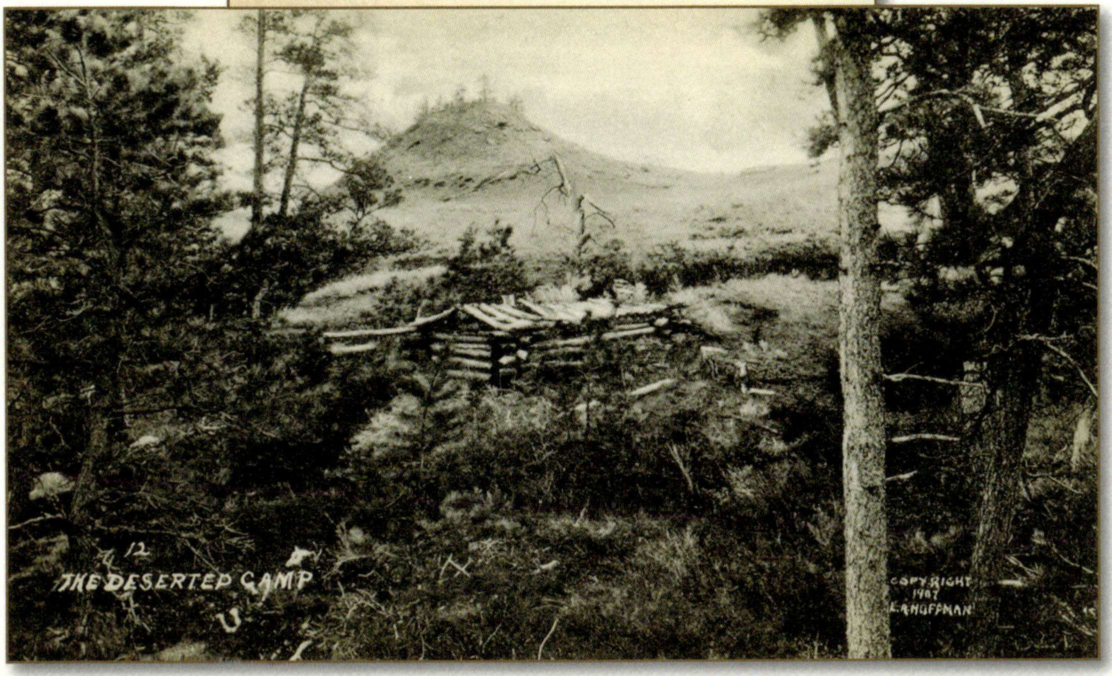

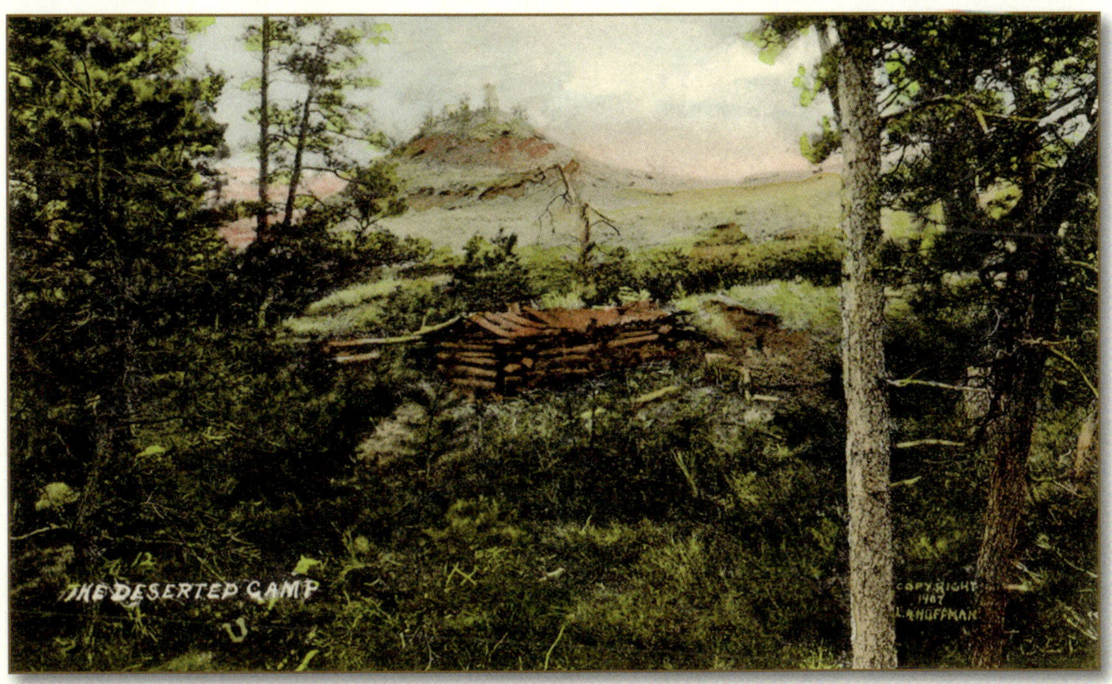

ABOVE: No. 12, *The Deserted Camp*—hand colored

TOP: No. 12, *The Deserted Camp*

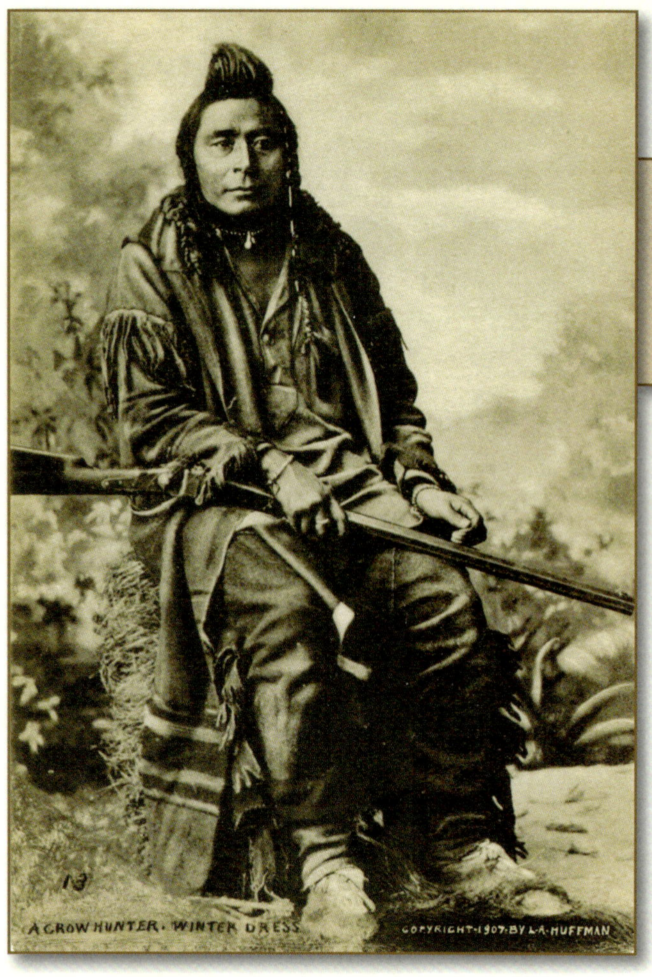

A CROW HUNTER, WINTER DRESS. I made this picture at Fort Keogh, Montana, in 1879 or 1880, when a large band of Crows were hunting, trading, racing horses and bartering buffalo skins and their women with the white hunters and rivermen wintering near Fort Keogh. The pompadour foretop is peculiar to the Crow Indians.

ABOVE: No. 13, *A Crow Hunter, Winter Dress*

RIGHT: No. 13, *A Crow Hunter, Winter Dress*—hand colored

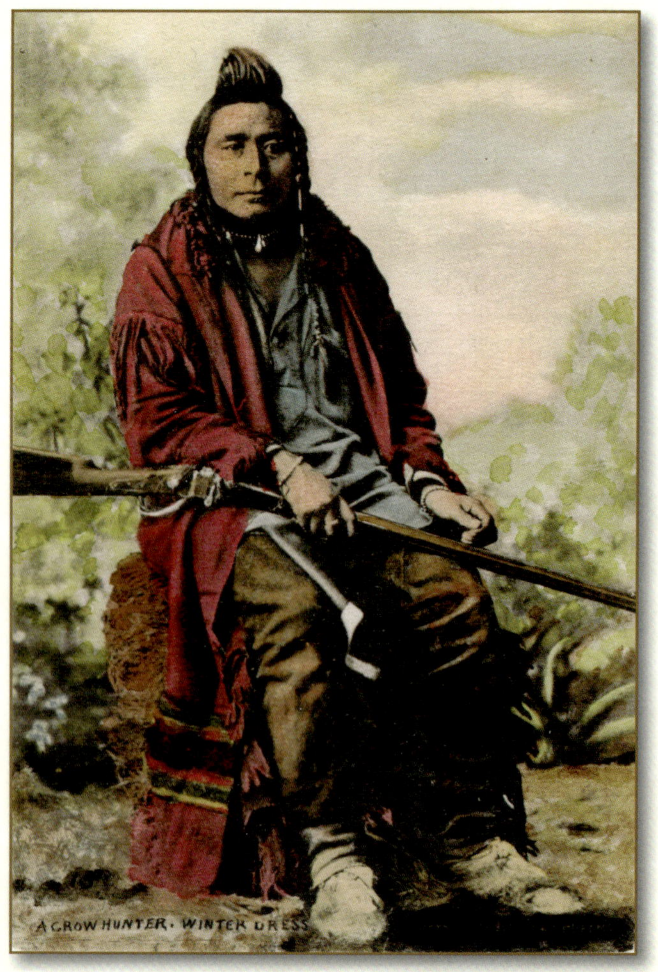

MRS. BAD GUN, A CHEYENNE GROS-VENTRE SQUAW. This woman got her strange name during the late seventies by having killed, with an old Winchester, four Indians who had murdered her husband. She was tried and promptly acquitted.

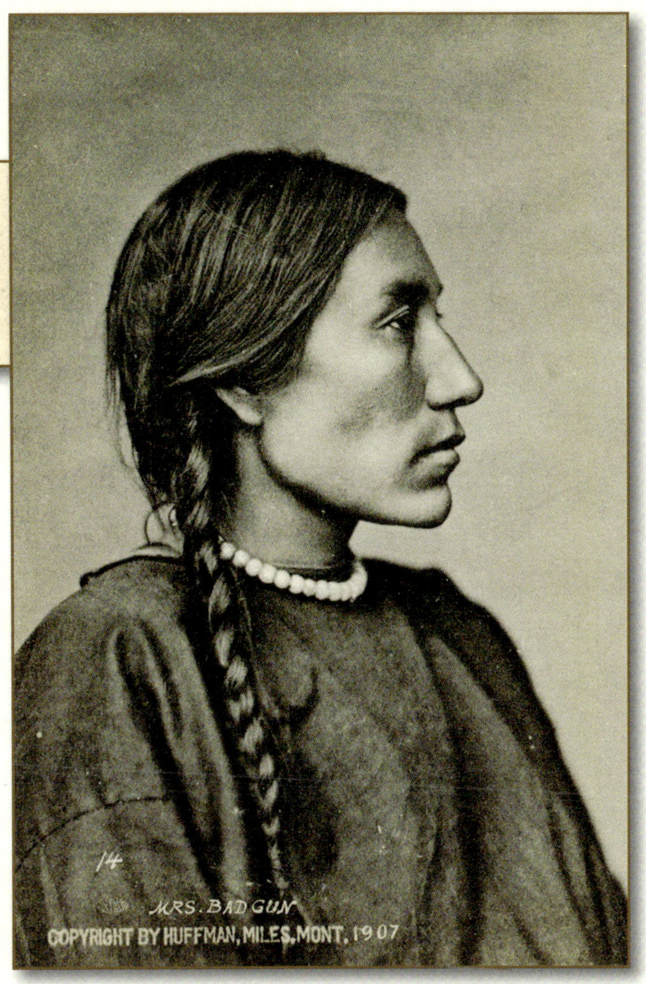

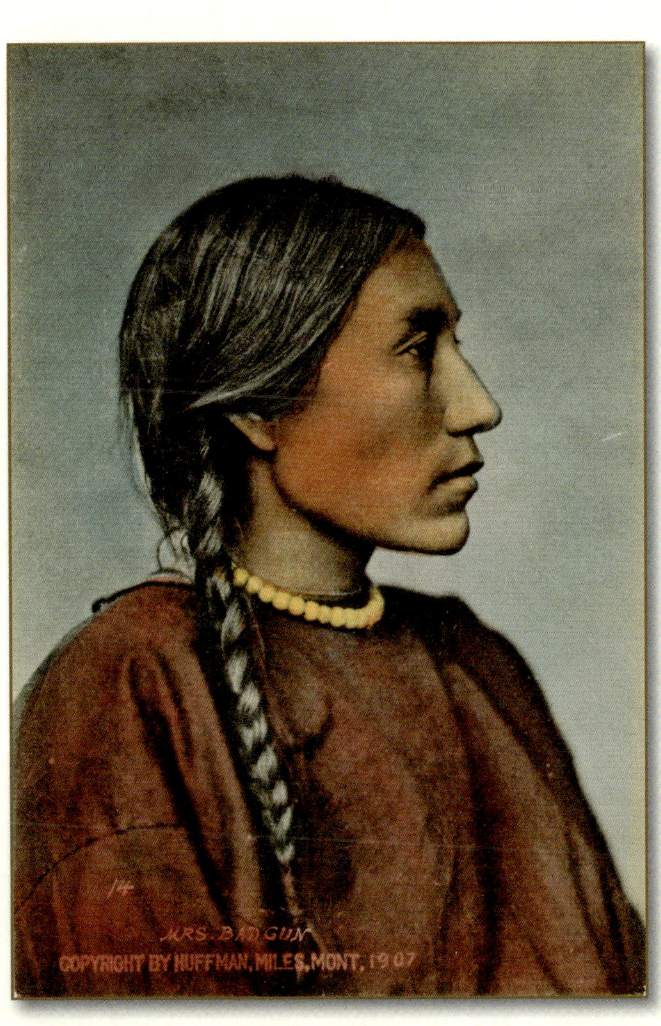

ABOVE: No. 14, *Mrs. Bad Gun*

LEFT: No. 14, *Mrs. Bad Gun*—hand colored

A FIERCE OLD CROW BUCK, named Good Eye. Photographed in my old log studio at Fort Keogh, in 1880.

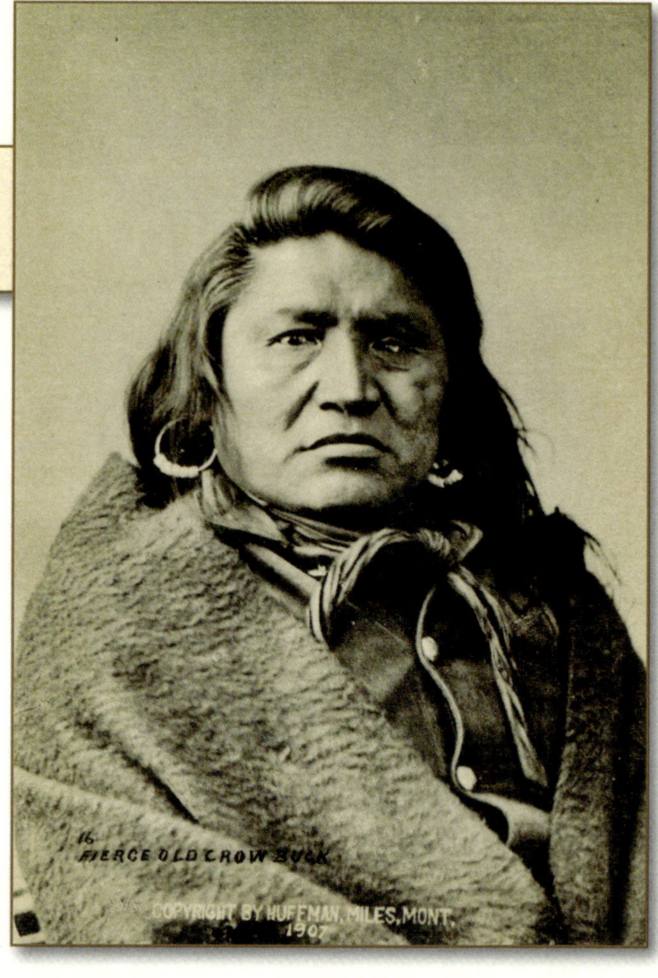

ABOVE: No. 16, *Fierce Old Crow Buck*

LEFT: No. 16, *Fierce Old Crow Buck*—hand colored

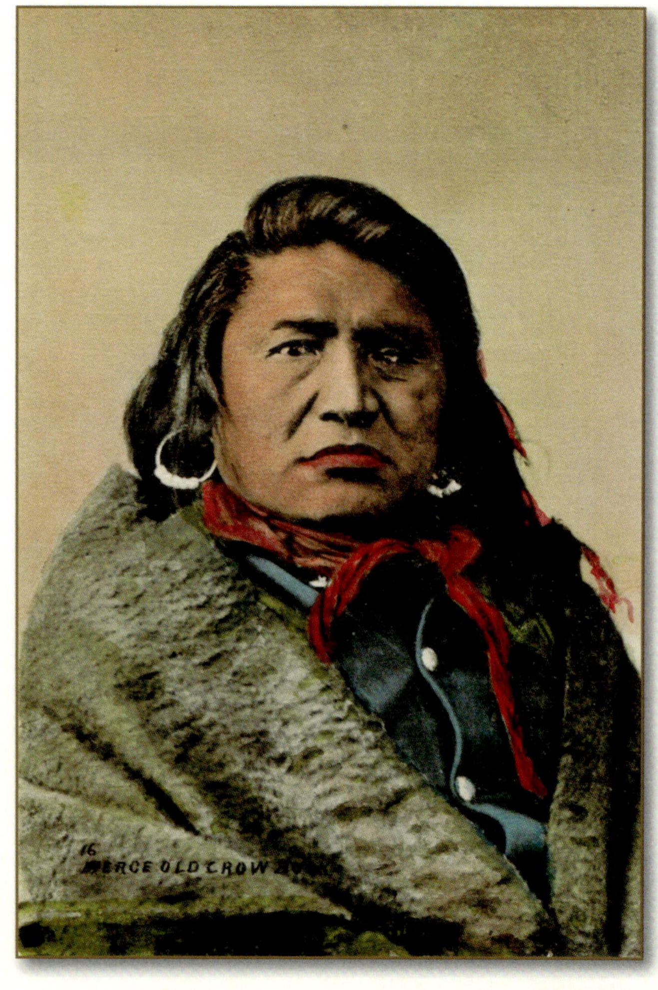

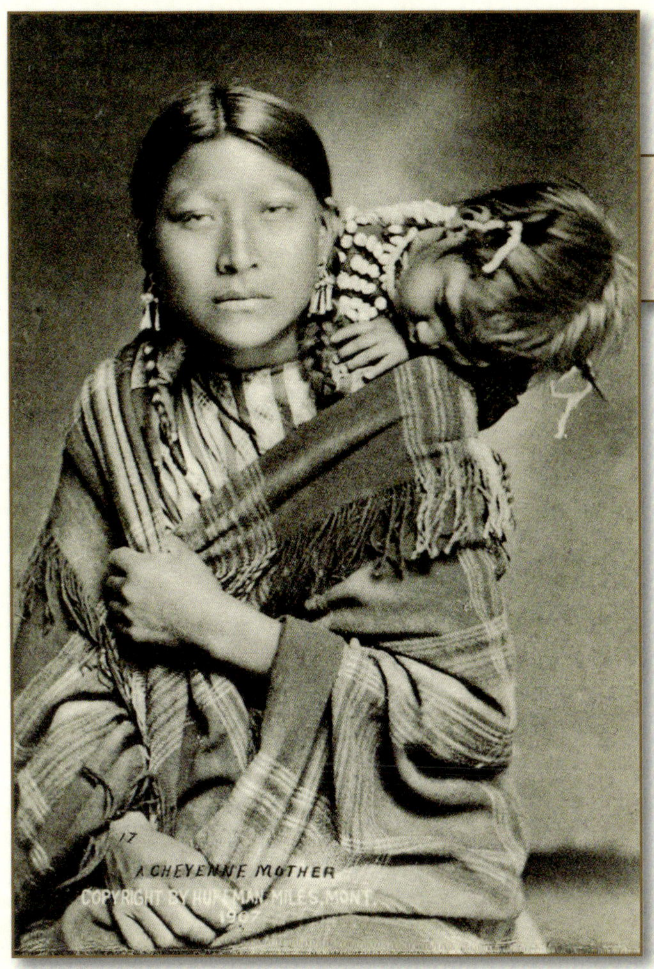

A CHEYENNE MOTHER AND PAPOOSE ASLEEP ON HER BACK. The agency of the Northern Cheyennes is 60 miles southwest of Milestown, Montana.

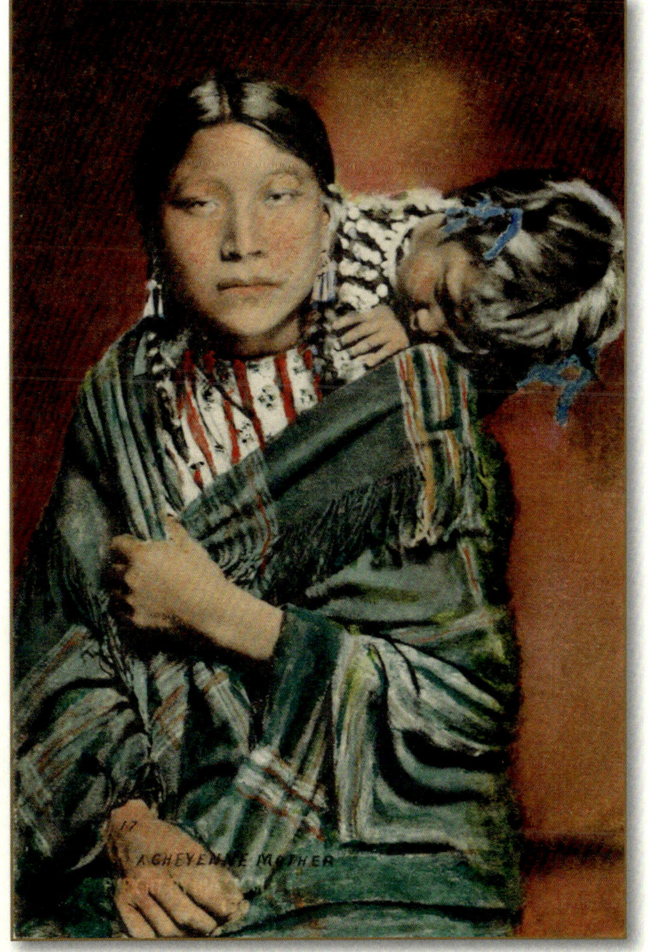

ABOVE: No. 17, *A Cheyenne Mother*

RIGHT: No. 17, *A Cheyenne Mother*—hand colored

MRS. WHITE ELK is a pure type of Cheyenne women of the better class; shy, graceful and modest. The Cheyennes, both men and women, were the purest, most savage, bravest red people of the plains and had kept their blood the purest of any Indians. I gave her a ring for posing.

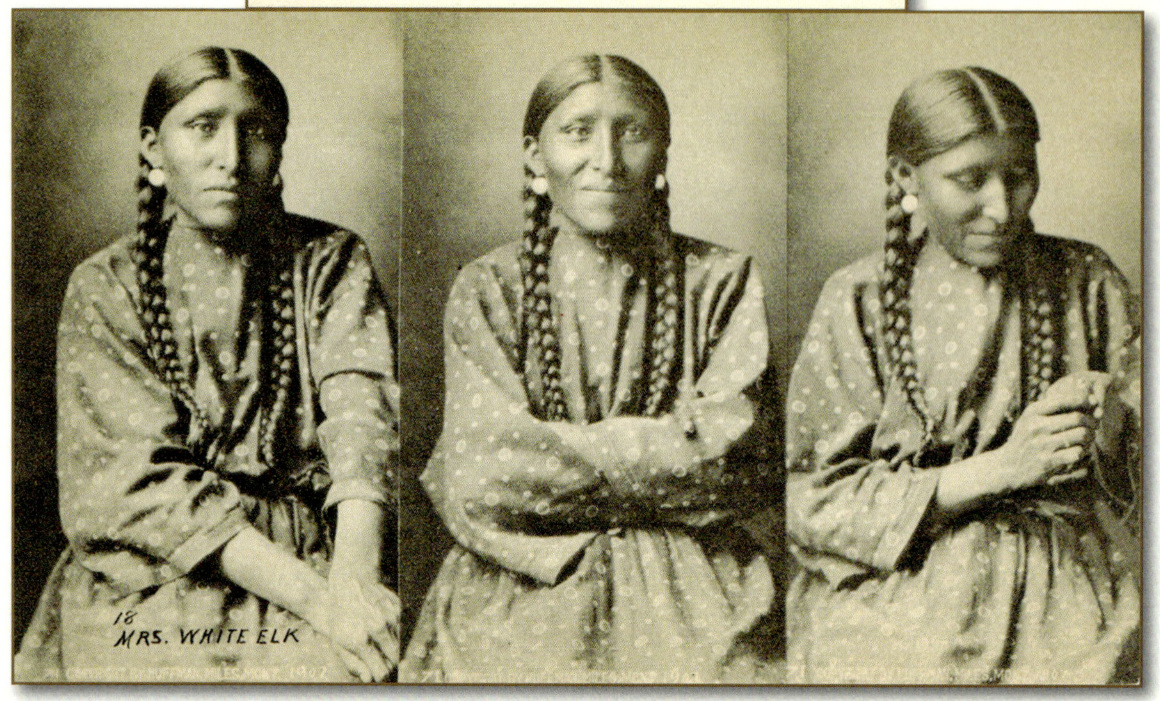

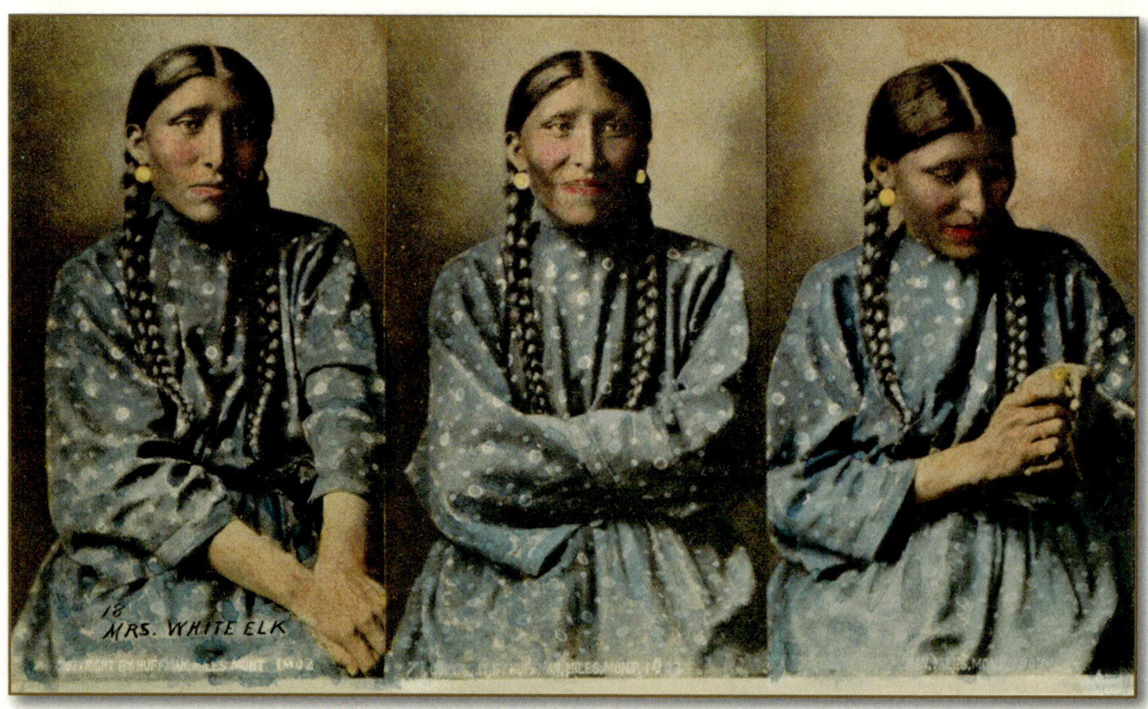

ABOVE: No. 18, *Mrs. White Elk*—hand colored

TOP: No. 18, *Mrs. White Elk*

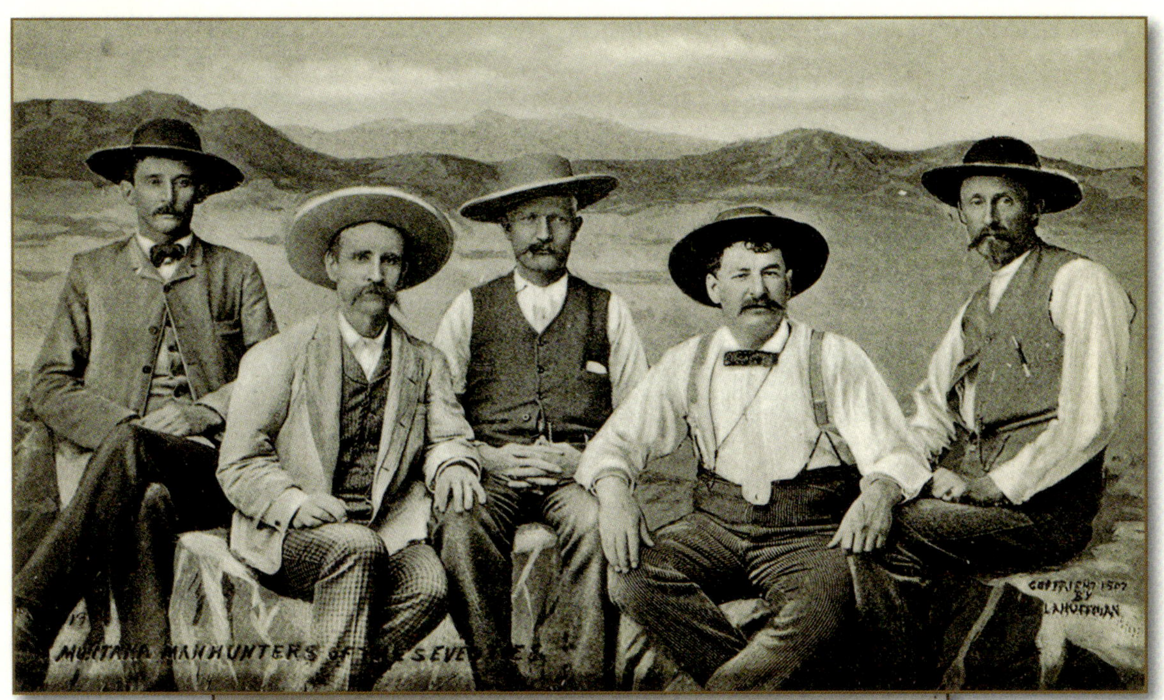

MONTANA MAN-HUNTERS OF THE SEVENTIES, before the railroad came. T. H. Irvine. now living in Alaska, was one of the old time sheriffs of Montana. The man at his right got his early education man-hunting with the Texas Rangers. He still lives in Milestown, Montana. At this writing only one of the five has passed in his checks. These men could write interesting stories, but are not built that way, they were men of action. They do not belong to our time and are soon to pass. Taken at Milestown in the early eighties.

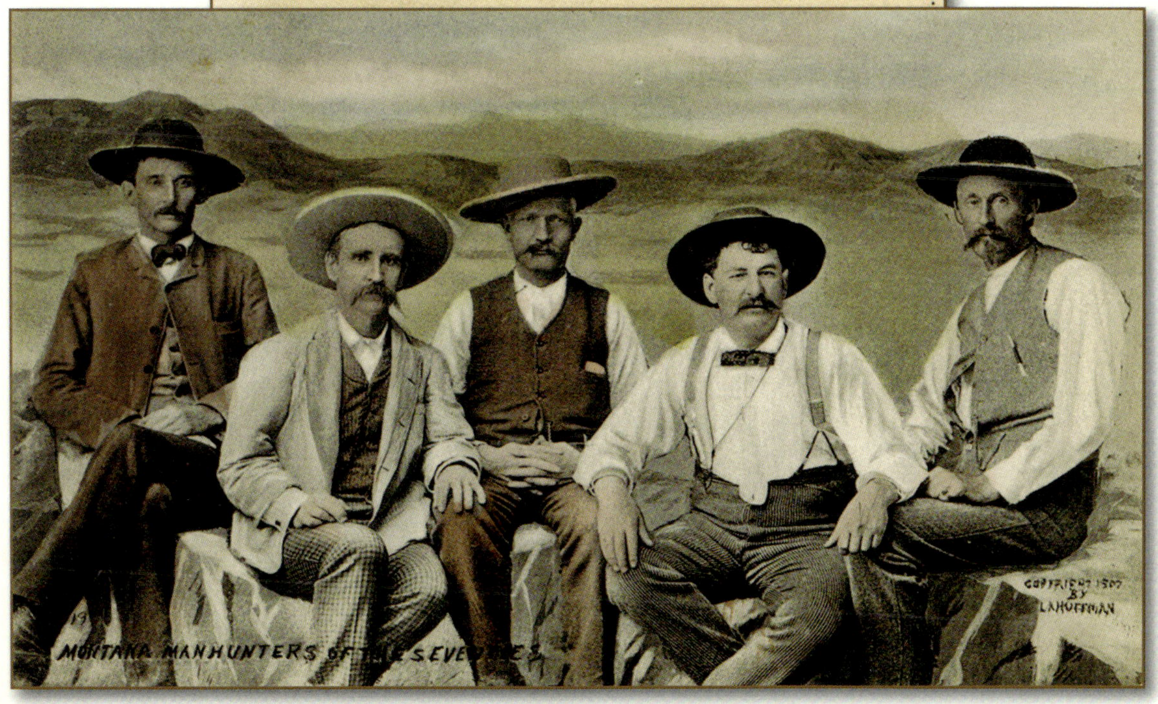

ABOVE: No. 19, *Montana Manhunters of the Seventies*—hand colored

TOP: No. 19, *Montana Manhunters of the Seventies*

PRETTY BIRD, a handsome young Cheyenne. He is going to take a sweat. His wife has placed inside this lodge some hot stones. A little later she will cover Mr. Bird's lodge with robes and blankets and pass him in a gourd of water, which he will sprinkle upon the hot stones, until he has had his Turkish bath, when he will duck out and take a souse in the creek and be rid of his ailments.

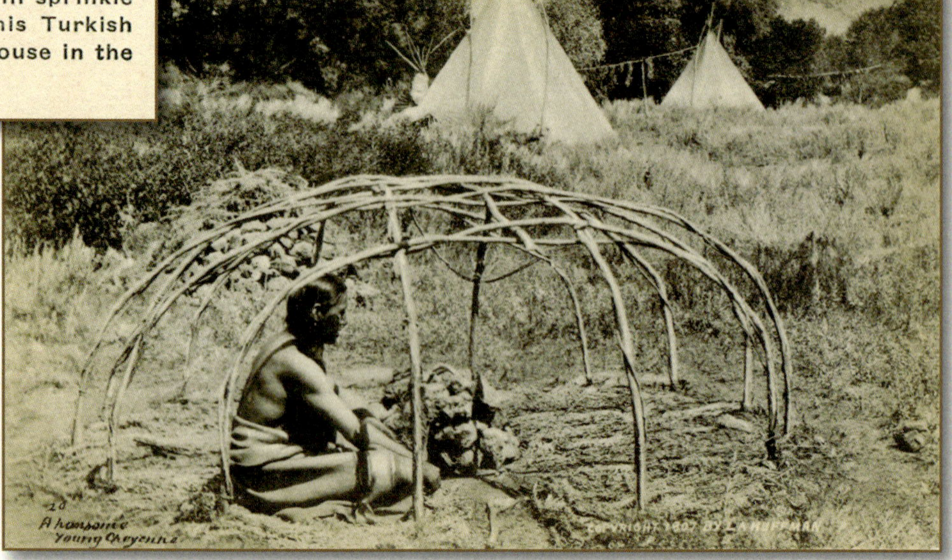

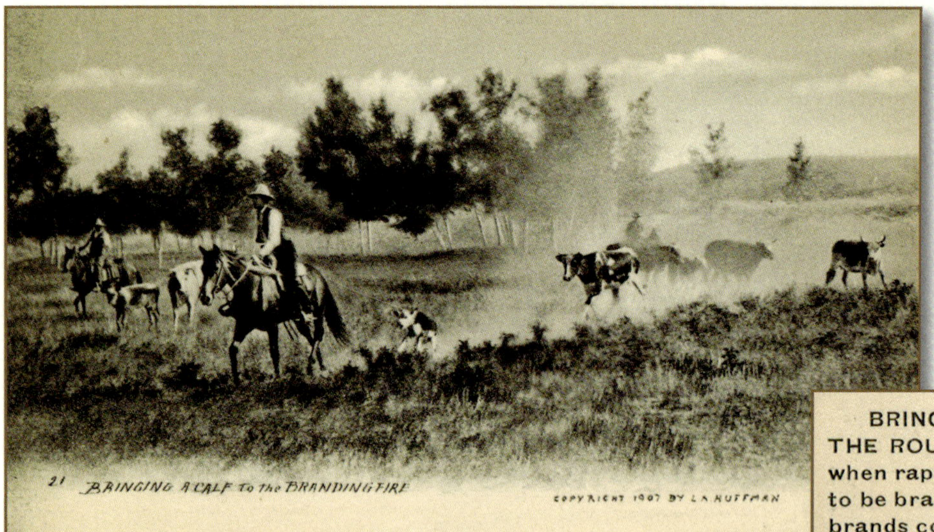

ABOVE: No. 20, *A Hansome Young Cheyenne*

LEFT: No. 21, *Bringing a Calf to the Branding Fire*

BOTTOM: No. 21, *Bringing a Calf to the Branding Fire*—hand colored

BRINGING A CALF TO THE BRANDING FIRE AT THE ROUND UP. This shows how the cowboys tell, when rapidly roping the calves where hundreds are to be branded, which mark, of the many marks and brands congregated in the round up, belongs to each particular calf, as he comes bucking and bellowing toward the fire at the end of the lariat. The cow, hearing her baby's bleat, dashes madly to the rescue.

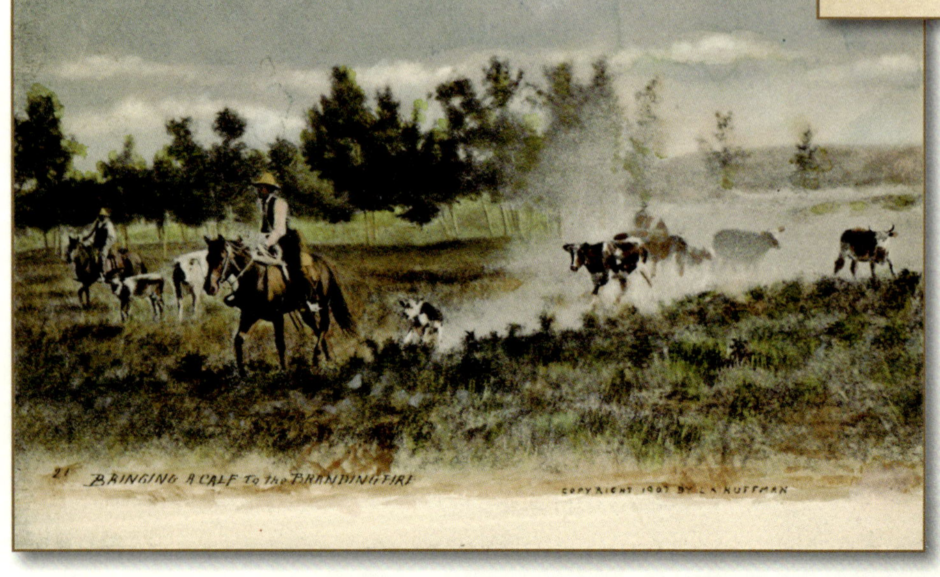

A BUFFALO FAMILY. A bull, cow and two yearlings, reproduced from the original wet plate negative, by yours truly,

L. A. HUFFMAN

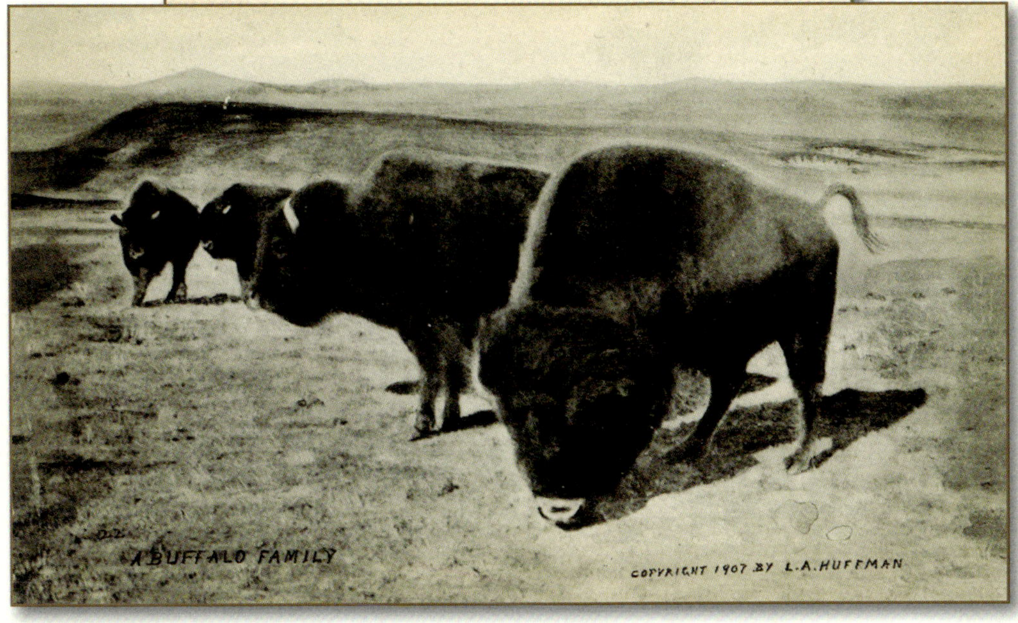

ABOVE: No. 22, *A Buffalo Family*

BELOW: No. 23, *An Old Time Tail Holt*

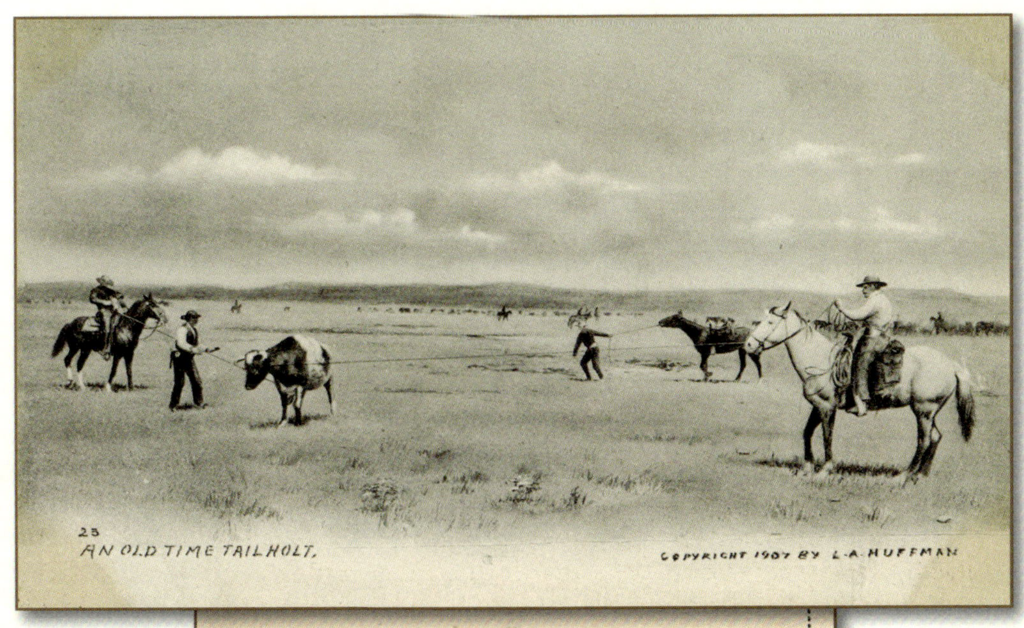

AN OLD TIME "TAIL HOLT" AT THE ROUND UP ON BIG POWDER RIVER, MONTANA. The man on the right has roped the steer by the neck; the man at the left by its hind foot. Old Andy Campbell, known to the cattle business of the early eighties, is about to "tail" the steer and throw him on his side, which he easily did, the two lariats keeping him taut.

A RELIC OF THE SEVENTIES, near Miles City, Montana. These old time dirt roofed cabins, that sheltered the pioneer, are rapidly passing away. This was the old Bender ranch and is about to be replaced by a modern house, costing many thousands of dollars.

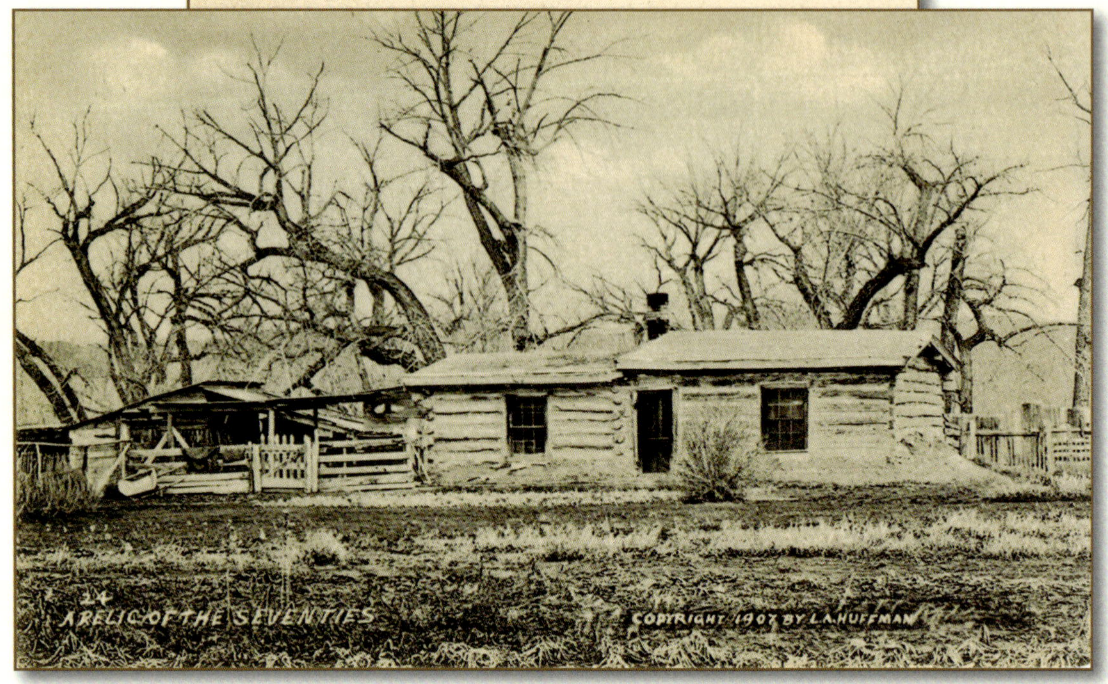

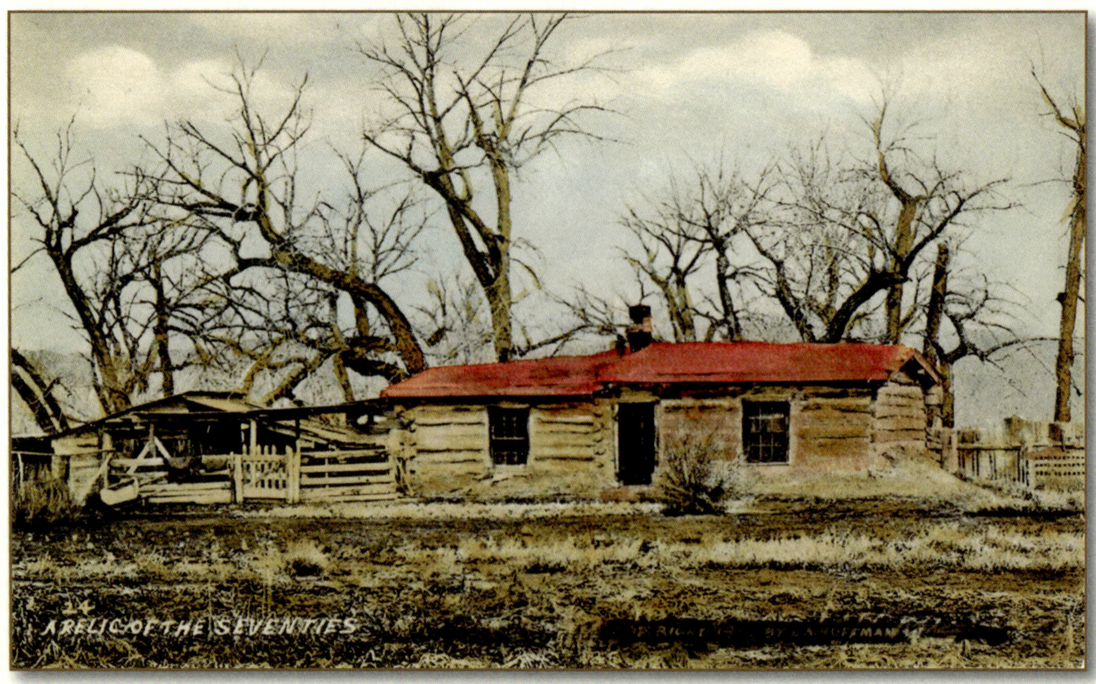

ABOVE: No. 24, *A Relic of the Seventies*—hand colored

TOP: No. 24, *A Relic of the Seventies*

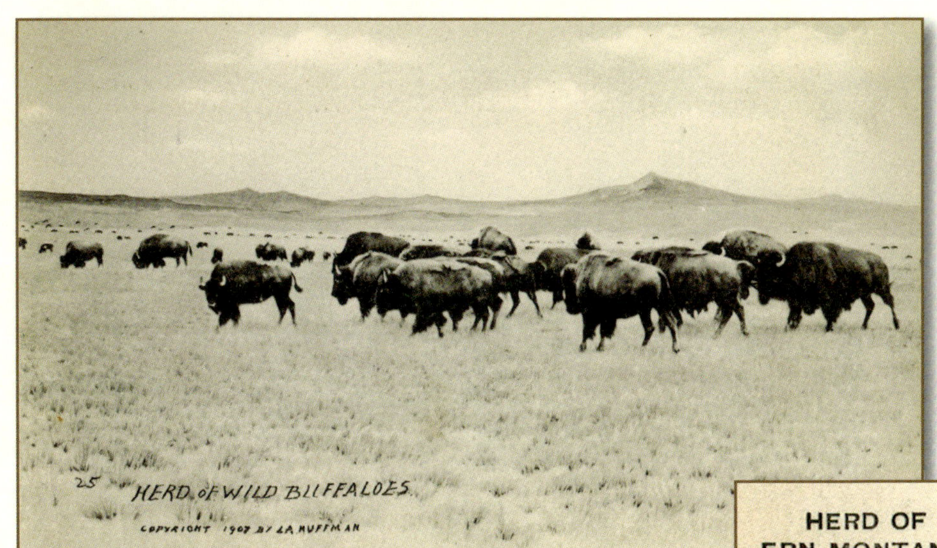

HERD OF WILD BUFFALOES ON THE NORTHERN MONTANA PRAIRIES. In the eighties it was still possible to see herds of six hundred to one thousand buffalo in many of the smaller valleys or on the high plateaus, between the Yellowstone and MIssouri Rivers.

FIFTEEN WILD BUFFALOES (count them), quietly grazing on the prairies of Northern Montana. Photographed in the early eighties.

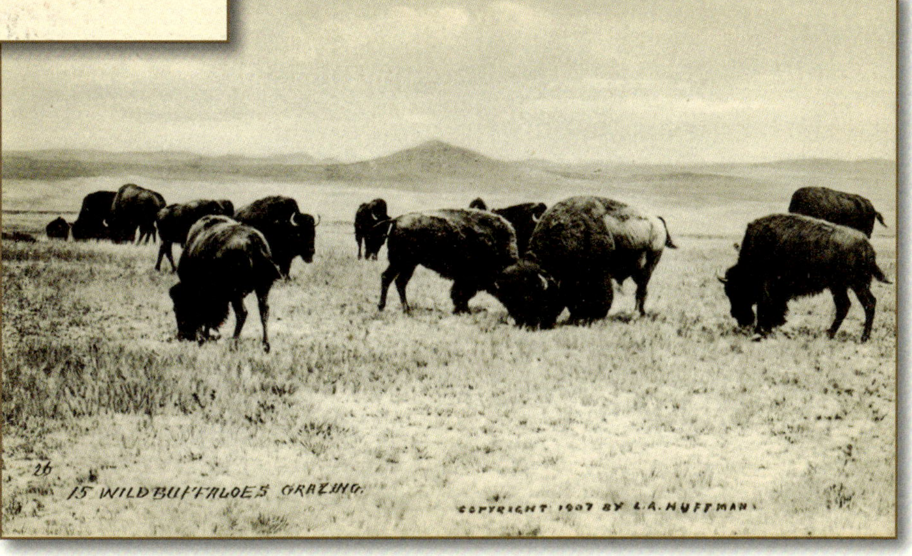

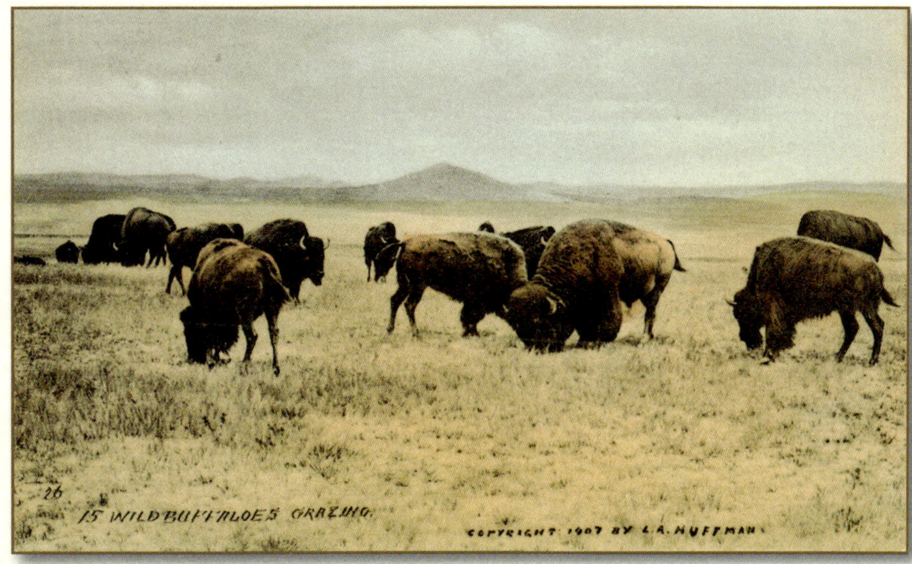

TOP: No. 25, *Herd of Wild Buffaloes*

MIDDLE RIGHT: No. 26, *15 Wild Buffaloes Grazing*

RIGHT: No. 26, *15 Wild Buffaloes Grazing*—hand colored

A HOT NOON AT THE ROUND UP, on the lower Big Dry Hat X Camp, Northern Montana. The saddle horses when turned loose come to the water, drink, roll and cool off. (See Scribner's Magazine, July, 1907.)

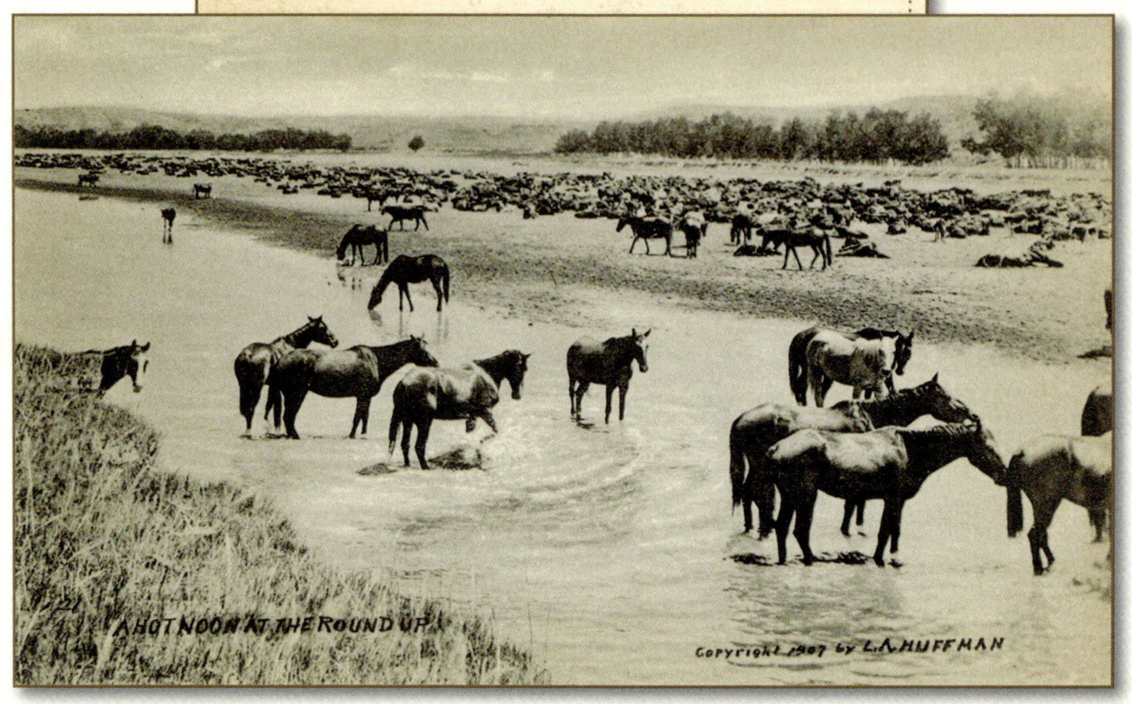

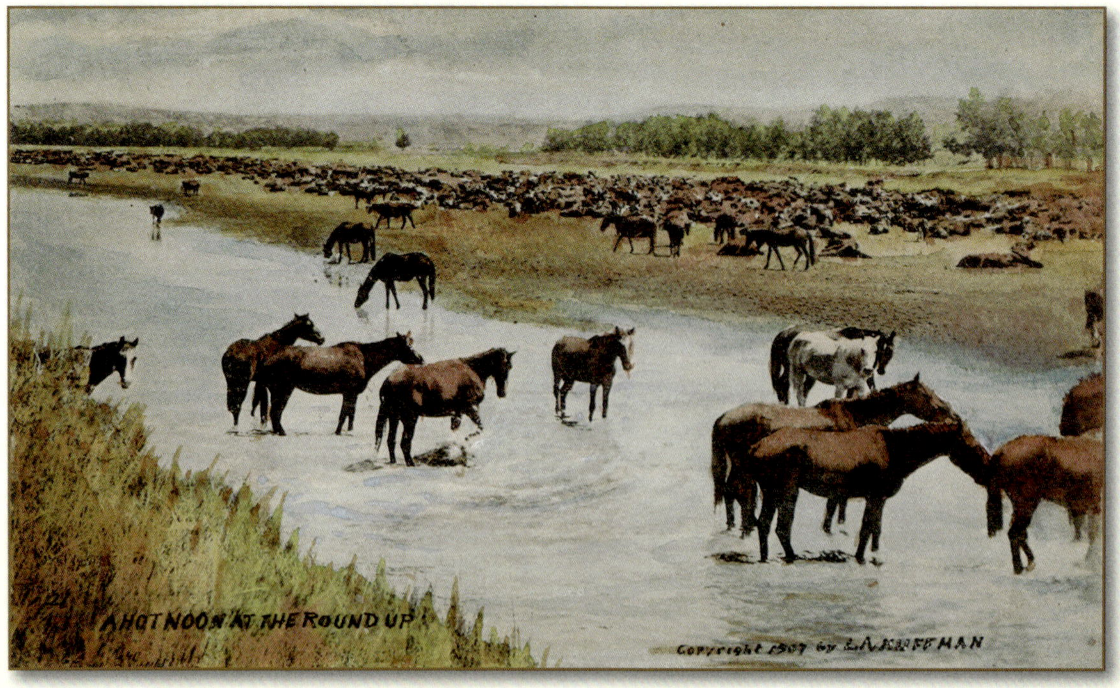

ABOVE: No. 27, *A Hot Noon at the Round Up*—hand colored

TOP: No. 27, *A Hot Noon at the Round Up*

1907 Notes

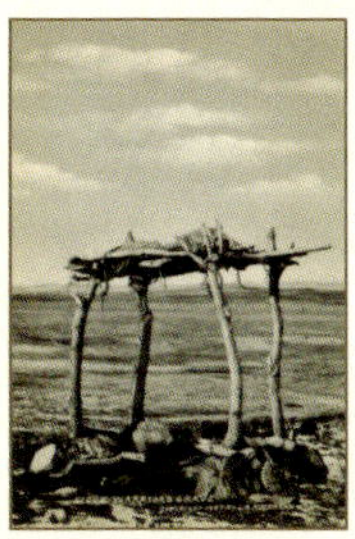

No. 1, A SIOUX WARRIOR'S GRAVE: Date of the photo is probably 1880 or 1881.

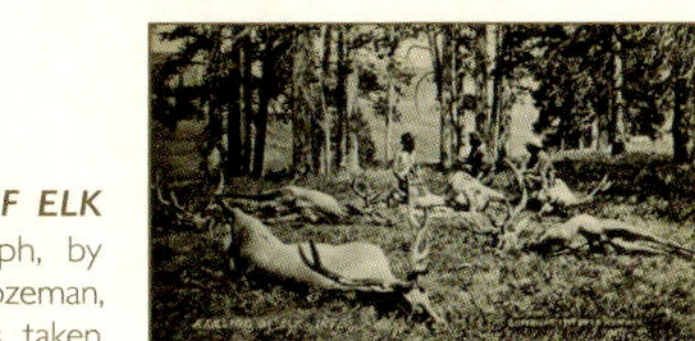

No. 3, A KILLING OF ELK 1875: This photograph, by Joshua Crissman of Bozeman, Montana Territory, was taken August 7, 1872, in an area that would soon become part of Yellowstone National Park. Crissman accompanied F. V. Hayden's first Geological Survey of the area in 1871 as a guest. He returned to the Yellowstone area in 1872 to take more photographs and was already there when Hayden's second survey crew arrived in late July. W. H. Jackson was the survey's official photographer. It is unknown when Huffman acquired the negative for this image; he is only one of several photographers to whom Crissman sold his negatives.

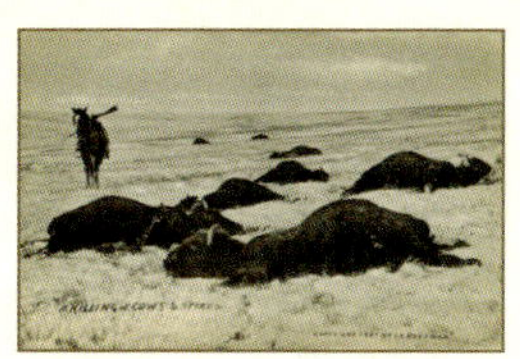

No. 5, A KILLING OF COWS AND SPIKES: The title on an original stereoview shows the date of this photo to be January 1882.

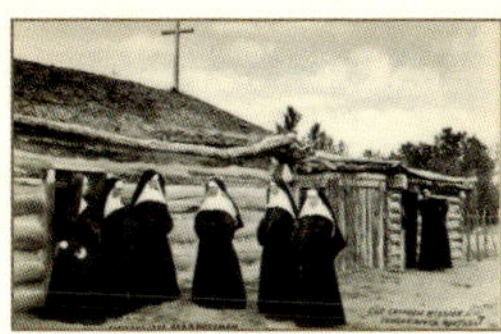

No. 7, OLD CATHOLIC MISSION: This photo was taken in 1898. The sisters' names (left to right) are Gertrude, Barbara, Monica, Mary of Angels (Superior), Thecla, and Hildegarde. On the right is Fr. Vermatt. (from a letter from Margaret Daily to W. R. Felton c. early 1950s).

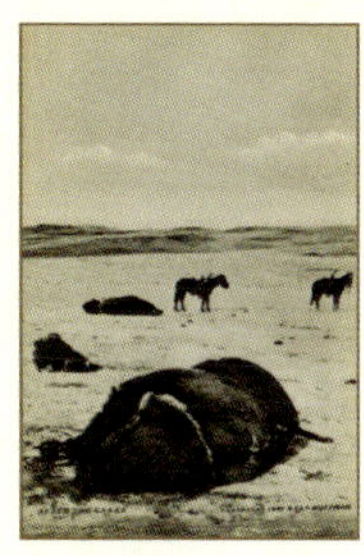

No. 8, AFTER THE CHASE: Date of this photo is January 1882.

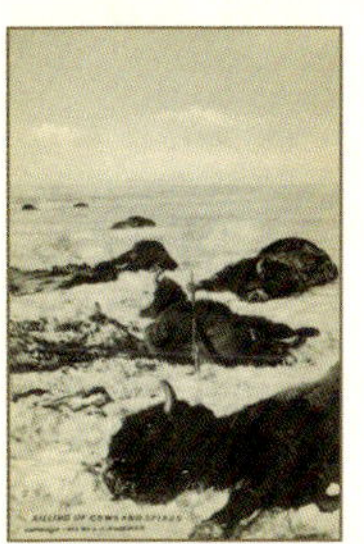

No. 9, KILLING COWS AND SPIKES: Date of this photo is January 1882.

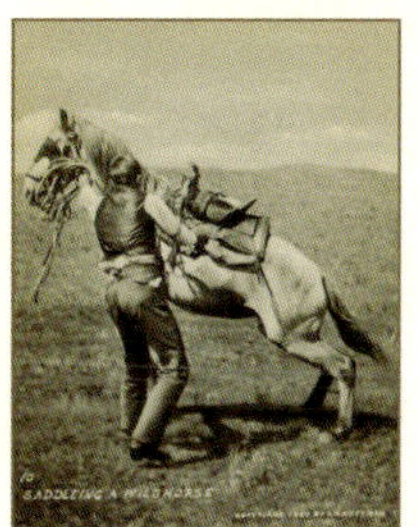

No. 10, SADDLEING A WILD HORSE: This photo taken in 1894; the cowboy is Andy Speelmon of Ekalaka, Montana.

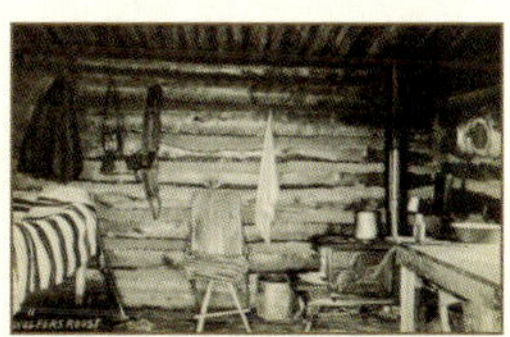

No. 11, A WOLFER'S ROOST: This photo taken during a 1901 hunt with William Hornaday to the Hell Creek area of north central Montana.

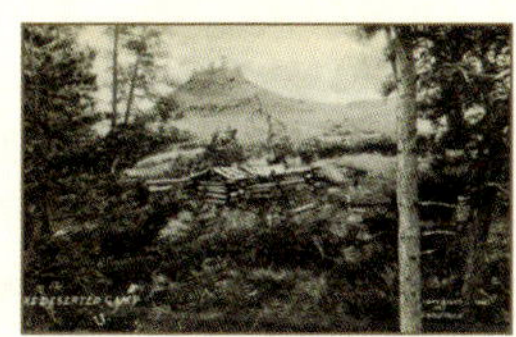

No. 12, THE DESERTED CAMP: This photo taken during a 1901 hunt with William Hornaday to the Hell Creek area of north central Montana.

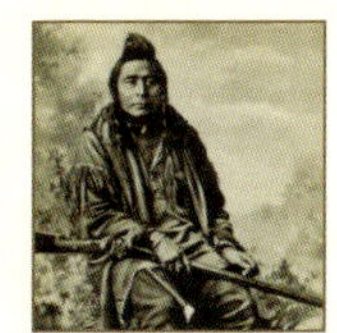

No. 13, A CROW HUNTER—WINTER DRESS: "This is a picture of Carries His Food who died in 1888. He was an expert hunter who always succeeded in providing food for his family." (From a letter from Gordon Powers to Mark Brown, 1951).

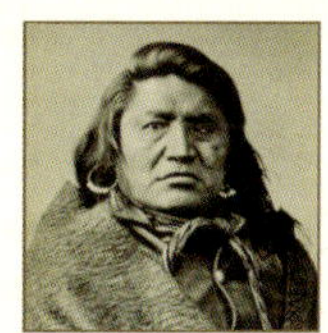

No. 16, FIERCE OLD CROW BUCK: "The Indian pictured on the postcard was Deaf Bull . . . Deaf Bull died on the Reservation in 1905 at the age of 59." (from a letter from Gordon Powers to W. R. Felton, 1950).

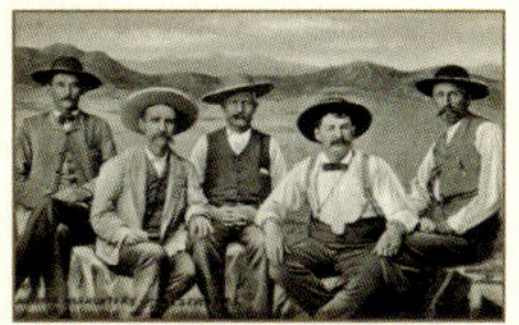

No. 19, MONTANA MANHUNTERS OF THE SEVENTIES: Left to right, manhunters: Billy Smith, Jack Hawkins, Tom Irvine, Louis King, and Eph Davis.

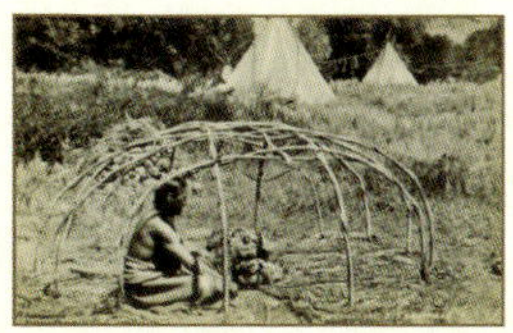

No. 20, A HANSOME YOUNG CHEYENNE: The Indian's name is Plenty Bird.

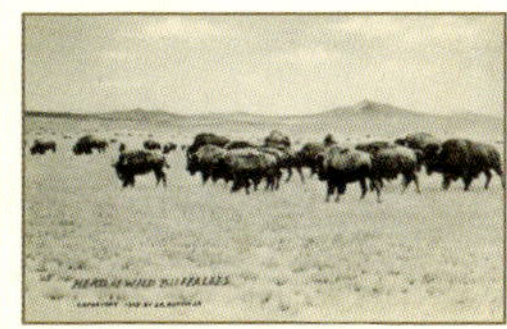

No. 25, HERD OF WILD BUFFALOES: Photo taken 1900 in Western Montana (see *Huffman Collotype Book* for more details).

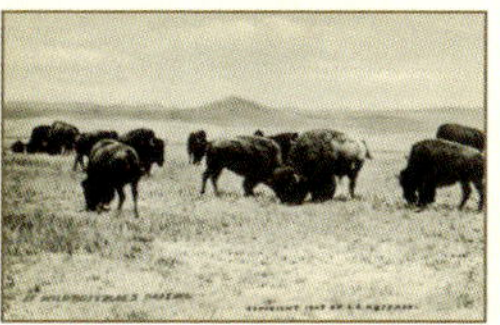

No. 26, 15 WILD BUFFALOES: Photo taken 1900 in Western Montana (see *Huffman Collotype Book* for more details).

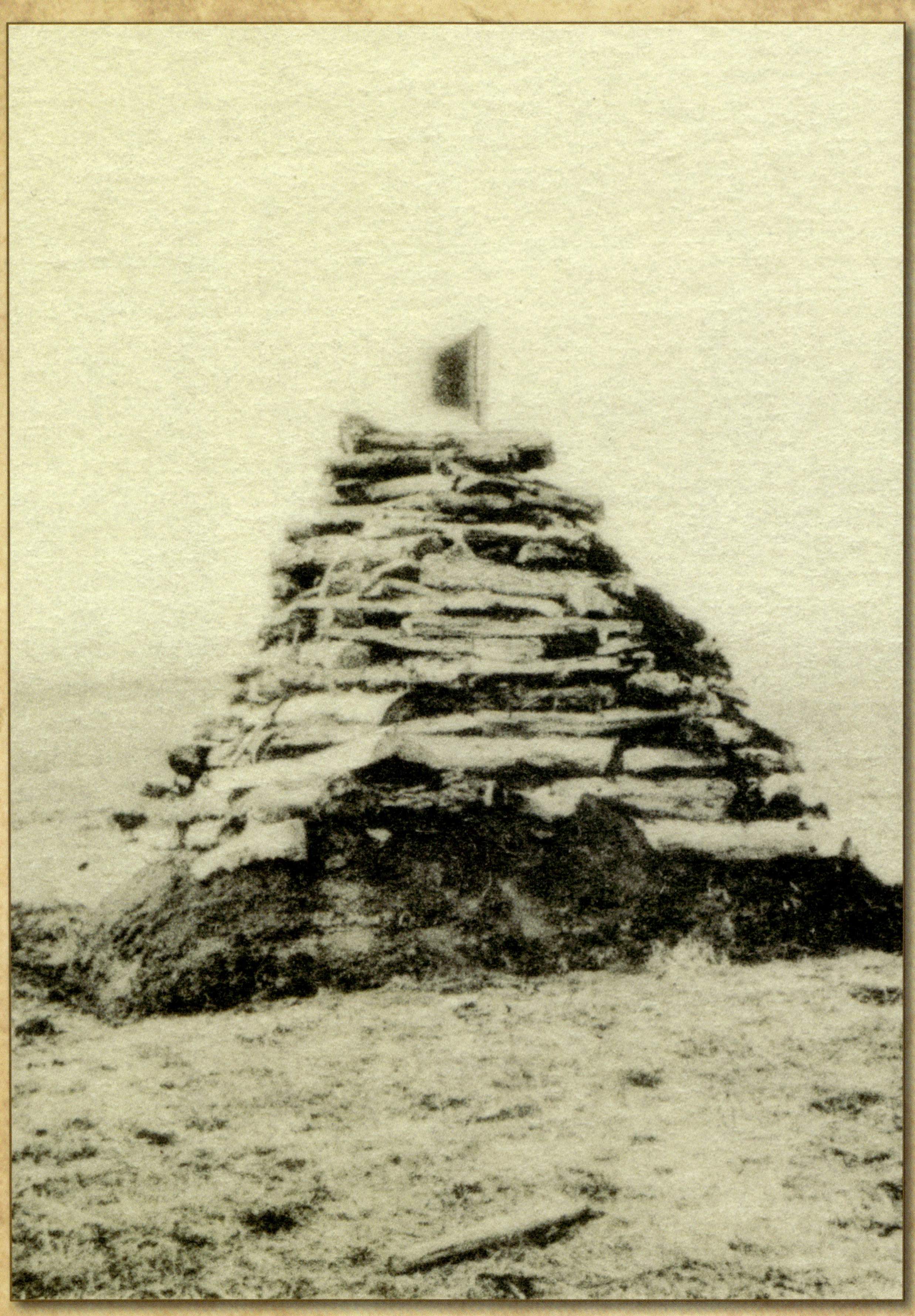

ABOVE: *No. 2, The First Monument on Custer's Hill.*

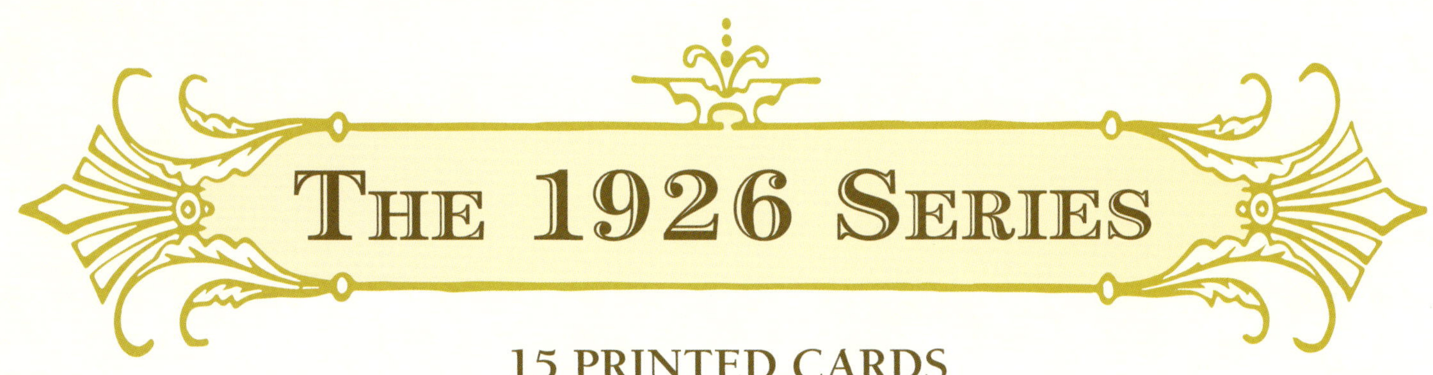

The 1926 Series

15 PRINTED CARDS

June 25, 1926, would be the 50th anniversary of the Battle of the Little Bighorn and a large celebration was being planned. Sometime in the spring, Huffman corresponded with the Hoffman Photogravure Company in Chicago regarding the printing of a set of postcards that would be available to the large crowds expected during the celebration. For some reason, he was tardy getting his material to the Hoffman Company. In a June 2nd letter he states, "I am about three days late in submitting copy for the run of fifteen thousand post cards as agreed some two weeks ago." He goes on to say that in the near future he will supplement this order with "orders for four or five additional series of cards." He also stresses that, while for those future series they will have ample time to run them, for this first series "I must ask you to make a very special effort to have them ready by the 12th or 15th of this month at the latest . . . Please also note that the tremendous crowd to whom these cards are to be offered are due on the battle field June 21st, 22nd and 23rd, where the second immense crowd will assemble over the 24th and 25th." In spite of Huffman's efforts and urgent request, the deadline was not met. A June 7th telegram from the Hoffman Photogravure Company delivers the bad news— "did not receive any negatives it will be too late now." Although not in time for the 50th anniversary celebration, the cards were printed and delivered later in the year.

This 15-card set was printed by a halftone process and reveals a dot pattern under magnification. A total of 15,000 cards (1,000 sets) was printed at a cost of $135.42,

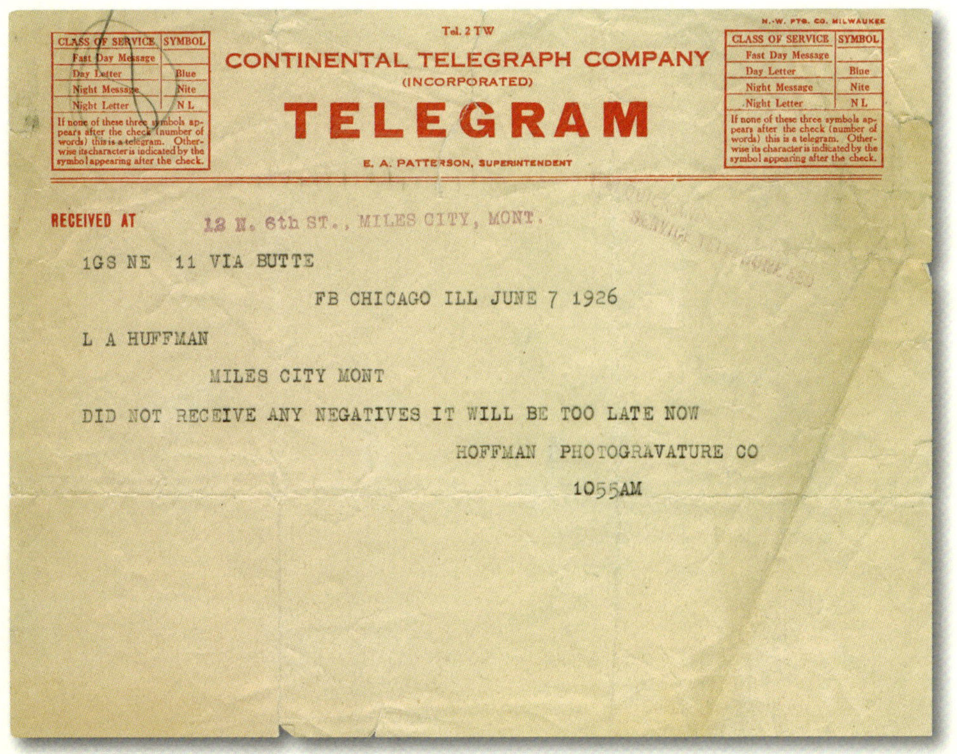

Tel. 2 TW

CONTINENTAL TELEGRAPH COMPANY
(INCORPORATED)

TELEGRAM

E. A. PATTERSON, SUPERINTENDENT

CLASS OF SERVICE	SYMBOL
Fast Day Message	
Day Letter	Blue
Night Message	Nite
Night Letter	N L

If none of these three symbols appears after the check (number of words) this is a telegram. Otherwise its character is indicated by the symbol appearing after the check.

RECEIVED AT 12 N. 6th ST., MILES CITY, MONT.

1GS NE 11 VIA BUTTE

FB CHICAGO ILL JUNE 7 1926

L A HUFFMAN

MILES CITY MONT

DID NOT RECEIVE ANY NEGATIVES IT WILL BE TOO LATE NOW

HOFFMAN PHOTOGRAVATURE CO

1055AM

LEFT: Telegram from Hoffman Photogravure Company.

slightly less than 1 cent each. They have a white border and were printed on basic, divided-back stock. A total of 19 images were used; two cards have two images each and one has three. The cards are numbered one through 15 and each has a title and Huffman credit; a few have a small amount of additional information.

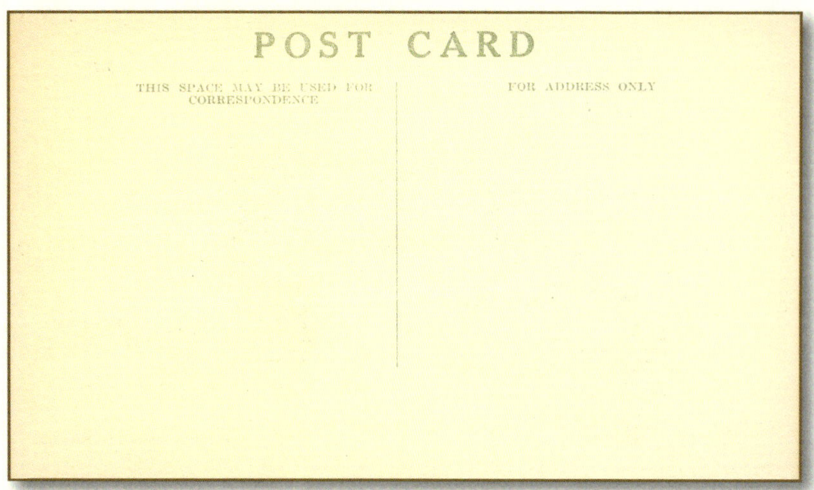

Most of the cards have images that relate to the 1876 Custer Command March and subsequent battle, many of them taken by Huffman in 1916 during the 40th anniversary celebration activities. As a prelude to the 1916 celebration, a select group retraced a portion of the Custer March trail. Among others, the group included General Godfrey (a member of the Custer command), Custer scholar Walter Camp and author and historian George Bird Grinnell. Huffman accompanied this excursion and took many photos, several of which are used on these cards. Both Sioux chief Rain-in-the-Face and Cheyenne chief Two Moon participated in the battle.

The 1926 series was sold as sets and issued in an envelope printed with two images and a statement that this was the first of what was going to be seven new series covering the "Huffman Line," to be issued before January 1927. Although the reasons are unclear, we know today that no other series were issued. The absence of additional cards, and envelopes that have the "new series" statement lined out, are both indicators that Huffman changed his mind.

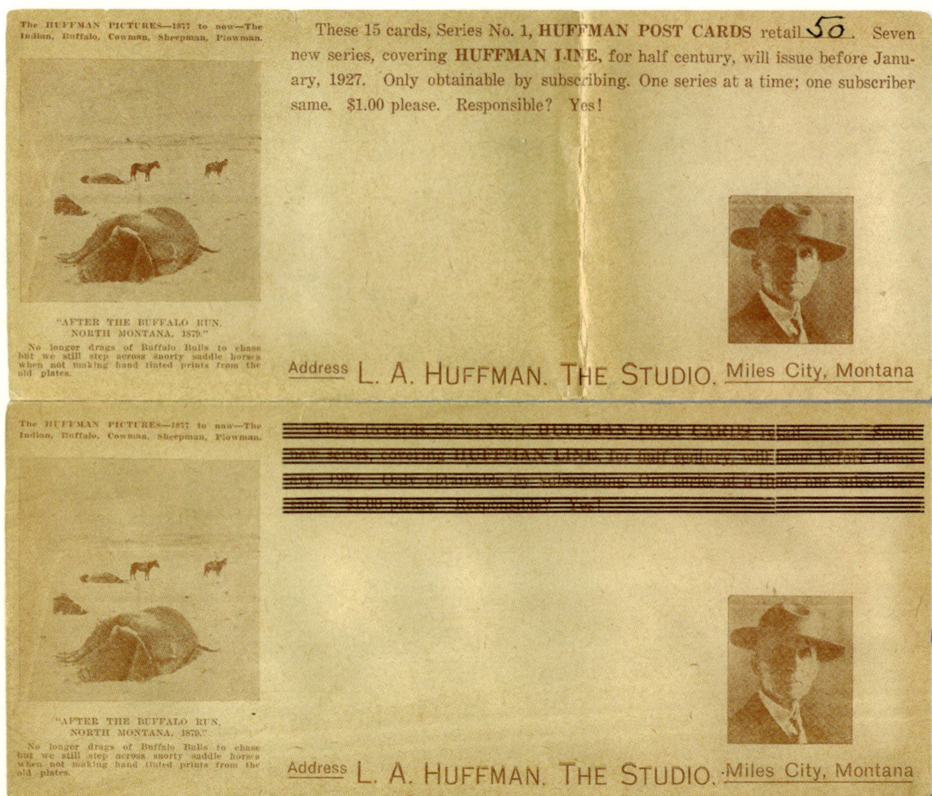
The HUFFMAN PICTURES—1877 to now—The Indian, Buffalo, Cowman, Sheepman, Plowman.

"AFTER THE BUFFALO RUN. NORTH MONTANA, 1879."

No longer drags of Buffalo Bulls to chase but we still step across snorty saddle horses when not making hand tinted prints from the old plates.

These 15 cards, Series No. 1, **HUFFMAN POST CARDS** retail 50. Seven new series, covering **HUFFMAN LINE**, for half century, will issue before January, 1927. Only obtainable by subscribing. One series at a time; one subscriber same. $1.00 please. Responsible? Yes!

Address L. A. HUFFMAN. THE STUDIO. Miles City, Montana

The HUFFMAN PICTURES—1877 to now—The Indian, Buffalo, Cowman, Sheepman, Plowman.

~~These 15 cards, Series No. 1, HUFFMAN POST CARDS retail . Seven new series, covering HUFFMAN LINE, for half century, will issue before January, 1927. Only obtainable by subscribing. One series at a time; one subscriber same. $1.00 please. Responsible? Yes!~~

"AFTER THE BUFFALO RUN. NORTH MONTANA, 1879."

No longer drags of Buffalo Bulls to chase but we still step across snorty saddle horses when not making hand tinted prints from the old plates.

Address L. A. HUFFMAN. THE STUDIO. Miles City, Montana

TOP: Reverse of postcard showing divided back.

RIGHT: Envelopes with "Additional Series" statement, original and lined out.

These original envelopes are relatively scarce today; the total number printed was probably less than 100 (assuming one envelope for each 15-card set). Envelopes in their original, unaltered condition are much scarcer than those with the new series statement lined out.

While it is unknown how many sets of these postcards were sold during Huffman's lifetime, it is clear there wasn't much profit from their sale. Postcard display boards from the Huffman Studio show he sold this set of postcards for 50 cents, making about 35 cents profit per set. Even in 1926, 35 cents was not a great deal of money. At this point in his career, Huffman was concentrating on enlarged,

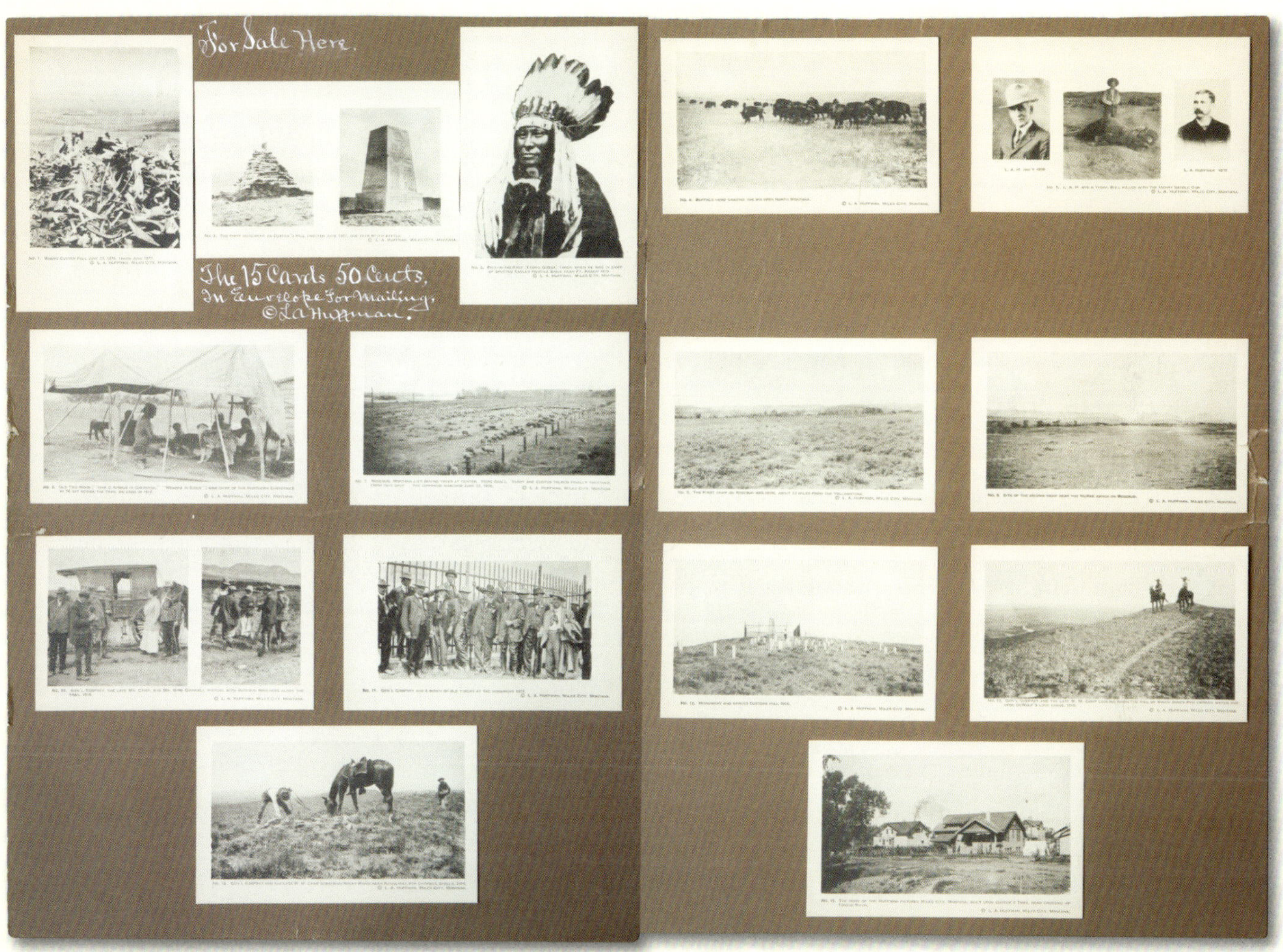

ABOVE: Postcard display boards from the Huffman Studio.

hand-tinted prints of his early images. A typical and popular size was approximately 12 x 24 that he sold for $20—about $200 in today's money and financially equivalent to 40 sets of postcards. Even if they sold well, sales of these postcards did not contribute a great deal to Huffman's financial welfare. Realization of this fact may have contributed to his decision to abandon plans for six more series.

We have a hand-colored card from this series—*No. 15, The Home of The Huffman Pictures.* It is shown with the standard No. 15 card in the following 1926 Postcards section.

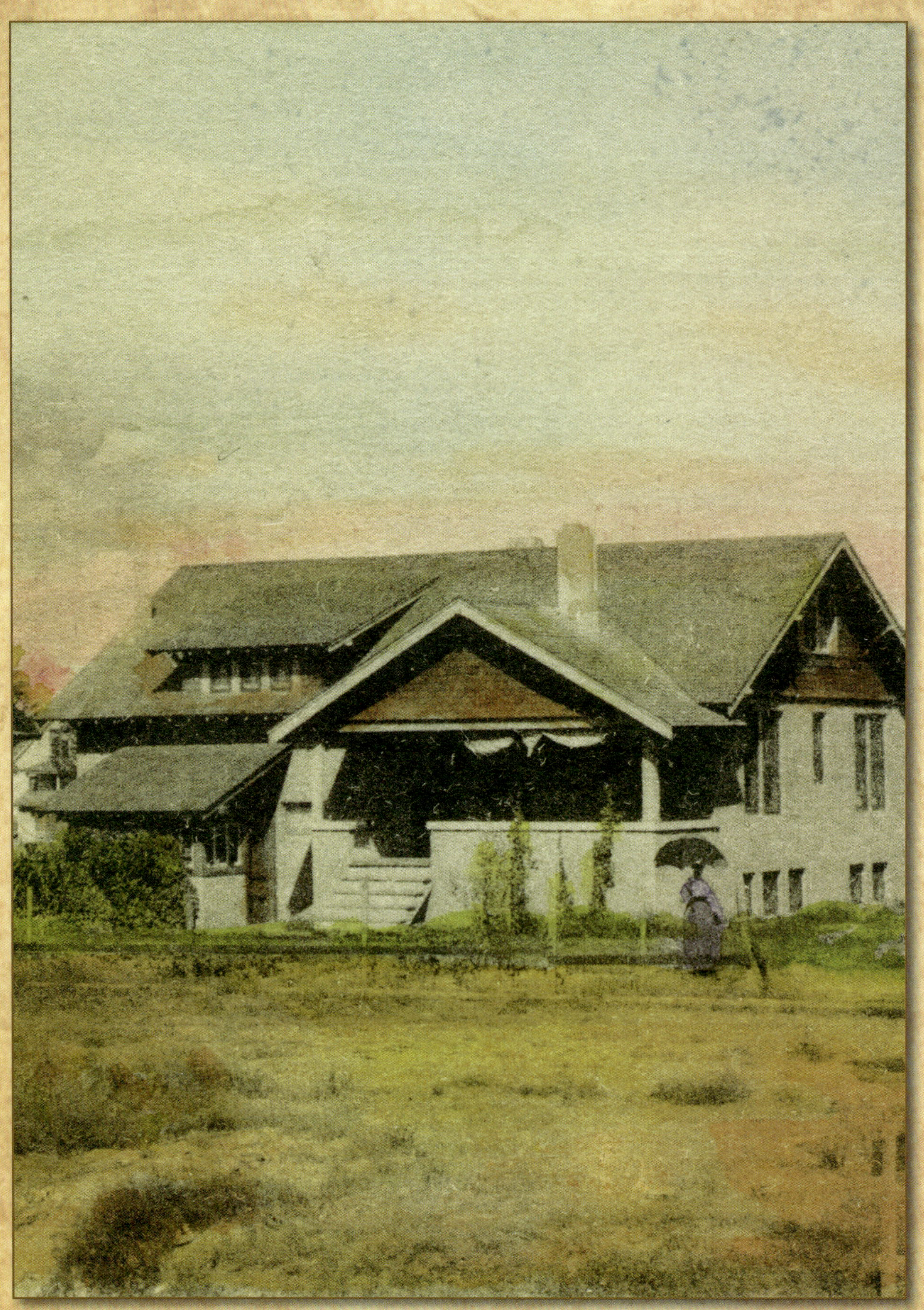

ABOVE: *No. 15, The Home of the Huffman Pictures*—hand colored

The 1926 Postcards

Following are the 15 cards in the 1926 series.

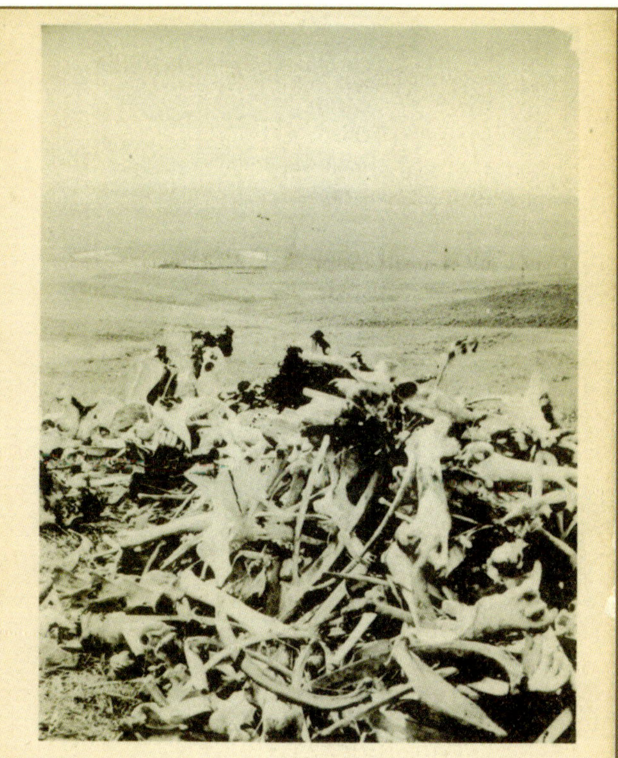

No. 1. Where Custer Fell June 25, 1876, taken June 1877.
© L. A. Huffman, Miles City, Montana.

LEFT: *No. 1, Where Custer Fell*

BELOW: *No. 2, The First Monument on Custer's Hill*

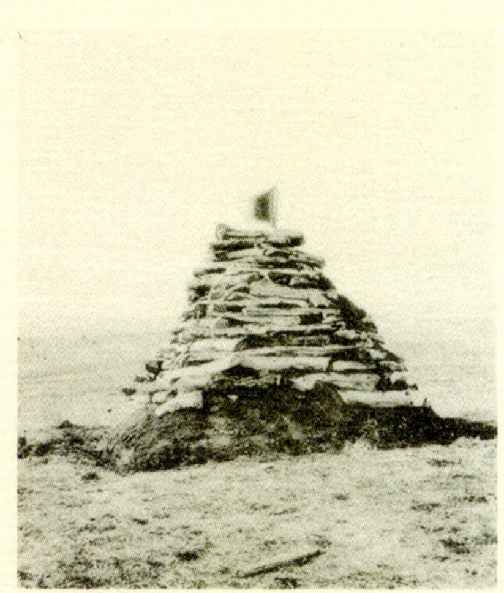

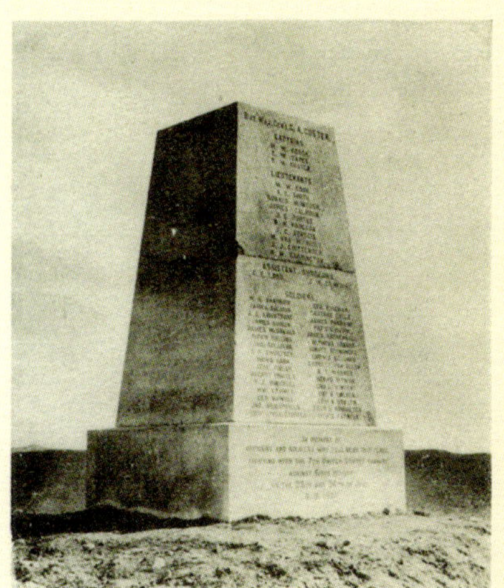

No. 2. The first monument on Custer's Hill erected June 1877, one year after battle.
© L. A. Huffman, Miles City, Montana.

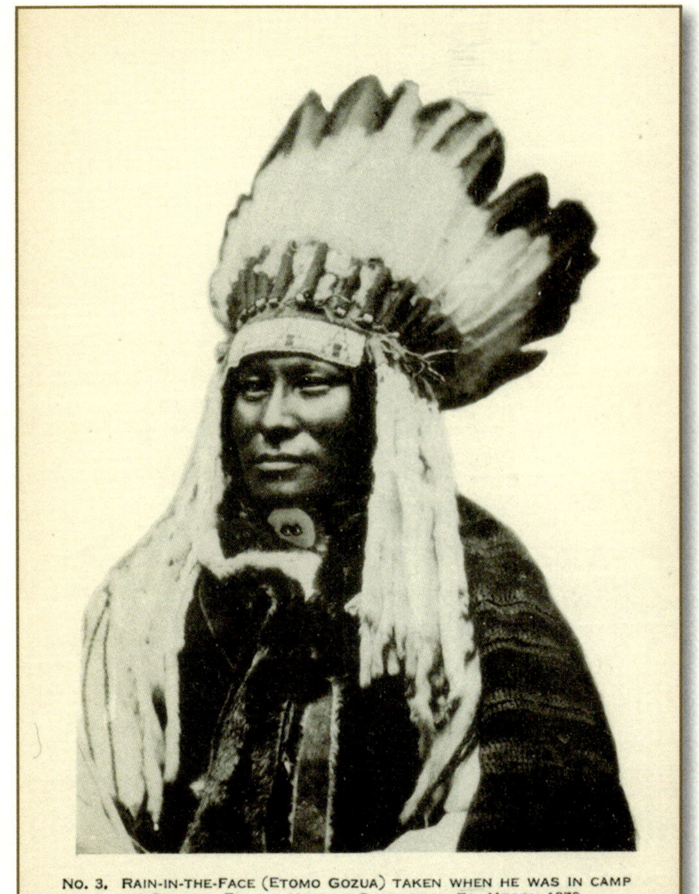

NO. 3. RAIN-IN-THE-FACE (ETOMO GOZUA) TAKEN WHEN HE WAS IN CAMP OF SPOTTED EAGLES HOSTILE SIOUX NEAR FT. KEOGH 1879.
© L. A. HUFFMAN, MILES CITY, MONTANA.

LEFT: *No. 3, Rain-in-the-Face*

BELOW: *No. 4, Buffalo Herd Grazing the Big Open*

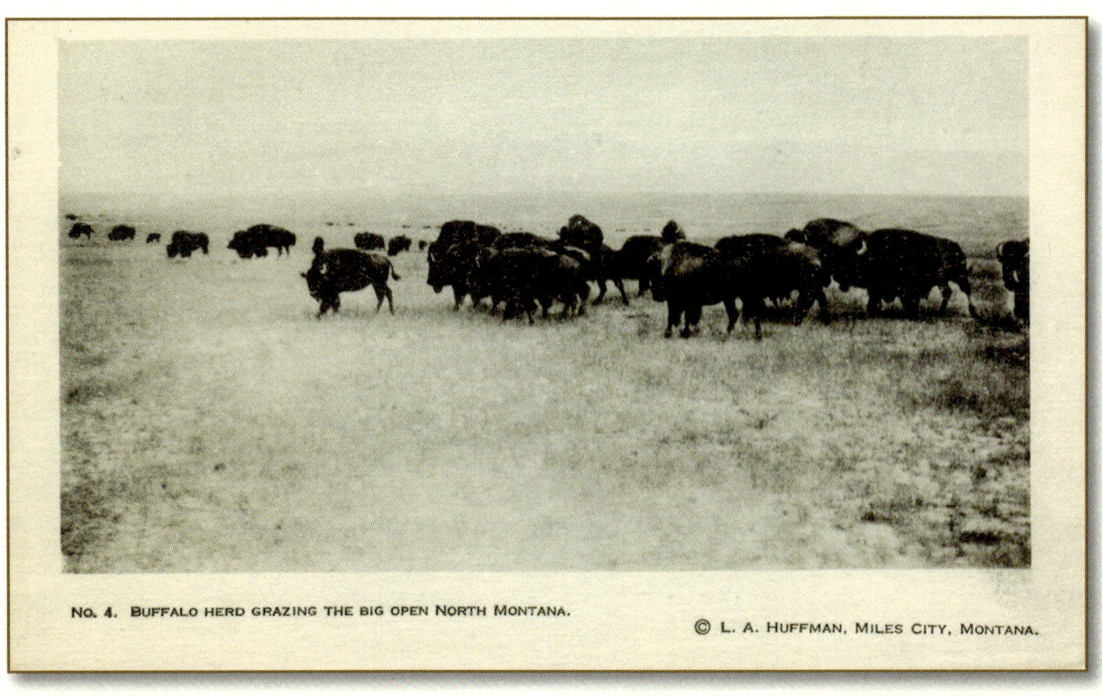

NO. 4. BUFFALO HERD GRAZING THE BIG OPEN NORTH MONTANA.
© L. A. HUFFMAN, MILES CITY, MONTANA.

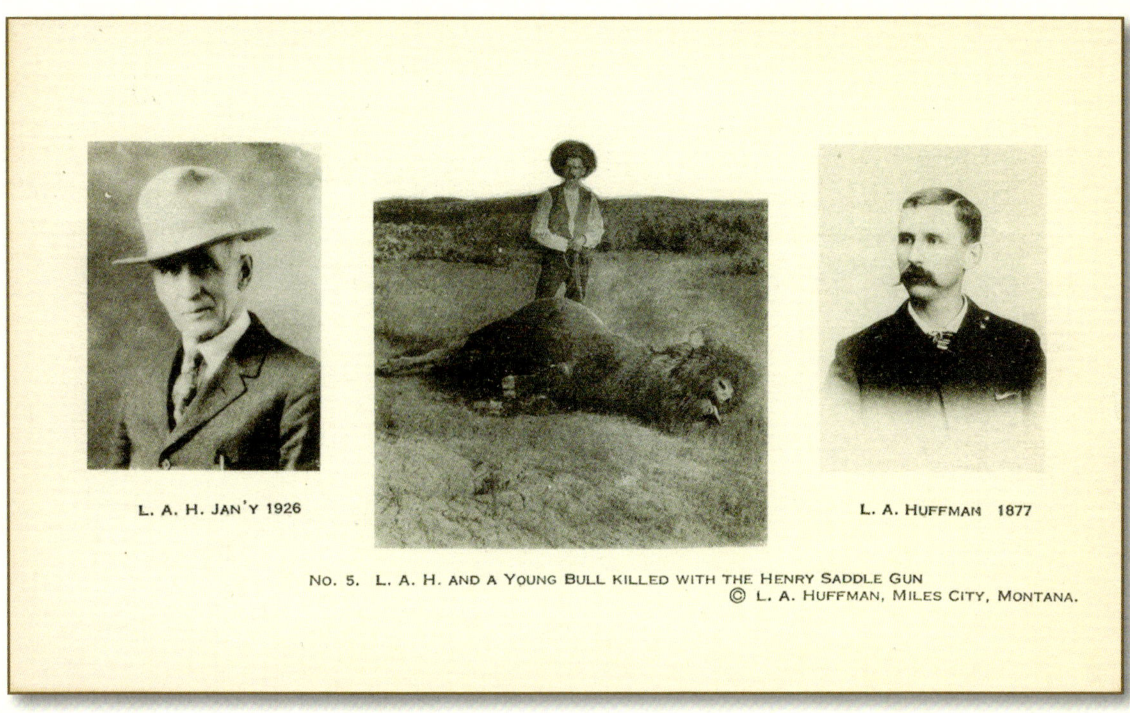

L. A. H. JAN'Y 1926

L. A. HUFFMAN 1877

NO. 5. L. A. H. AND A YOUNG BULL KILLED WITH THE HENRY SADDLE GUN
© L. A. HUFFMAN, MILES CITY, MONTANA.

ABOVE: *No. 5, L. A. H. and a Young Bull*

BELOW: *No. 6, Old Two Moon*

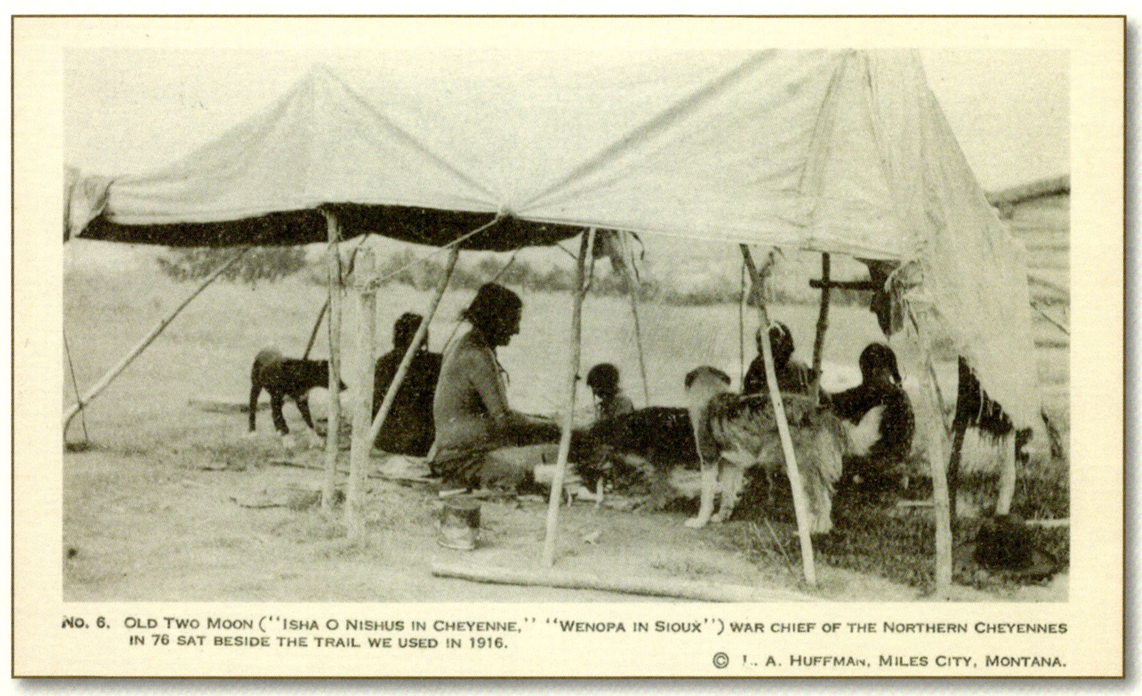

NO. 6. OLD TWO MOON ("ISHA O NISHUS IN CHEYENNE," "WENOPA IN SIOUX") WAR CHIEF OF THE NORTHERN CHEYENNES IN 76 SAT BESIDE THE TRAIL WE USED IN 1916.
© L. A. HUFFMAN, MILES CITY, MONTANA.

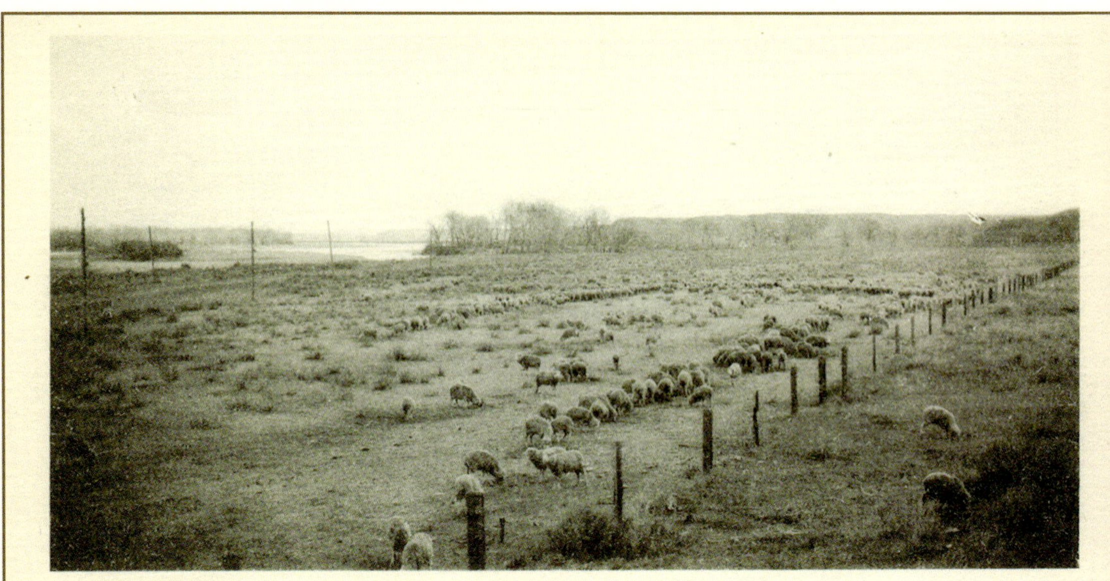

ABOVE: *No. 7, Rosebud, Montana Lies Behind Trees*

BELOW: *No. 8, The First Camp on the Rosebud*

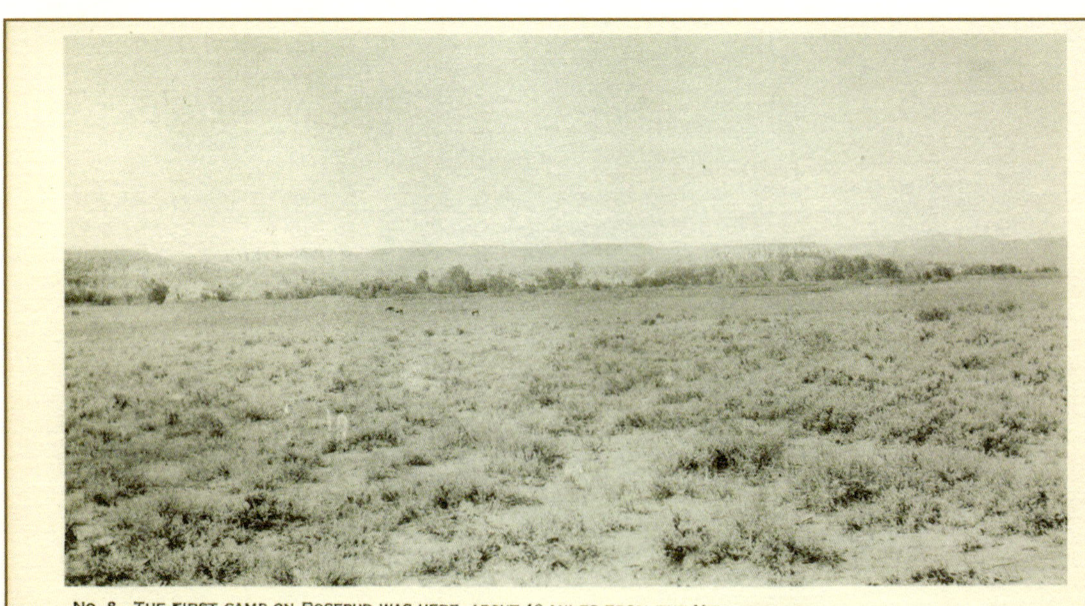

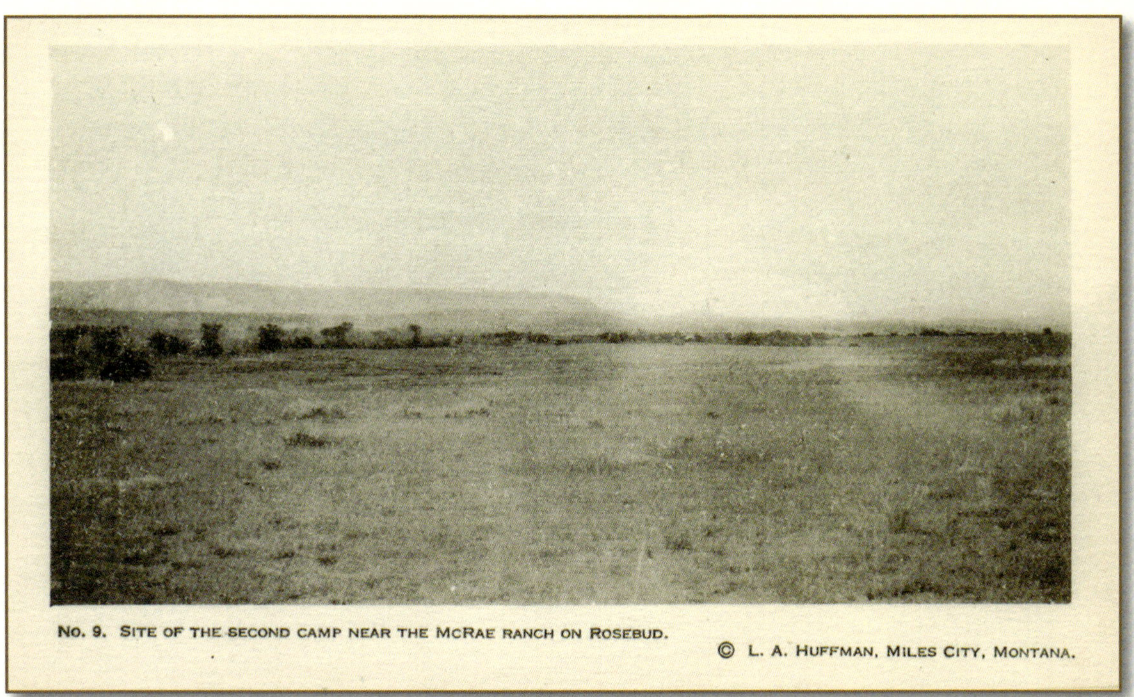

ABOVE: *No. 9, Site of the Second Camp*

BELOW: *No. 10, Gen'l Godfrey, Mr. Camp, and Mr. Bird Grinnell*

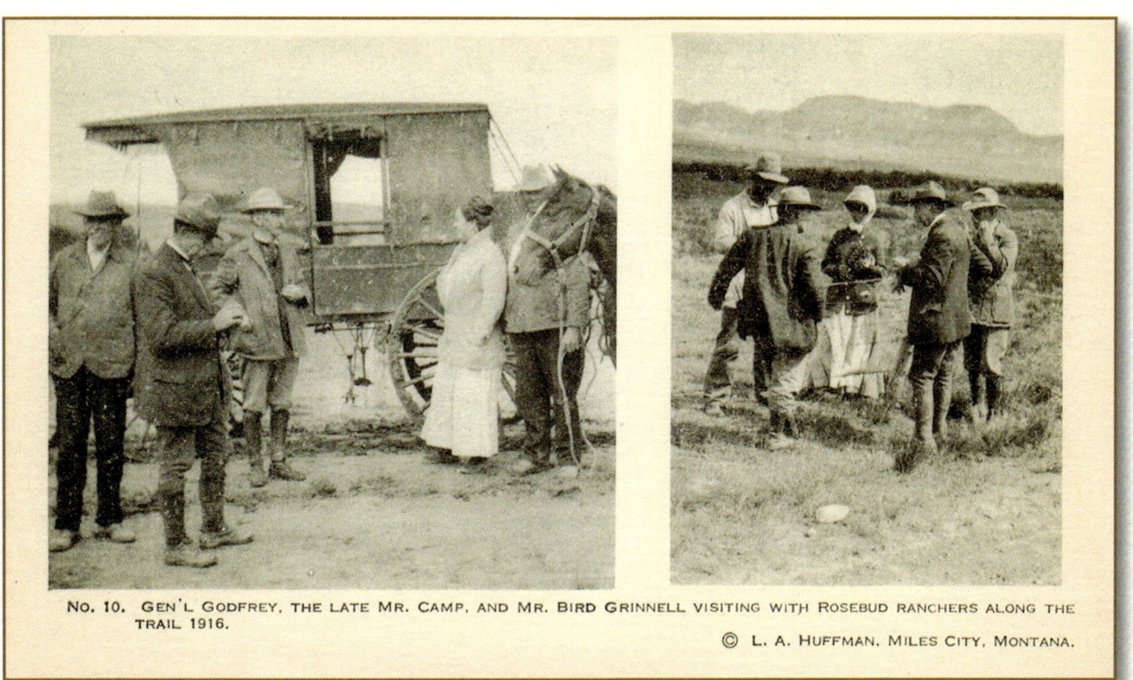

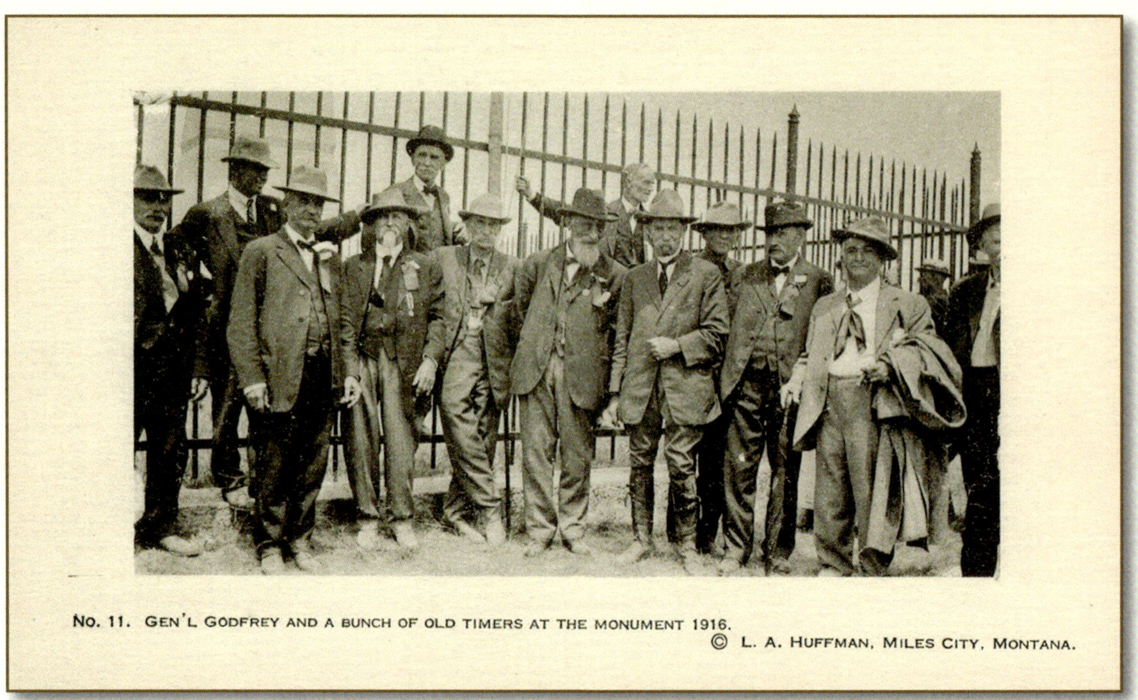

ABOVE: *No. 11, Gen'l Godfrey and a Bunch of Old Timers*

BELOW: *No. 12, Monument and Graves Custers Hill*

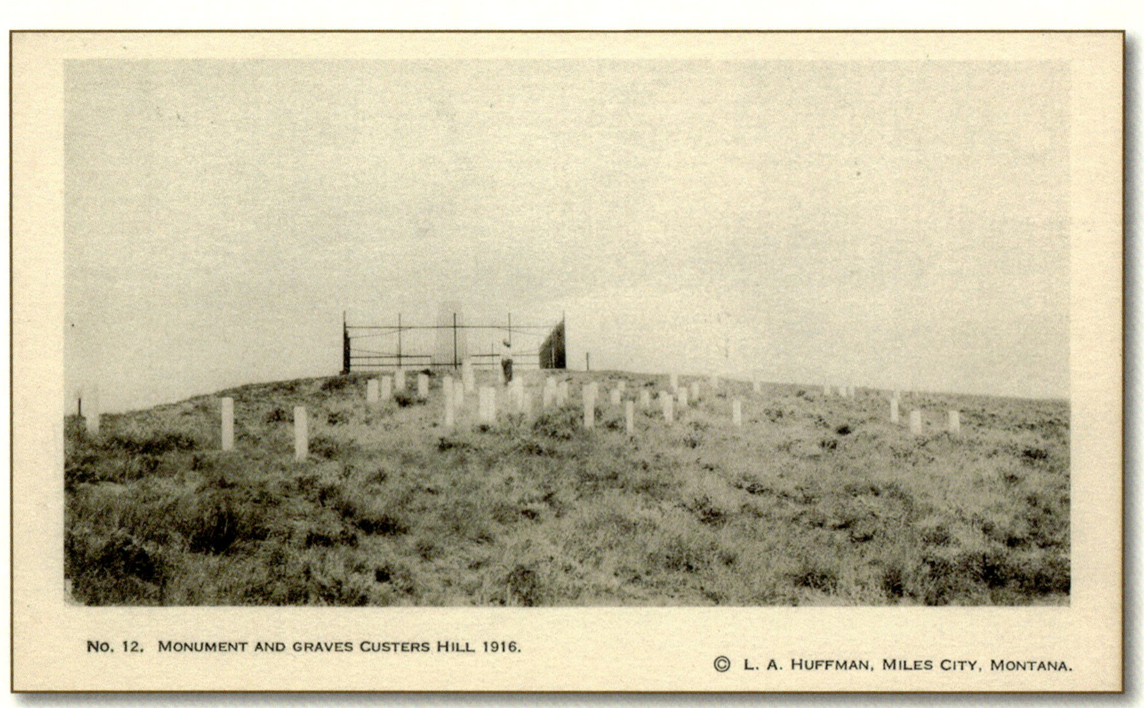

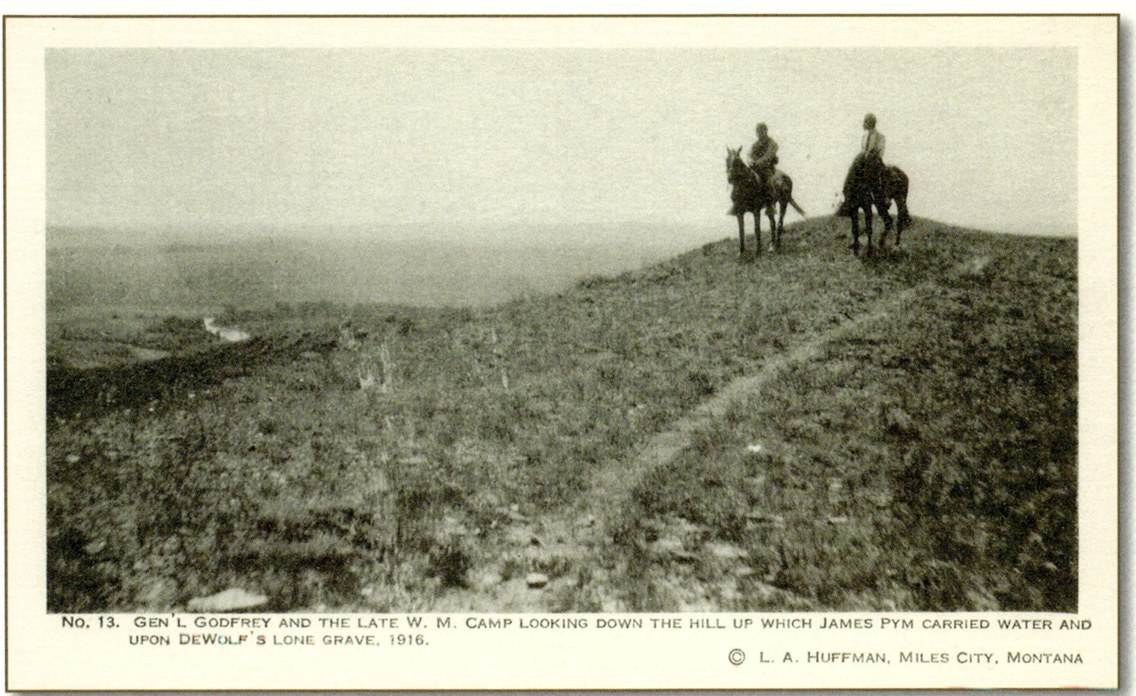

ABOVE: *No. 13, Gen'l Godfrey and the Late W. M. Camp*

BELOW: *No. 14, Gen'l Godfrey and W. M. Camp Searching for Cartridge Shells, 1916*

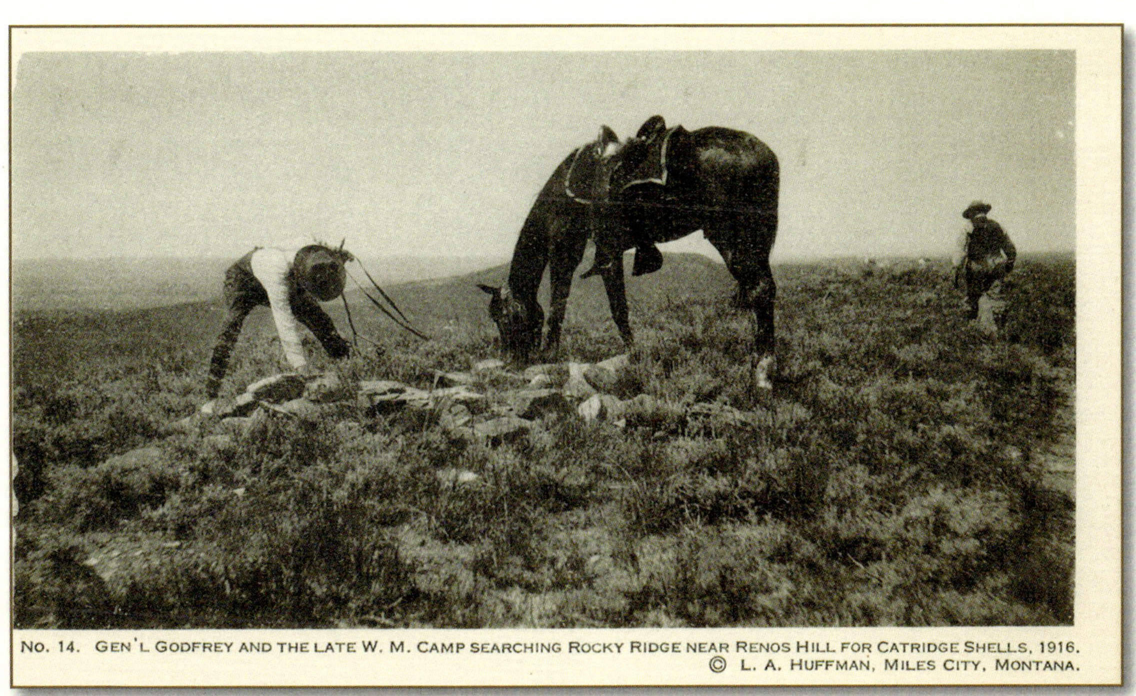

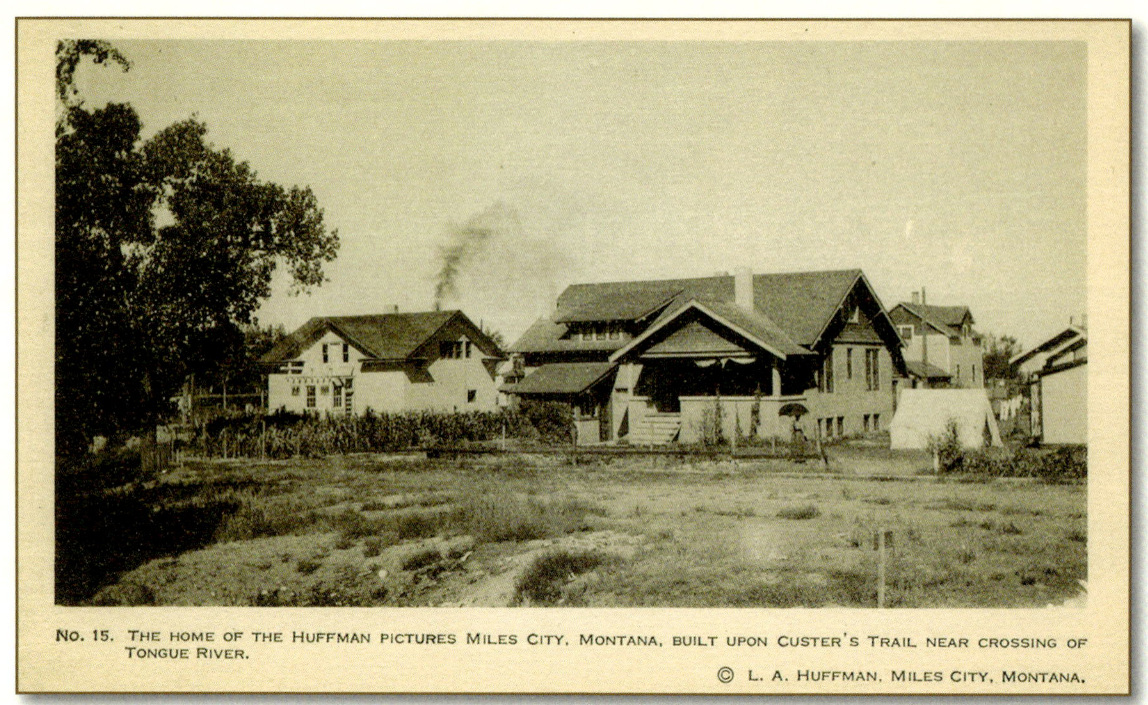

ABOVE: *No. 15, The Home of the Huffman Pictures*

BELOW: *No. 15, The Home of the Huffman Pictures*—hand colored

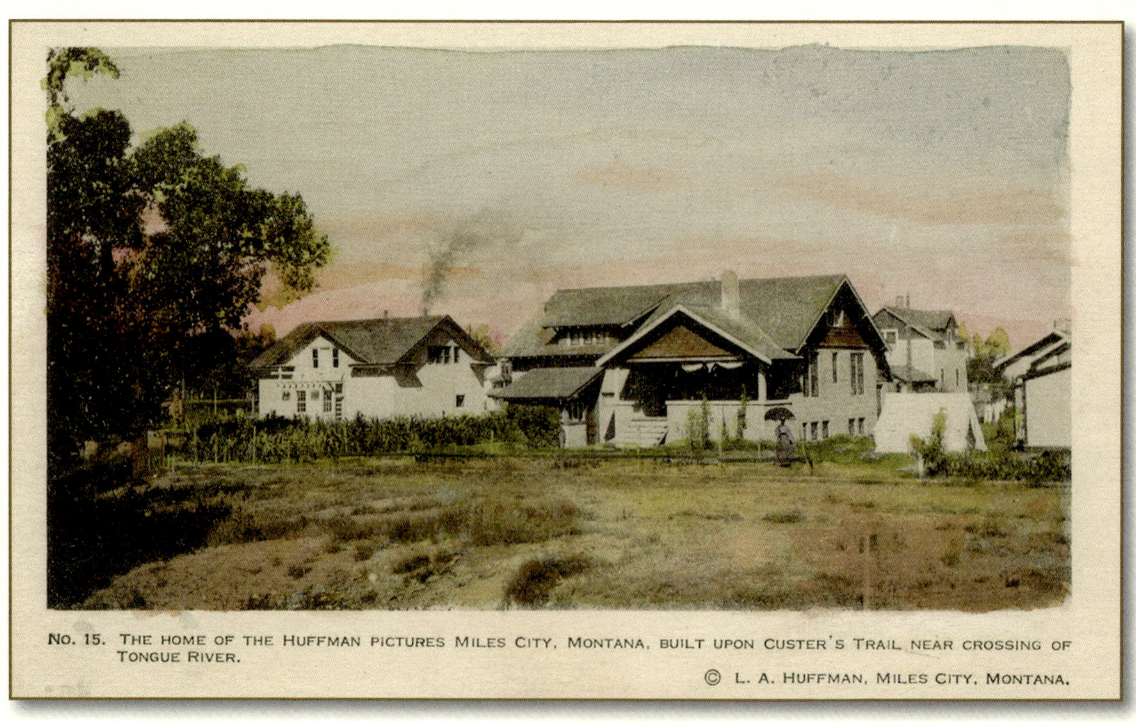

1926 Notes

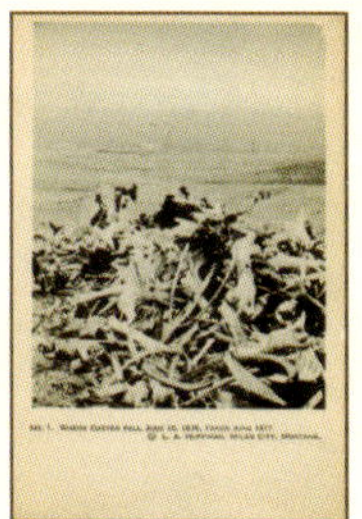 **No. 1, WHERE CUSTER FELL:** Date of the photo is 1879.	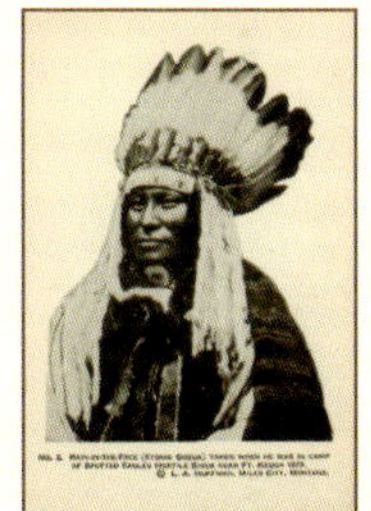 **No. 3, RAIN-IN-THE-FACE:** Date of the photo is 1880.	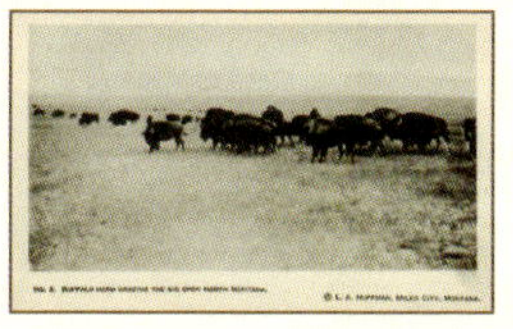 **No. 4, BUFFALO GRAZING THE BIG OPEN:** Photo taken in 1900 in Western Montana. (See *Huffman Collotype Book* for details.)

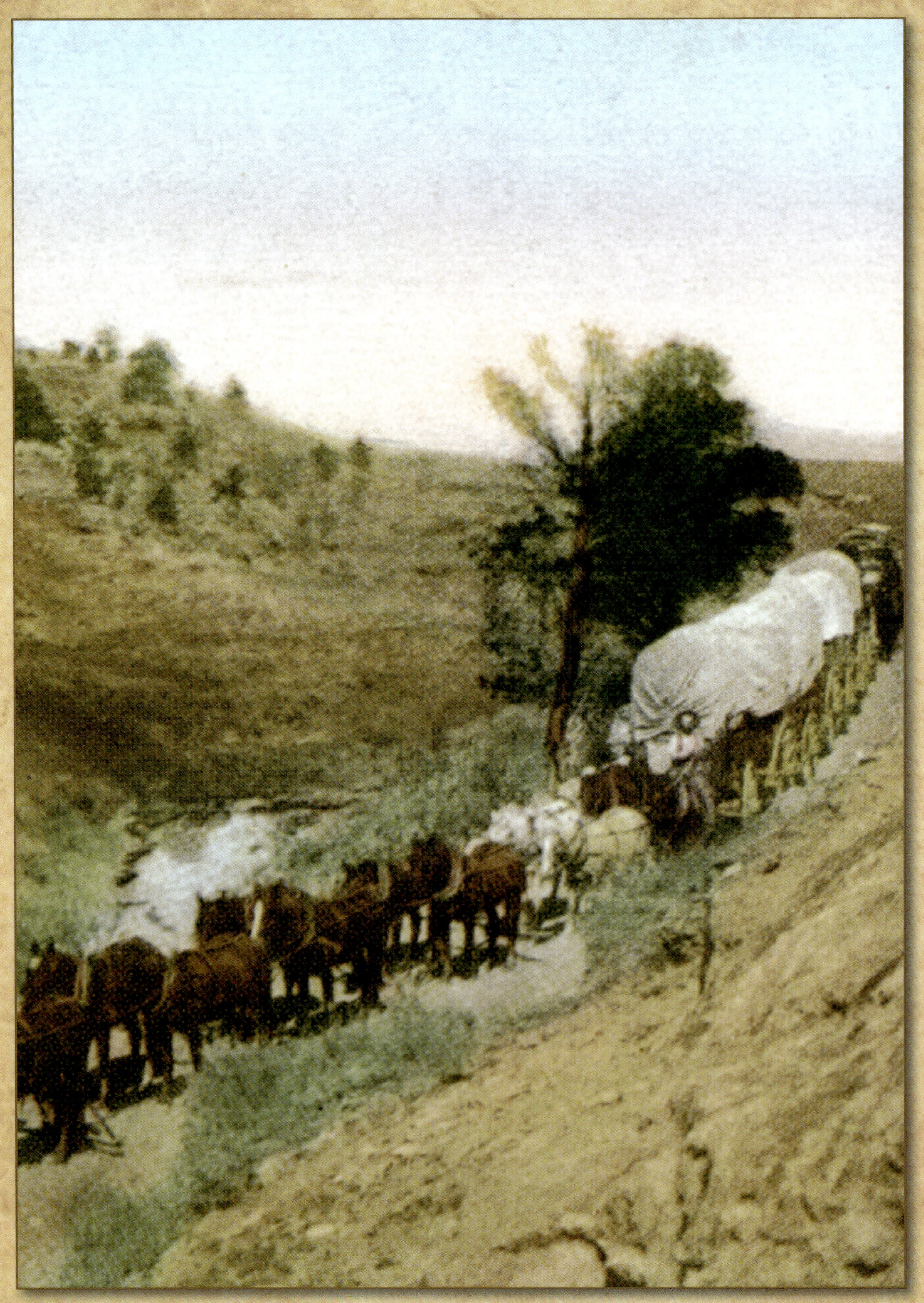

ABOVE: *"Jerk-line twelve" on the Old Freight Road Before the Railroad Came*

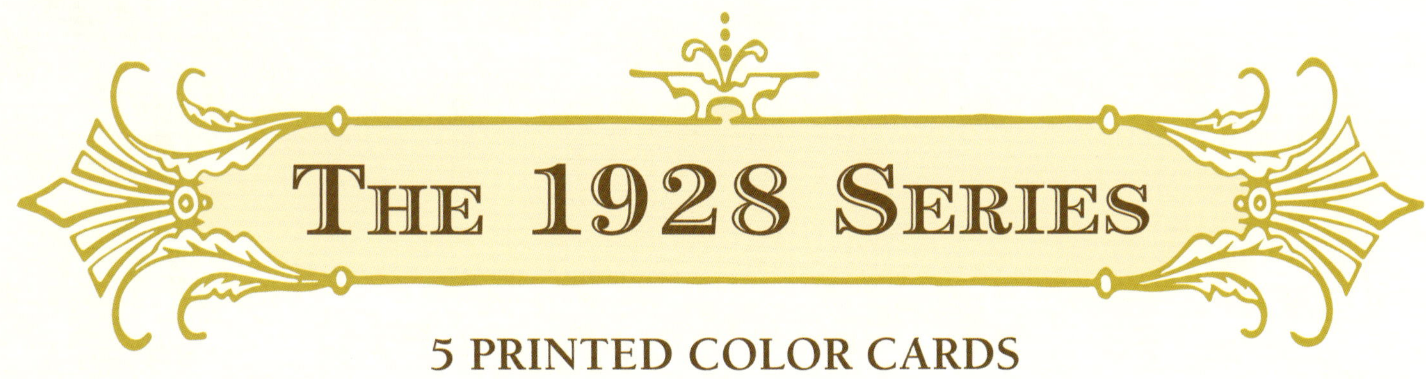

The 1928 Series

5 PRINTED COLOR CARDS

Huffman's last venture into the realm of postcards was a cooperative effort with the Northern Pacific Railroad. Discussions during the waning months of 1927 between Huffman and representatives of the Railroad resulted in an agreement to produce five cards. They would be printed in color based on hand-colored prints provided by Huffman. In a letter dated November 25, 1927, Northern Pacific representative A. B. Smith acknowledges receipt of the five colored photo examples sent by Huffman and offers to pay Huffman a royalty of ½ cent per printed card, an offer accepted by Huffman. In another letter five days later he informs Huffman that the first printing of the "postal cards" will be 5,000 each, or a total of 25,000 cards.

The cards were printed in color using the standard 4-color process and reveal a dot pattern under magnification. The cards have a white border with the title printed in black under the image. A copyright credit and Huffman's name appears in the lower right corner. The reverse side of the card is a basic divided back format with a stamp box in the upper right corner. The top half of the message side is used for a brief description of the image and the lower half is blank except for a small Northern Pacific logo in the lower left corner. Centered along the bottom is "6220—Printed in U.S.A."

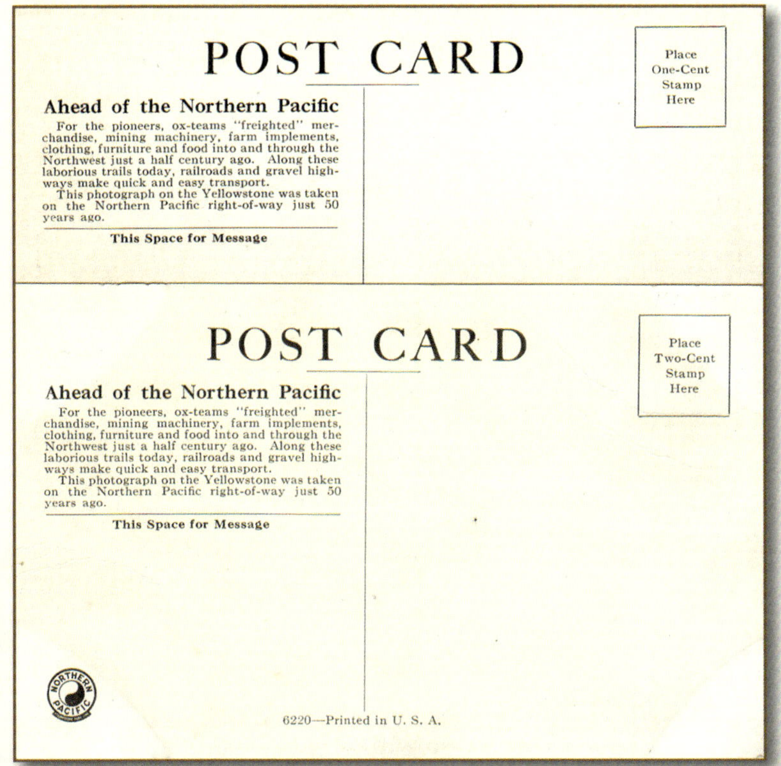

POST CARD

Place One-Cent Stamp Here

Ahead of the Northern Pacific

For the pioneers, ox-teams "freighted" merchandise, mining machinery, farm implements, clothing, furniture and food into and through the Northwest just a half century ago. Along these laborious trails today, railroads and gravel highways make quick and easy transport.

This photograph on the Yellowstone was taken on the Northern Pacific right-of-way just 50 years ago.

This Space for Message

POST CARD

Place Two-Cent Stamp Here

Ahead of the Northern Pacific

For the pioneers, ox-teams "freighted" merchandise, mining machinery, farm implements, clothing, furniture and food into and through the Northwest just a half century ago. Along these laborious trails today, railroads and gravel highways make quick and easy transport.

This photograph on the Yellowstone was taken on the Northern Pacific right-of-way just 50 years ago.

This Space for Message

6220—Printed in U. S. A.

ABOVE: Cards with one- and two-cent stamp blocks.

The cards were printed sometime in the spring of 1928. Huffman received his royalty check of $125 in a letter from the Northern Pacific dated May 14, 1928. General Passenger Agent M. M. Goodsill also states, "I am also attaching a few copies of the cards which I believe you will agree are excellent reproductions of your very fine photographs." In another letter dated June 12th, Goodsill informs Huffman "we are very much pleased with the way your pictures reproduced on our postal cards and the way they are moving, we will have to re-order a supply soon." Evidence indicates a second printing was made. The two printings are identical with one major exception

—one has a one-cent stamp box and the other has a two-cent box. Contrary to conventional logic, cards with the two-cent value were the first printing and those with one-cent were the second!

On May 19, 1898, Congress authorized the use of Private Mailing Cards at the rate of one cent each, the same rate charged for government issued Postal Cards. Except for two brief interludes of two and three years each, the cost to send a postcard was one cent until January 1, 1952. The first exception was a wartime measure when the rate was temporarily raised to two cents on both postcards and Postal Cards between November 2, 1917, and June 30, 1919. The second increase to two cents for postcards began April 1, 1925. This rate increase proved unpopular and on July 1, 1928, the one-cent rate was re-established. It was permanently raised to two cents on January 1, 1952.

The first printing of the Northern Pacific Huffman cards was in spring of 1928, towards the end of the second period of a brief two-cent rate and the cards were printed with a "Place two-cent stamp here" message in the stamp box. The second printing of cards occurred after July 1st when the rate had gone back to one cent and these cards carry a one-cent message.

While the number of cards produced in the second printing is unknown, it may have been larger than the first run of 5,000 each. Our personal experience with these cards suggests the one-cent cards are noticeably more abundant than the two-centers. The second printing also may have been printed on slightly lighter weight postcard stock.

An interesting card in our collection, given to us by postcard collector Tom Mulvaney, is one with a two-cent stamp block mailed only three days after the one-cent rate went back into effect. The sender did the logical thing—write an ink note under the stamp block, "no 1¢ stamps" and apply half of a two-cent stamp! This creativity apparently met with the approval of the postal clerk who cancelled it and sent it on its way.

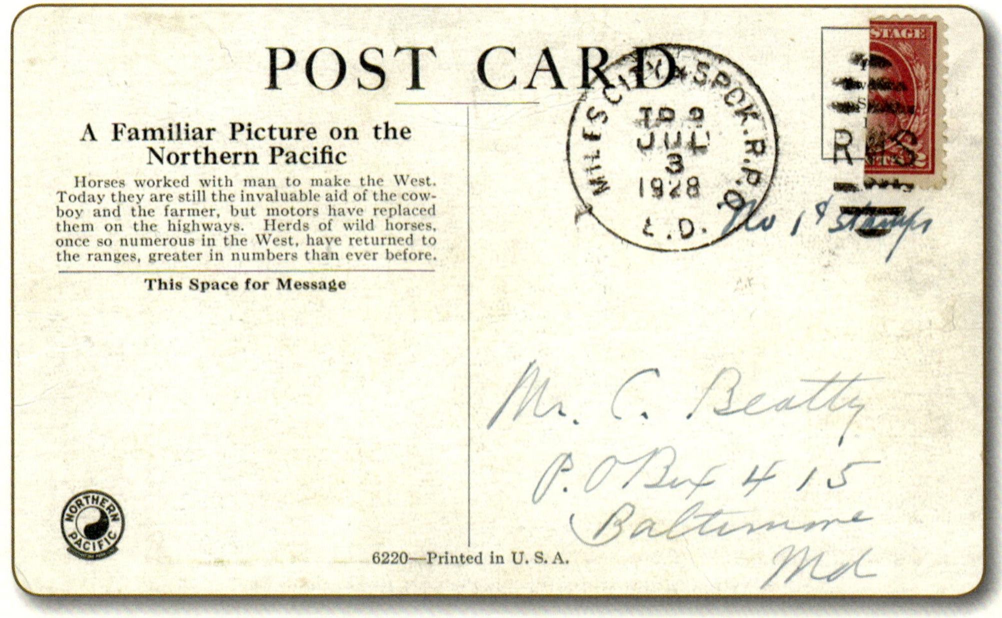

ABOVE: Postcard mailed with half a two-cent stamp.

The 1928 Postcards

Following are the five printed color cards in the 1928 series. Shown with each card is Huffman's description of the image as it appears on the back of the card.

The Indian Camp

Indian Camps in the Northwest are as picuresque today as they were before the Northern Pacific Railway, "First of the Northern Transcontinentals", was built. Braves, squaws, papooses, lodges of cowhide, campfires, cayuses, dogs, gay colors of costume, tepee and western sky —a picture of the romantic West which time does not change. Sioux, Crow, Cheyenne, Flathead, Mandan, Blackfeet, Chippewa, Yakima and a dozen other tribes live on the Northern Pacific.

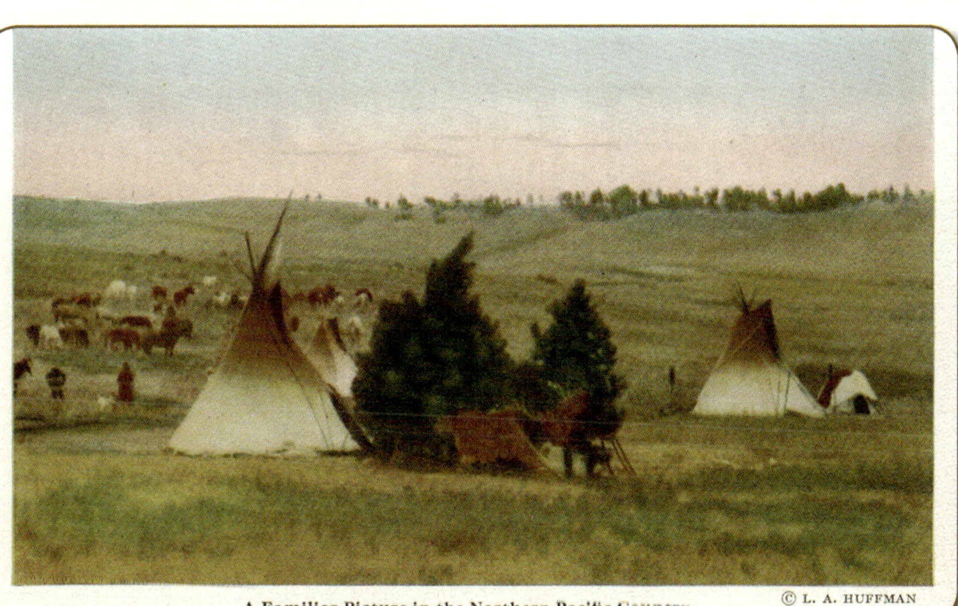

A Familiar Picture in the Northern Pacific Country © L. A. HUFFMAN

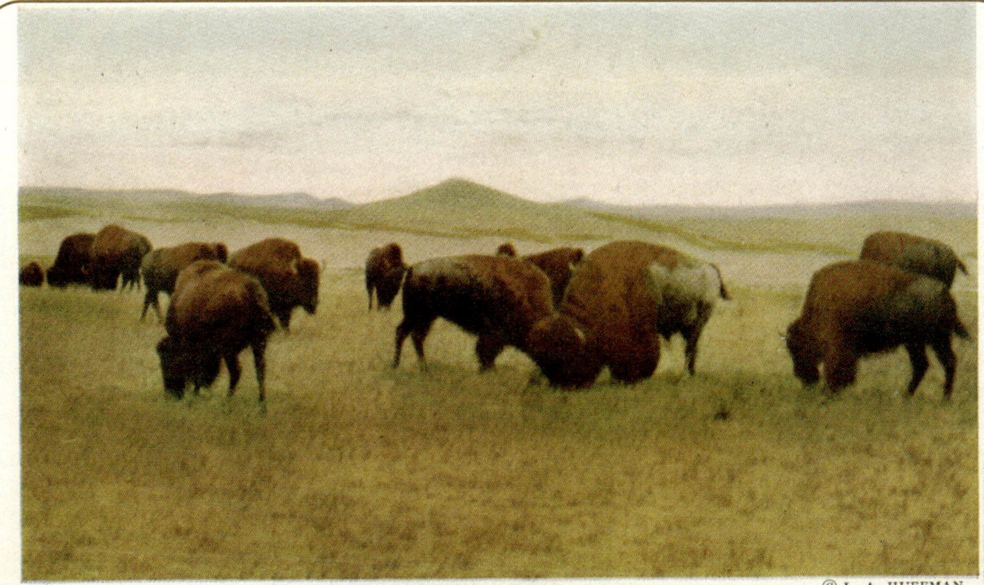

Buffalo Grazing the Big Open © L. A. HUFFMAN

The American Bison Saved

White hunters, Indians and wolves wiped out the great herds of buffalo, which roamed the ranges before and during the time the Northern Pacific Railway was building. A few survivors were brought to Yellowstone Park for protection; others to the U. S. Biological ranch in western Montana. Today a thousand buffalo thunder over the hills of these two reserves and the herds are rapidly multiplying. The American bison is saved.

The photograph reproduced on this card was made by Huffman, near Miles City, 50 years ago.

A Familiar Picture on the Northern Pacific

Horses worked with man to make the West. Today they are still the invaluable aid of the cowboy and the farmer, but motors have replaced them on the highways. Herds of wild horses, once so numerous in the West, have returned to the ranges, greater in numbers than ever before.

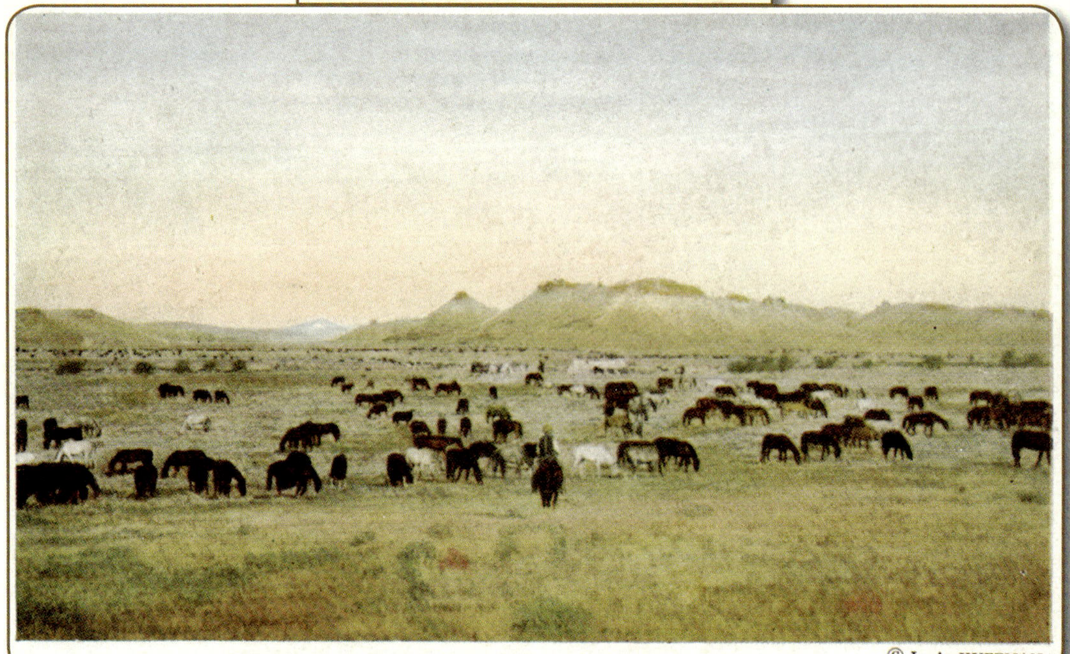

Evening at the Round-up, Big Pumpkin Creek, Montana

© L. A. HUFFMAN

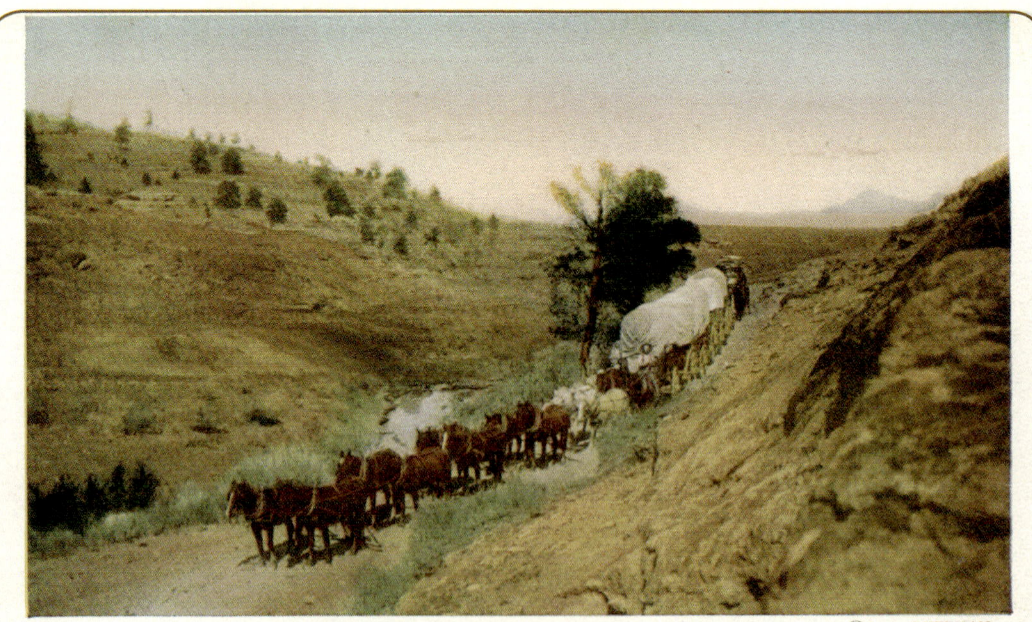

"Jerk-line twelve" on the Old Freight Road Before the Railroad Came

© L. A. HUFFMAN

Ahead of the Northern Pacific

For the pioneers, ox-teams "freighted" merchandise, mining machinery, farm implements, clothing, furniture and food into and through the Northwest just a half century ago. Along these laborious trails today, railroads and gravel highways make quick and easy transport.

This photograph on the Yellowstone was taken on the Northern Pacific right-of-way just 50 years ago.

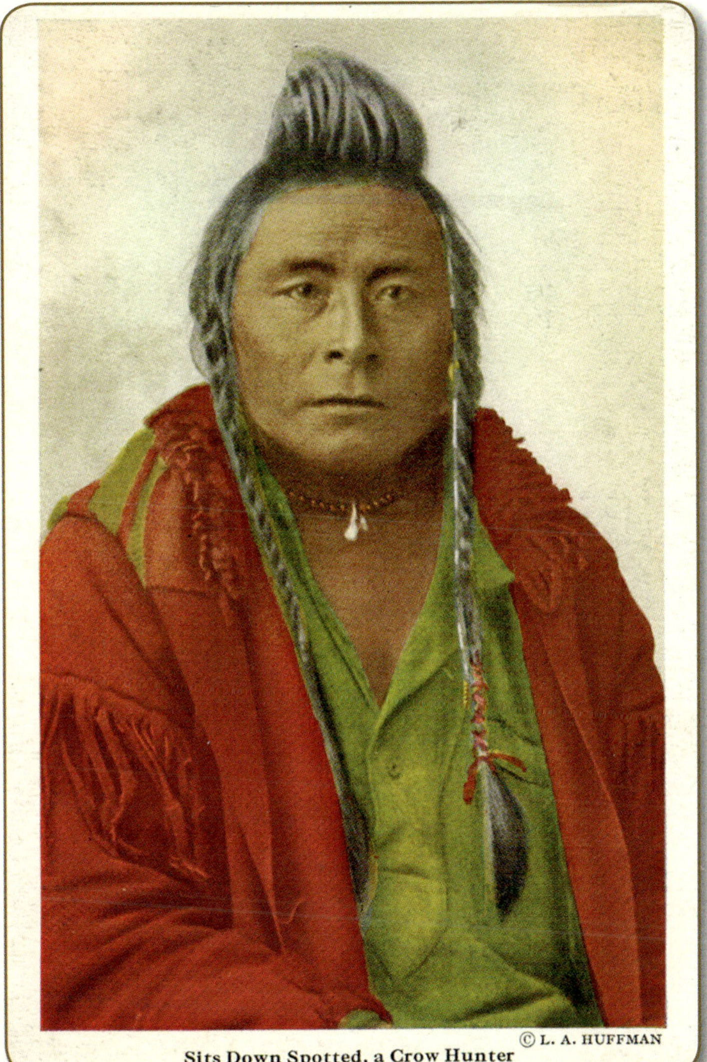
© L. A. HUFFMAN

Sits Down Spotted, a Crow Hunter

The First Americans

Nowhere can more splendid types of our first Americans be found than in the Northwest. At first, Indians fought the building of the Northern Pacific Railway, "First of the Northern Transcontinentals"; train rides and fair dealing won their friendship. Today Indians of the Northwest welcome the trains and their passengers. Sioux, Crow, Cheyenne, Flathead, Mandan, Blackfeet, Chippewa, Yakima and a dozen other tribes live on the Northern Pacific.

1928 Notes

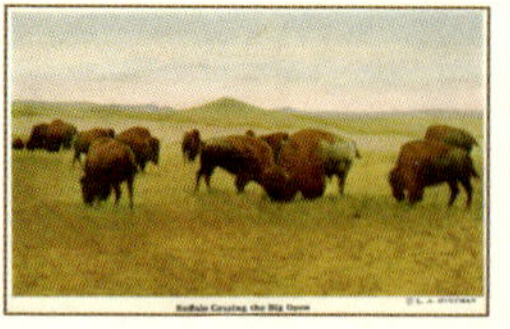

BUFFALO GRAZING THE BIG OPEN: This photo was taken in 1900 in Western Montana (see *Huffman Collotype Book* for details).

SITS DOWN SPOTTED, A CROW HUNTER: "This is a picture of Carries His Food who died in 1888. He was an expert hunter who always succeeded in providing food for his family." (From a letter from Gordon Powers to Mark Brown, 1951.)

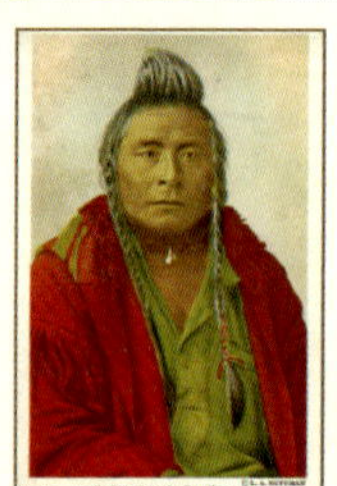

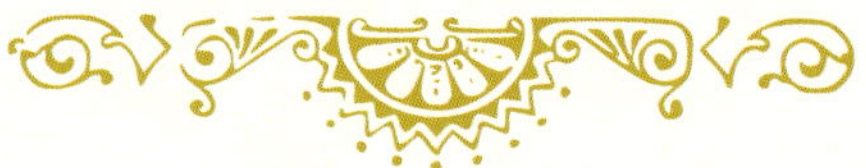

Real Photo Postcards

All of Huffman's real photo postcards (RPPC) must be considered scarce to rare. While we have more than 50 in our collection, we thought this discussion required a broader look that included examples from other collections. Our good friend Tom Mulvaney, one of Montana's most serious and longtime postcard collectors, provided additional contacts. A survey of the collections from more than a dozen institutions and collectors turned up 185 total cards representing 117 different images. Most cards are numbered and titled with observed numbers from 1–581. The numbers appear to be Huffman's negative numbers and unrelated to postcard sequence. Their collective information provides the basis for the following discussion.

Only about a third of the 185 cards were postally used, providing 58 readable cancellation dates. The earliest observed date was from August 1906, which appeared on three cards. More than 80 percent of the cancels occurred during the 1906–1908 period and 95 percent between 1906–1912. The latest observed date was from the year 1918, found on two cards. The copyright date "07" appears on several of the cards as part of the title.

More than 70 percent of the 117 known images appear on the earlier undivided back cards and 25 percent on the later divided back cards. Only four images appeared on both types of cards. Similarly, about 78 percent of the cancels appear on undivided backs and 22 percent on divided backs. Ninety seven percent of the cancels on undivided backs occurred between 1906–1908. Nearly 90 percent of the divided back cancels occurred between 1908–1912 with the earliest in July 1908.

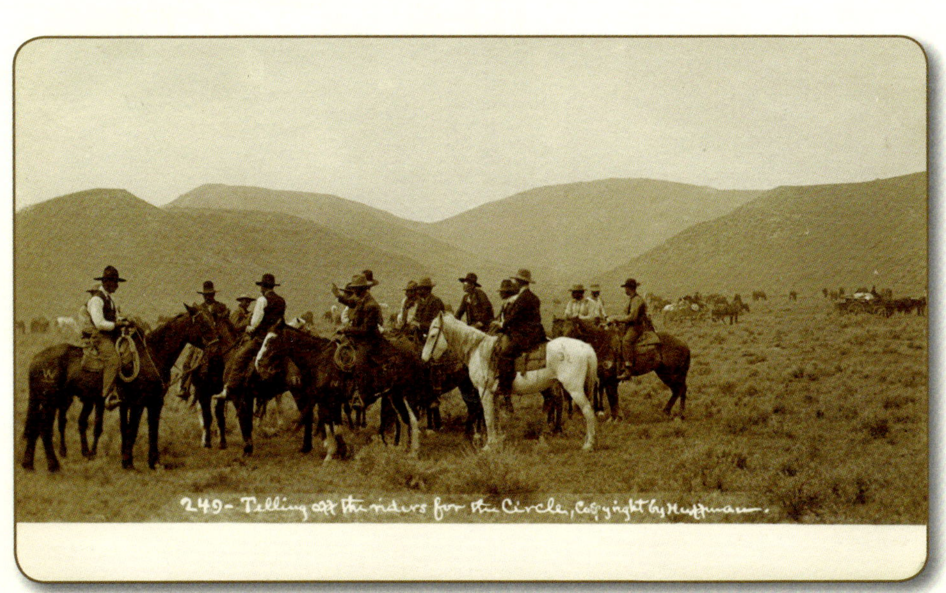

ABOVE: *Telling Off the Riders for the Circle*

Of the total 117 different images, 74, or about 60 percent, made one-of-a-kind appearances in our survey and were found in only one collection. About 25 percent appeared in two collections and only 15 percent in three. No image appeared in more than three collections. All of the undivided backs are on a single

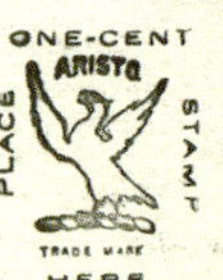

LEFT: Aristo undivided back (1905–1913)

BELOW: *AZO divided back (1904–1918)*

LEFT: Artura divided back (1908–1924)

FACING PAGE: *The Honyocker*

BELOW: *CYKO divided back (1904–1920s) courtesy Tom Mulvaney*

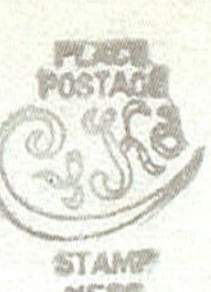

type of card, Aristo. Nearly all of the divided backs are on three types of cards—AZO 45 percent, Artura 33 percent and CYKO 22 percent (all shown with production dates).

Assuming there is a strong correlation between when the cards were made and when they were used, there are a number of general observations that can be drawn from the above information. Perhaps most significant, Huffman's active production of RPPCs didn't last very long, only four or five years. The general scarcity of his cards, and extreme scarcity of many of the images, suggests that he didn't print up a supply of cards to have on hand when someone stopped by his studio. By this time, Huffman's studio was no longer in a downtown storefront. He was in his new studio built next door to his house in a north side residential part of Miles City. It seems more likely that he only made a postcard when someone requested one. There are a few examples of cards with the same number and image but with slightly different hand-written titles, also suggesting he was making them one at a time. While several of his more popular images appear in two or three of the collections, it is interesting to note the absence of any examples of *The Honyocker,* arguably one of today's most iconic Huffman images. Apparently, some icons have long gestation periods.

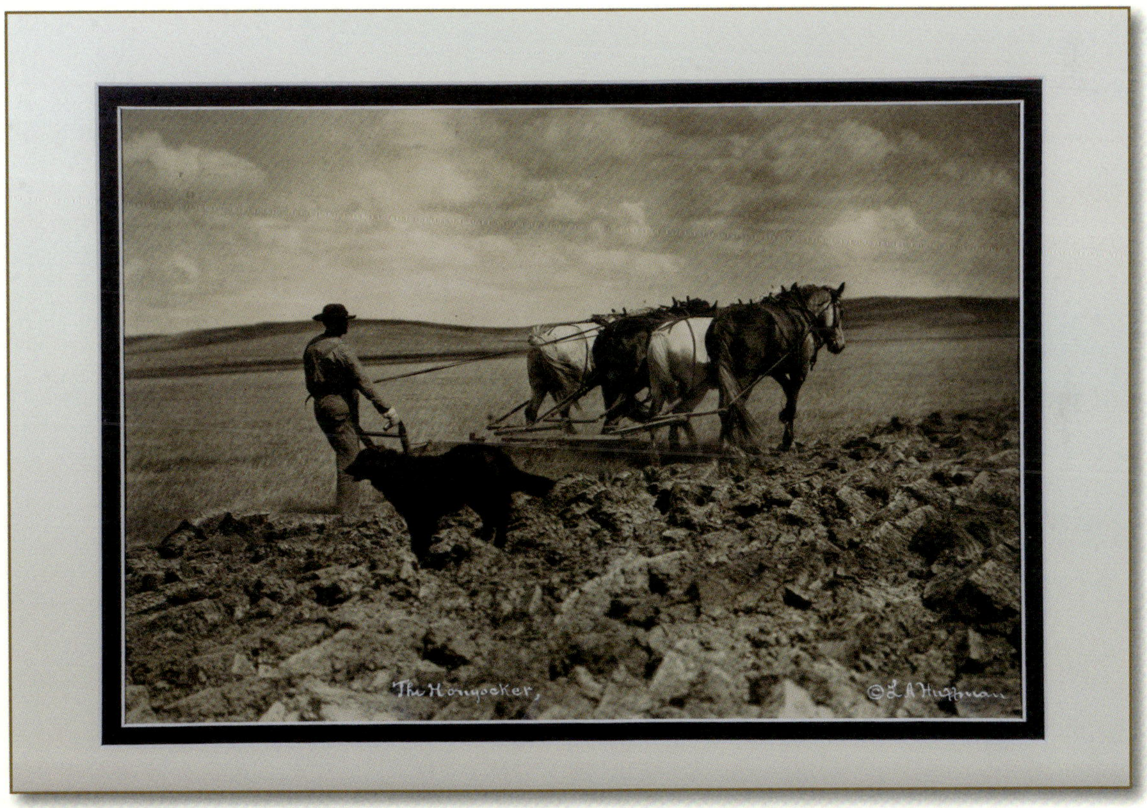

Huffman's first apparent use of postcards in mid 1906 was towards the end of the undivided card era; divided back use was authorized beginning March 1, 1907. Cancel evidence suggests he used his stock of Aristo undivided back cards until they were gone sometime in mid 1908 before going to divided backs. After a couple more years, Huffman's production of RPPCs was drastically reduced if not ended. It was an outcome one would not have expected during the Golden Age of postcard use. It wasn't because he didn't have interesting images to offer; he had great images. There were probably several factors that contributed to that outcome. His financial position was never good and he had just recently filed for bankruptcy. He had left his downtown location and moved his studio to a residential neighborhood, lessening the "walk in" potential for postcard customers. He probably recognized the small profit margin in individual postcards. He had just invested in his 1907 series, 81,000 printed cards, and perhaps thought that would be adequate to fill any demand for his postcards. Whatever his reasons, Huffman produced a very limited number of RPPCs and that explains the rarity of those postcards today.

Two cards were produced considerably later than the others. Both are of a street scene in Glendive, Montana, titled *Glendive Mont 1882*, and are of the same image as No. 26 on the checklist at the back of the book. One is on an EKC card (production 1939–1950) and would not have been produced during Huffman's lifetime. The other is on a later AZO card (production 1926–1940s) and could have been, but probably wasn't, produced during Huffman's lifetime.

There are two instances where two slightly different images were assigned the same number. The first is No. 580, *Bender's Ranch, a Relic of the Seventies,* where both close-up and distant views of the same ranch building have the same number. The other is No. 581, *Main St., Miles City, West of 8th,* where one view is looking down the street and another is looking across the street.

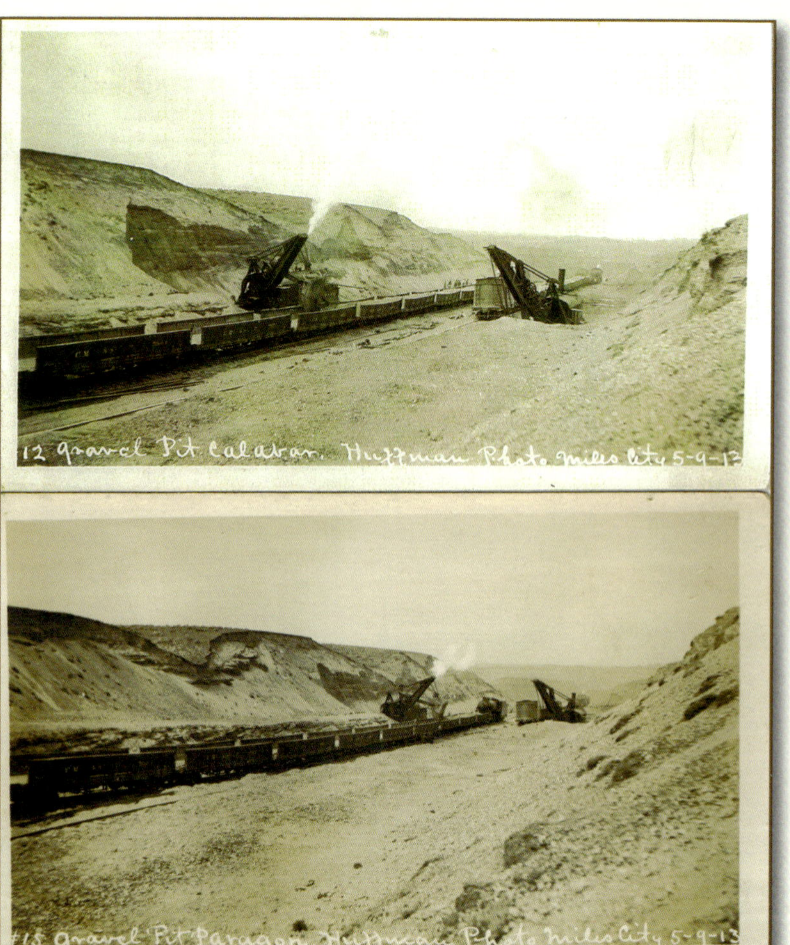

LEFT: Two Gravel Pit cards.

The Chicago, Milwaukee, St. Paul and Pacific Railroad (The Milwaukee Road) arrived in Miles City in 1907 on its westward trek across Montana. The railroad operated a number of gravel pits used in the construction and maintenance of their rail line. Two of those pits were just west of Miles City in the Yellowstone Valley near the small settlements of Paragon (8 miles west) and Calabar (20 miles west). Four cards in the collection (Nos. 8, 11, 12, 15) carry gravel pit images, three titled "Calabar" and one titled "Paragon." Three of them indicate they were taken the same day, "5–9–13." Two of the cards are slightly different views of the same site but one is titled "Calabar" and the other "Paragon."

We're not sure which is correct. All four photos may have been taken at the same site, at least three of them on the same day. Two of the cards carry 1918 postmarks, one in August and the other in October. As mentioned earlier, these are the latest postmarks observed on any of Huffman's RPPCs. At least three of the cards have a three-line stamp across the message end of the card that reads "From the Holmboe Studio, 611 Main St., Miles City, Montana." A Mrs. Marion Holmboe operated a photo studio at that address during that time period.

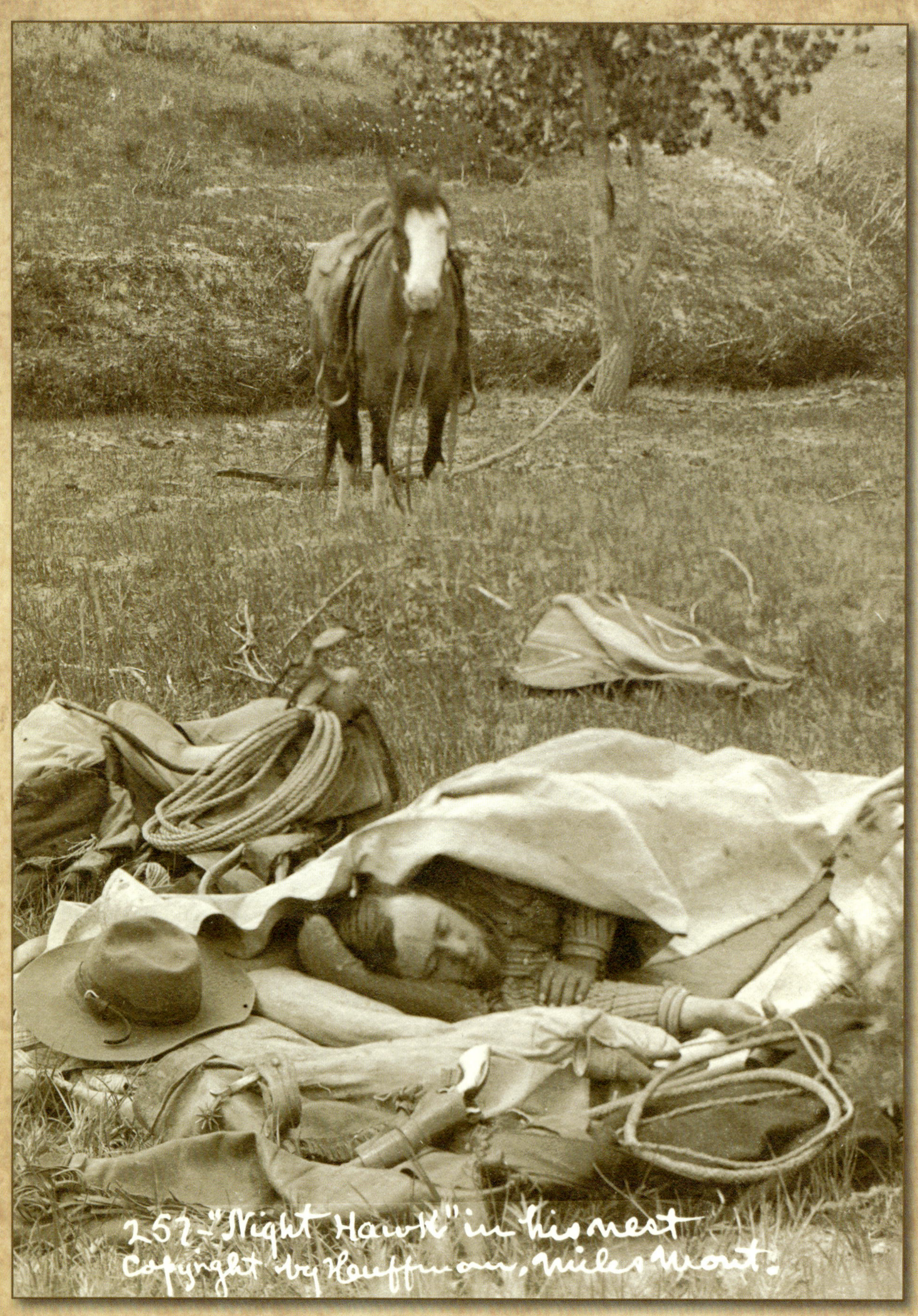
252-"Night Hawk" in his nest
Copyright by Huffman, Miles Mont.

The Real Photo Postcards

A variety of Huffman's real photo postcards are shown on the following pages. Those with numbers are arranged in numerical order. A complete listing of the known images can be found in the checklist at the back of the book.

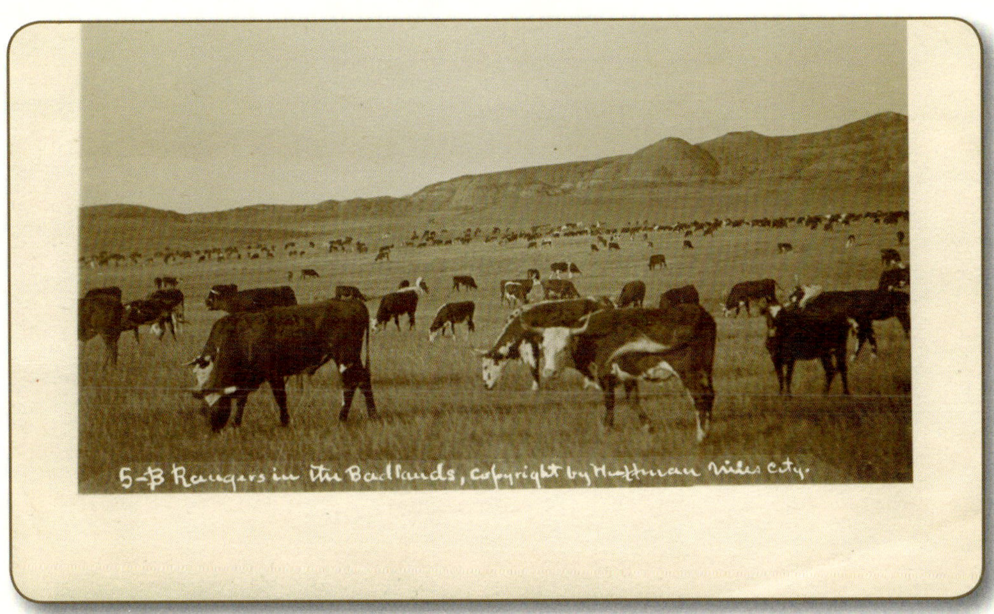

ABOVE: *5-B Rangers in the Badlands*

BELOW: *8 Cheyenne Agency Lamedeer*

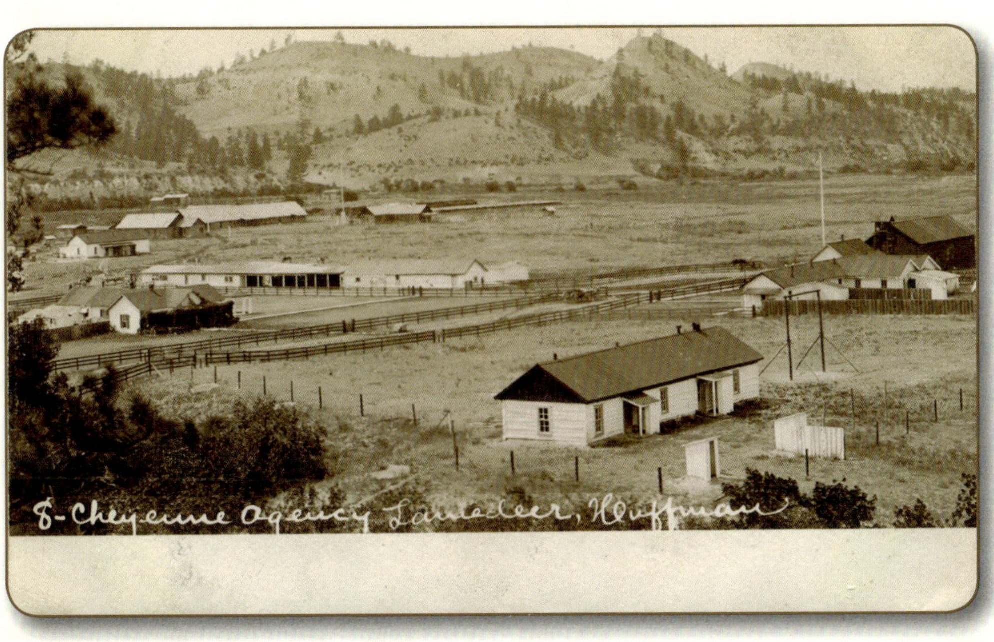

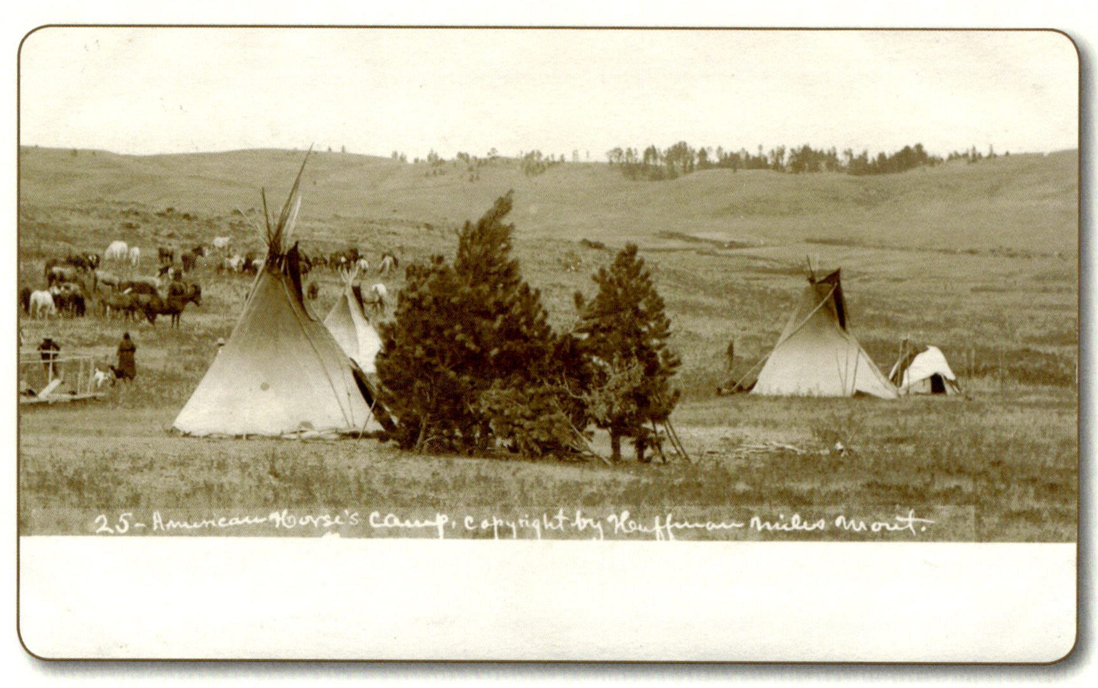

ABOVE: *25 American Horse's Camp*

BELOW: *41 Squaw Fleshing Hide*

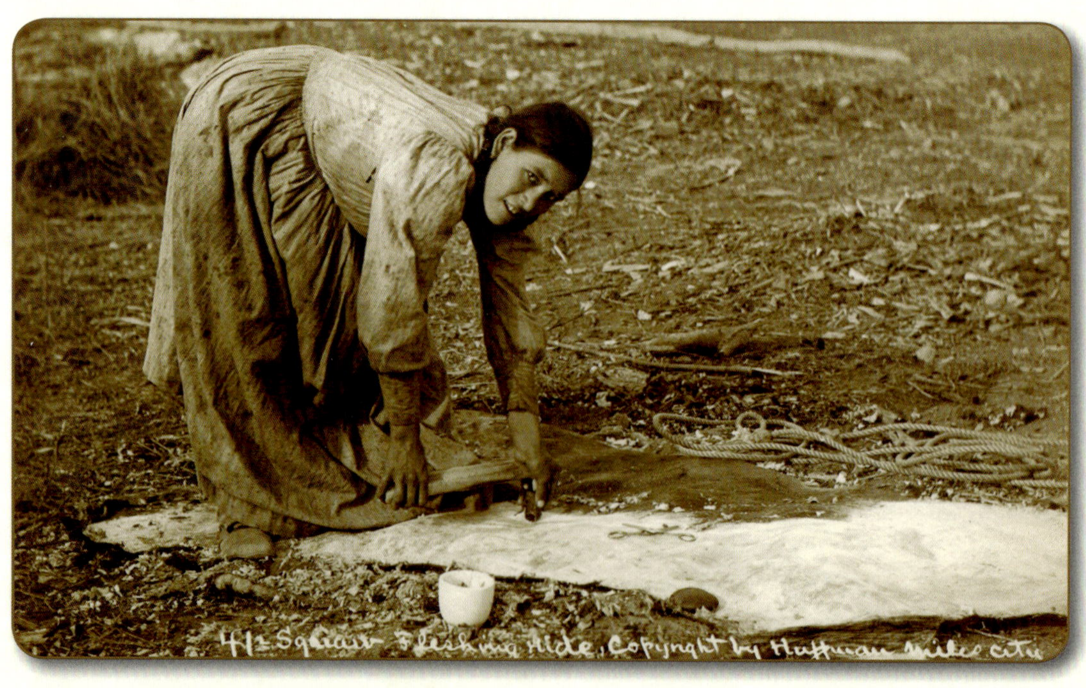

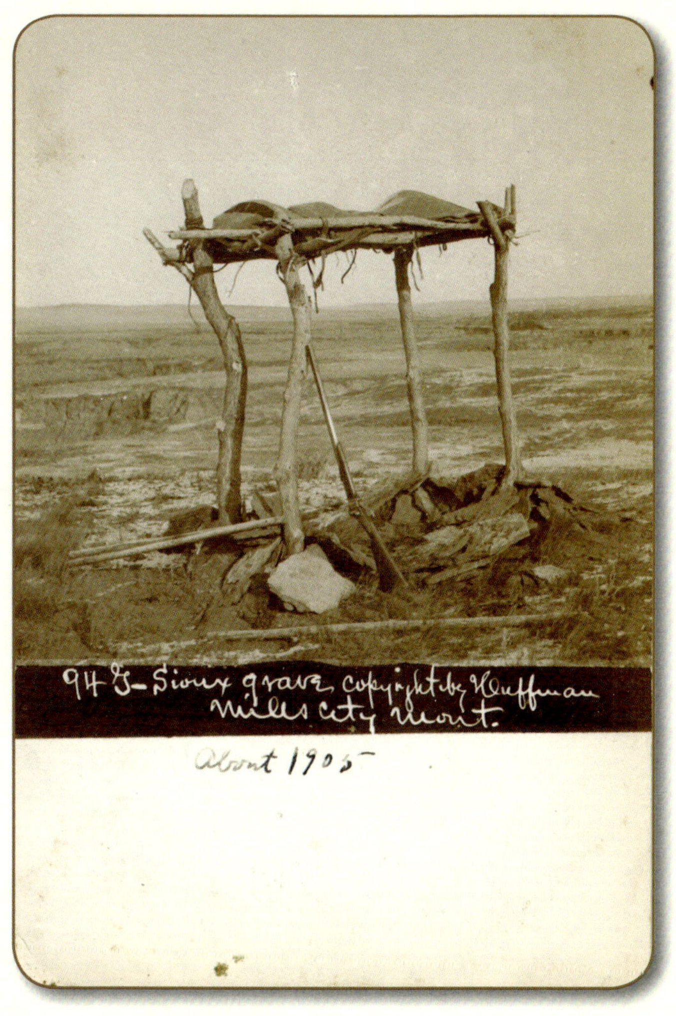

ABOVE: *94G Sioux Grave*

BELOW: *151 Hunters Horse Ranch*

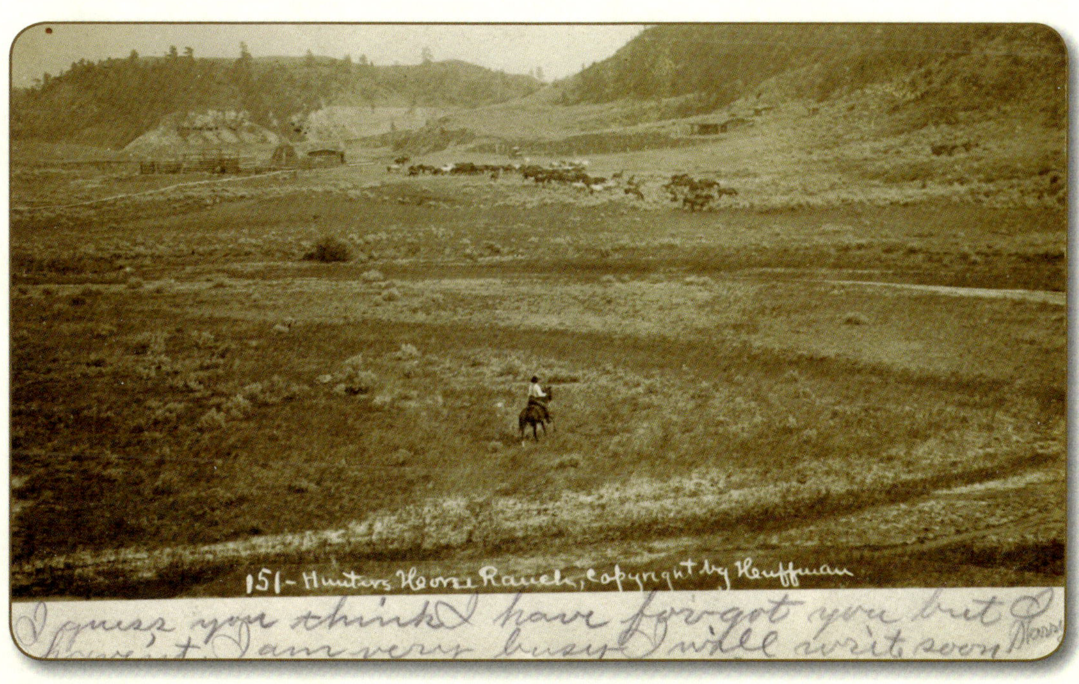

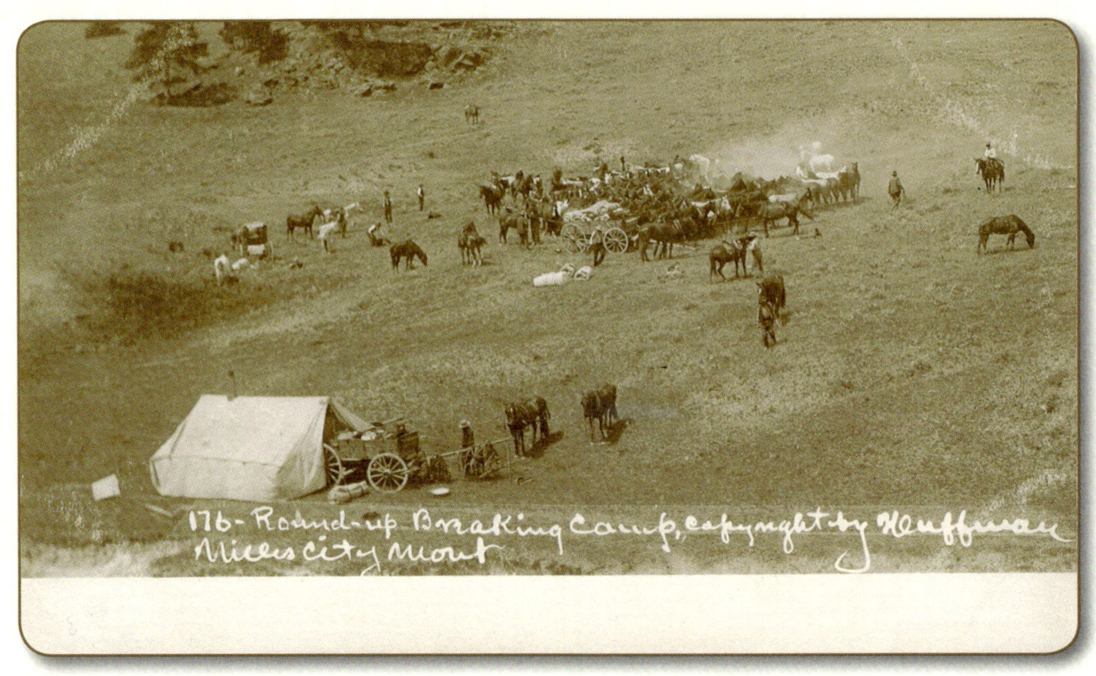

ABOVE: *176 Round-up Breaking Camp*

BELOW: *185 C. Horse Camp*

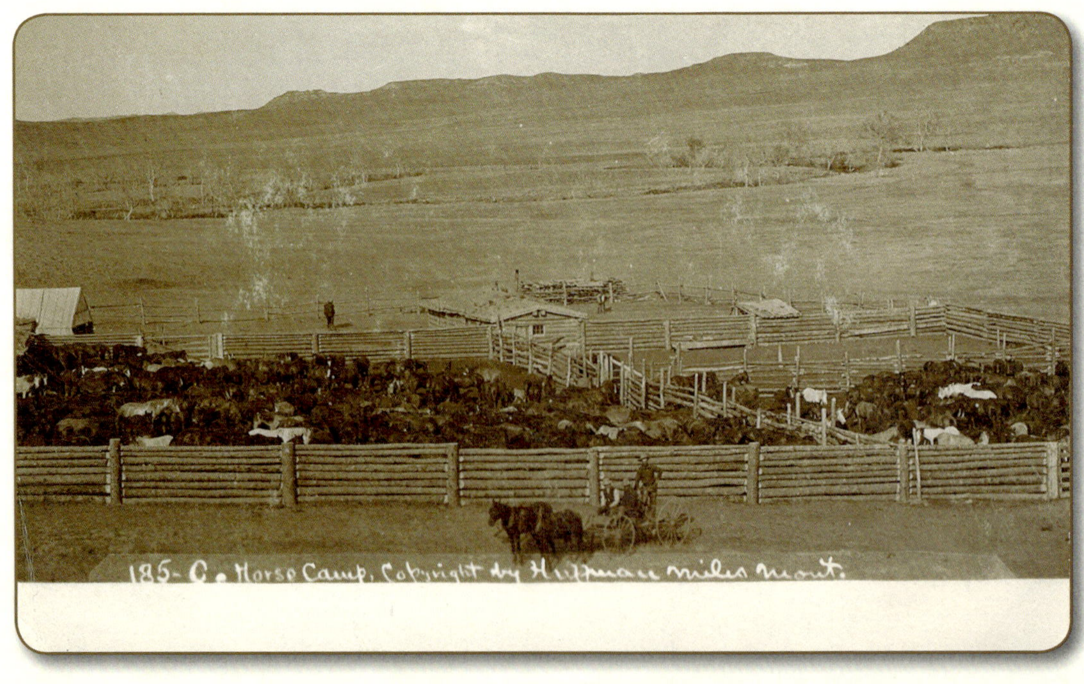

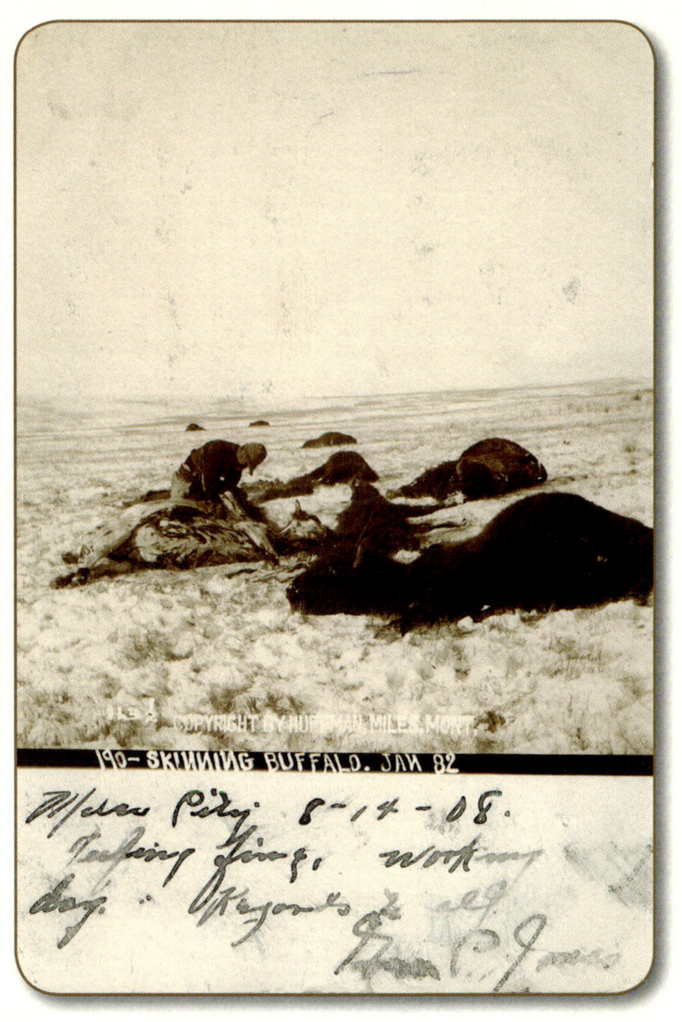

ABOVE: *190 Skinning Buffalo. Jan. 82*

BELOW: *203 Branding Calves in Corrall*

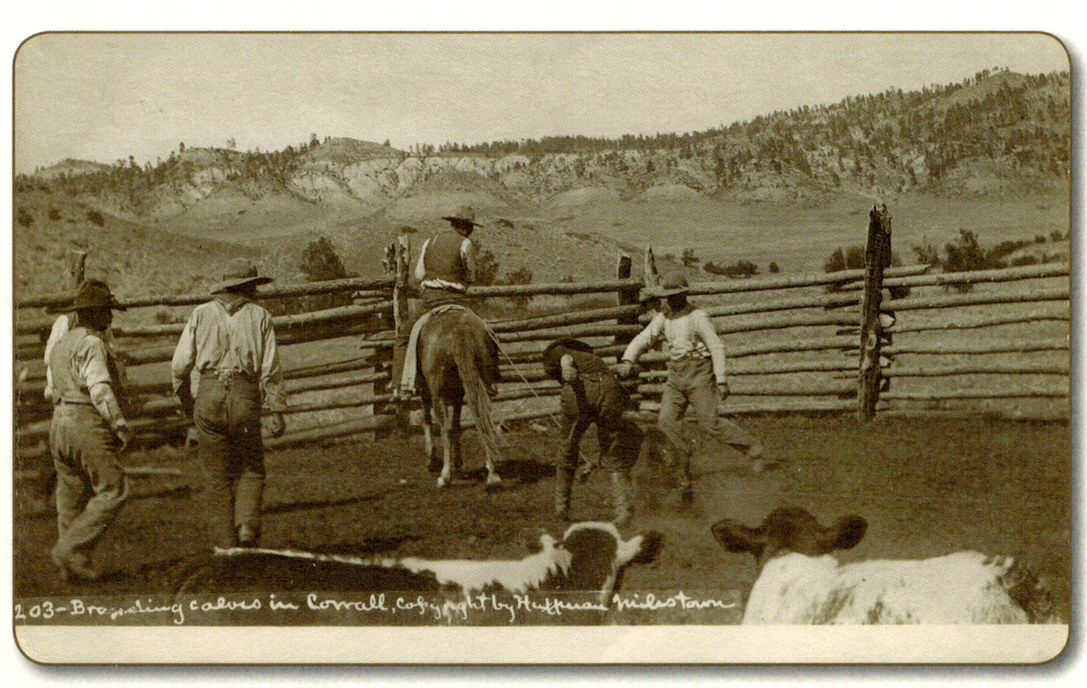

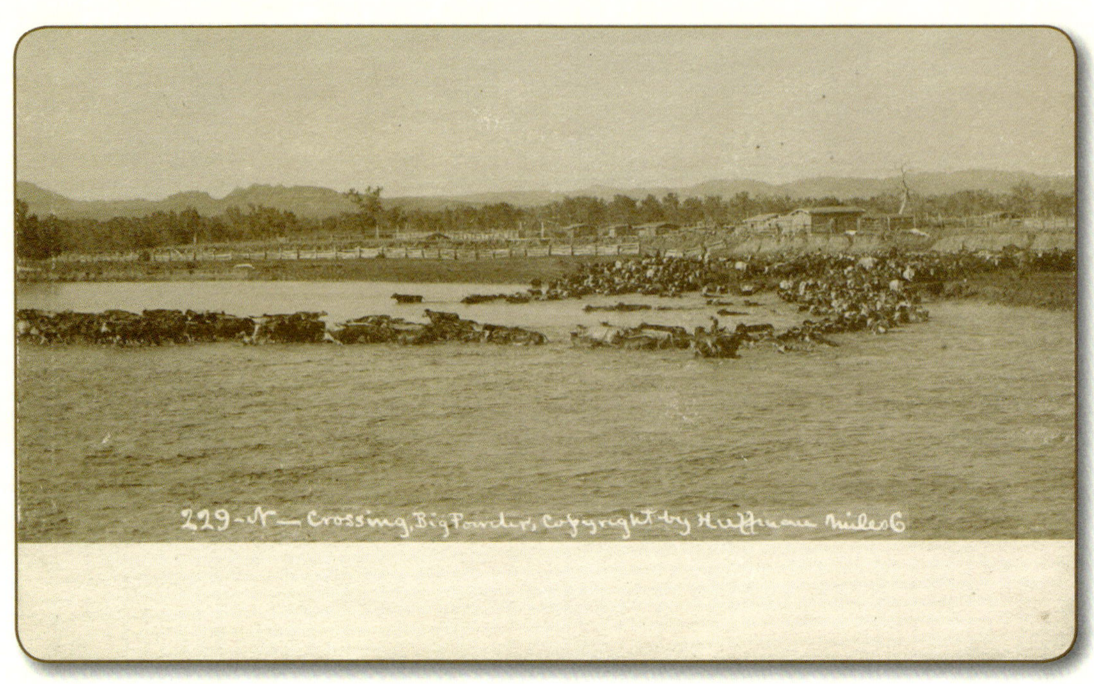

ABOVE: *229 N Bar Crossing, Big Powder*

BELOW: *231 SH Outfit on Trail*

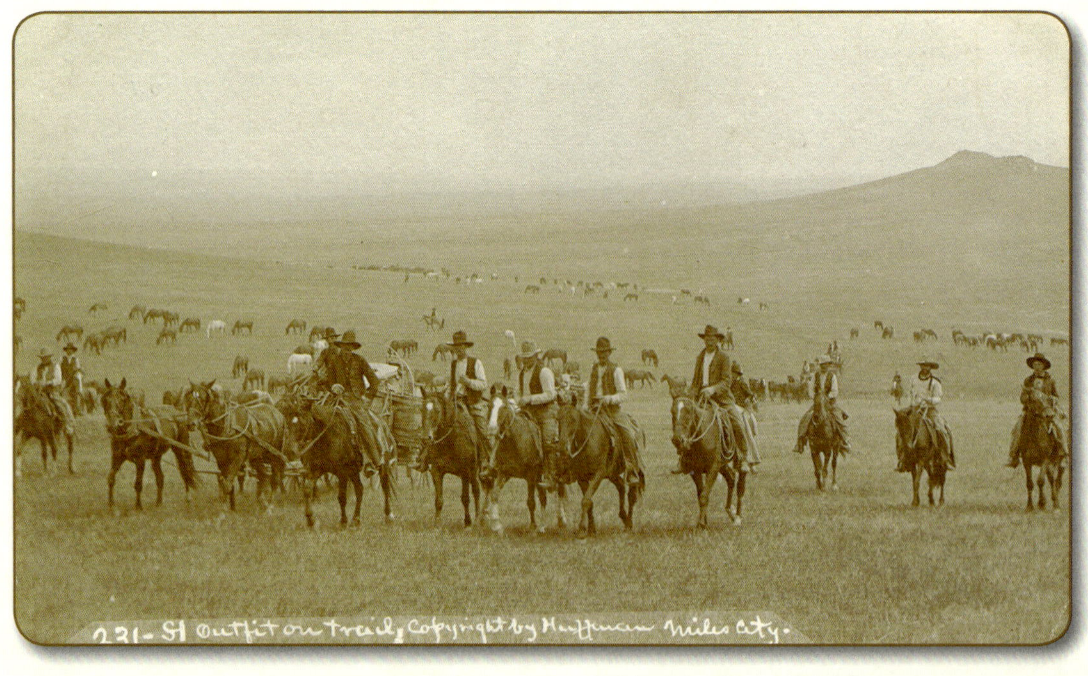

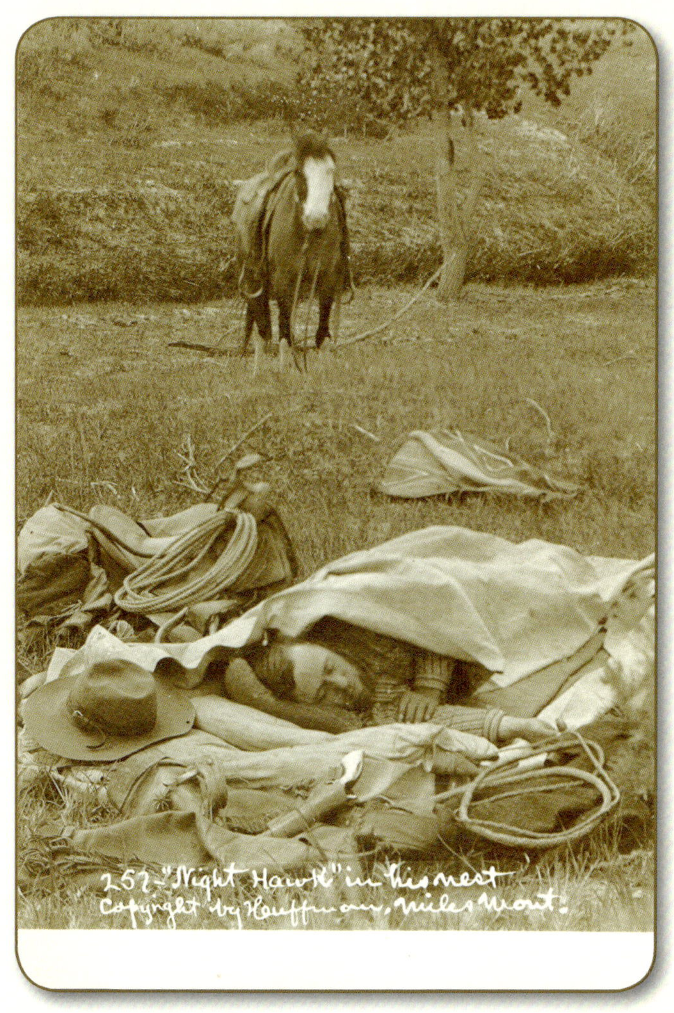

ABOVE: *257 "Night Hawk" in His Nest*

BELOW: *259 Round-up on the Move*

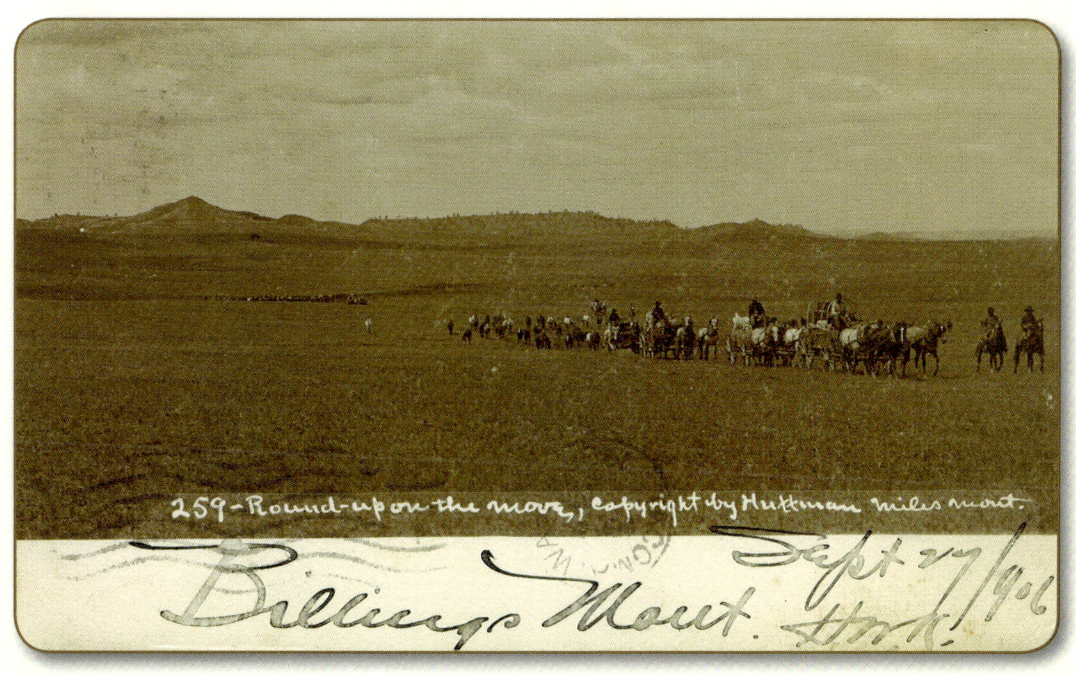

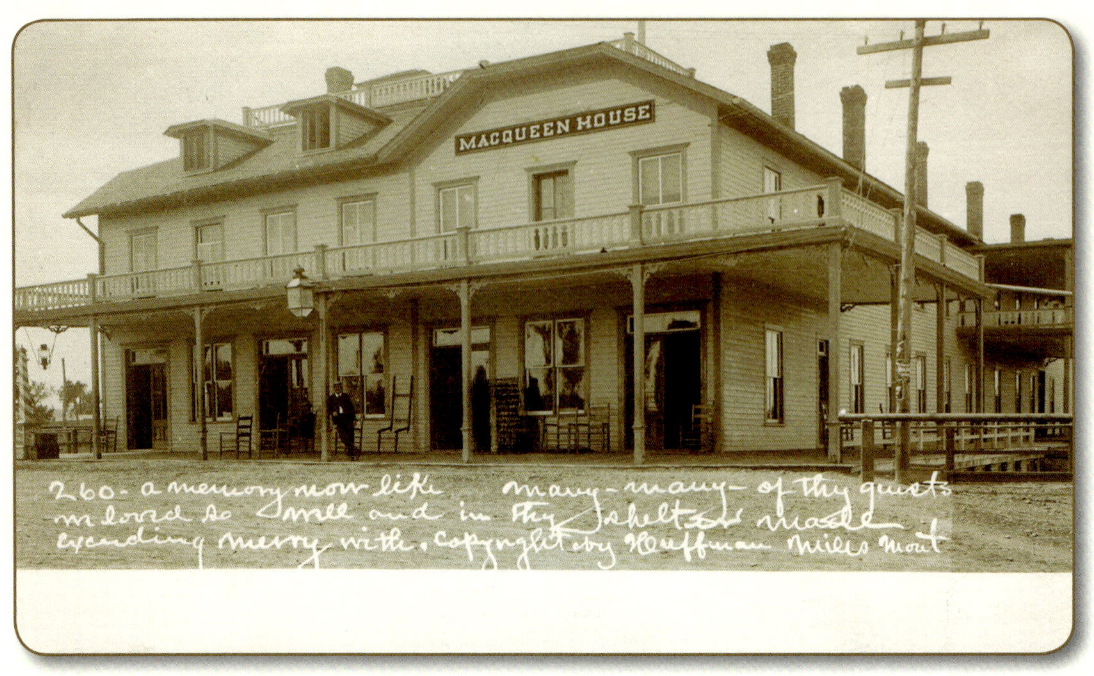

ABOVE: *260 MacQueen House*

BELOW: *274 Riding a Bronco*

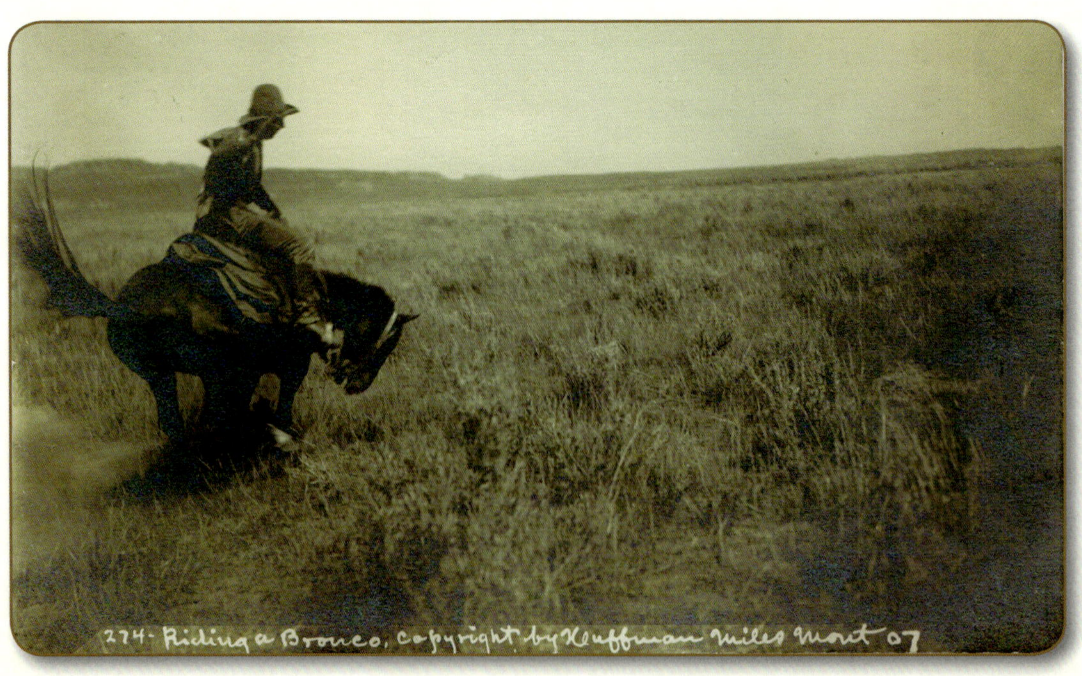

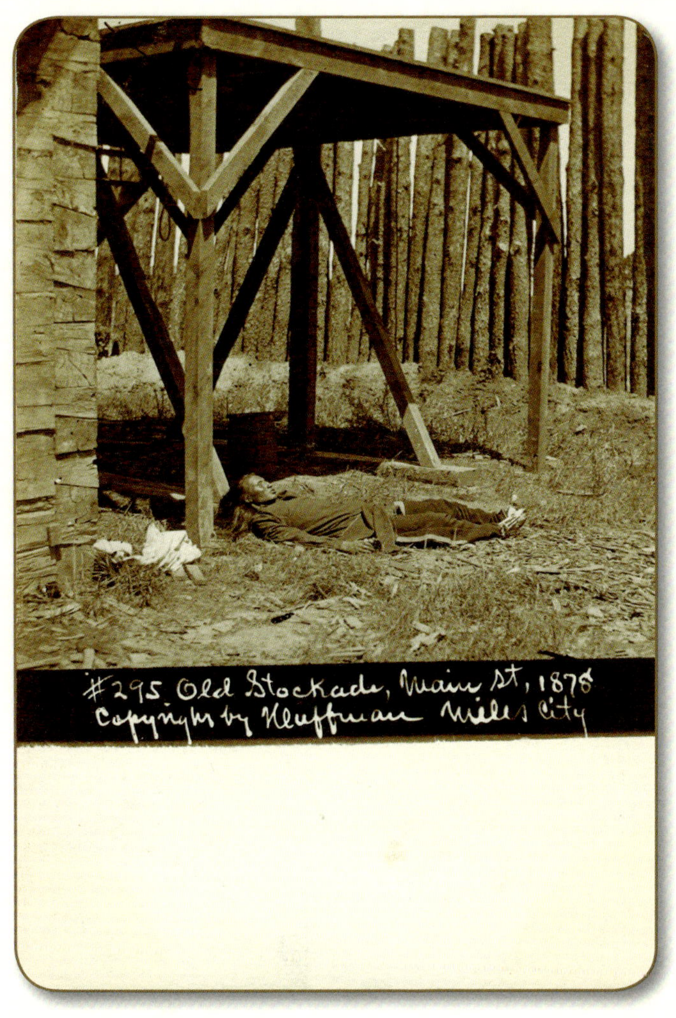

ABOVE: *295 Old Stockade, Main St. 1878*

BELOW: *298 Miles from North*

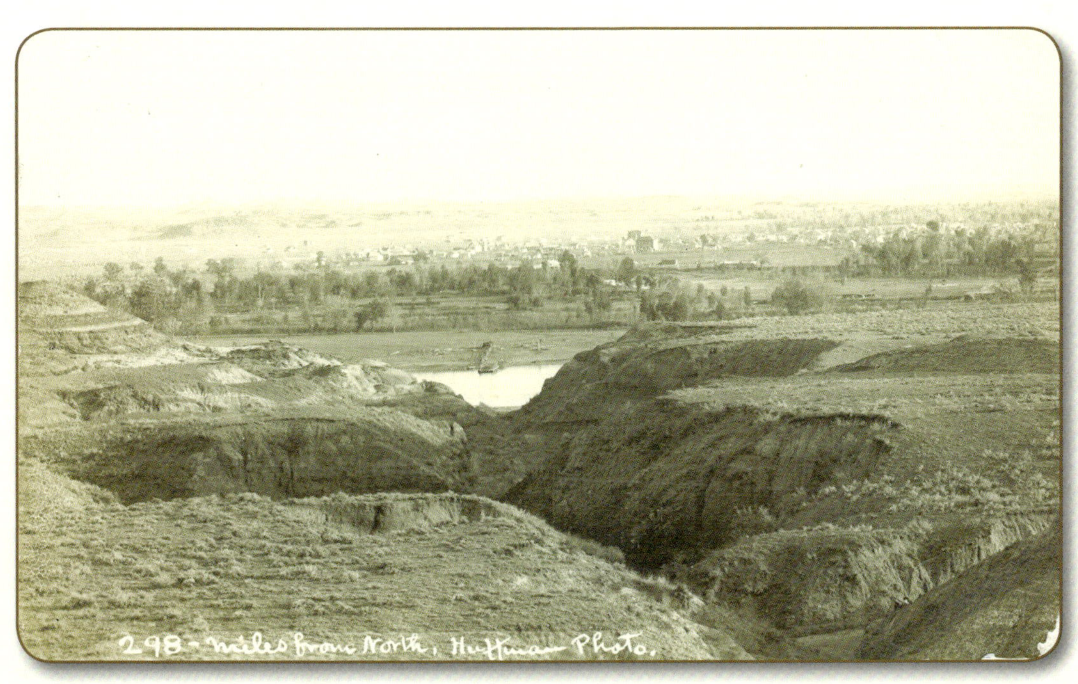

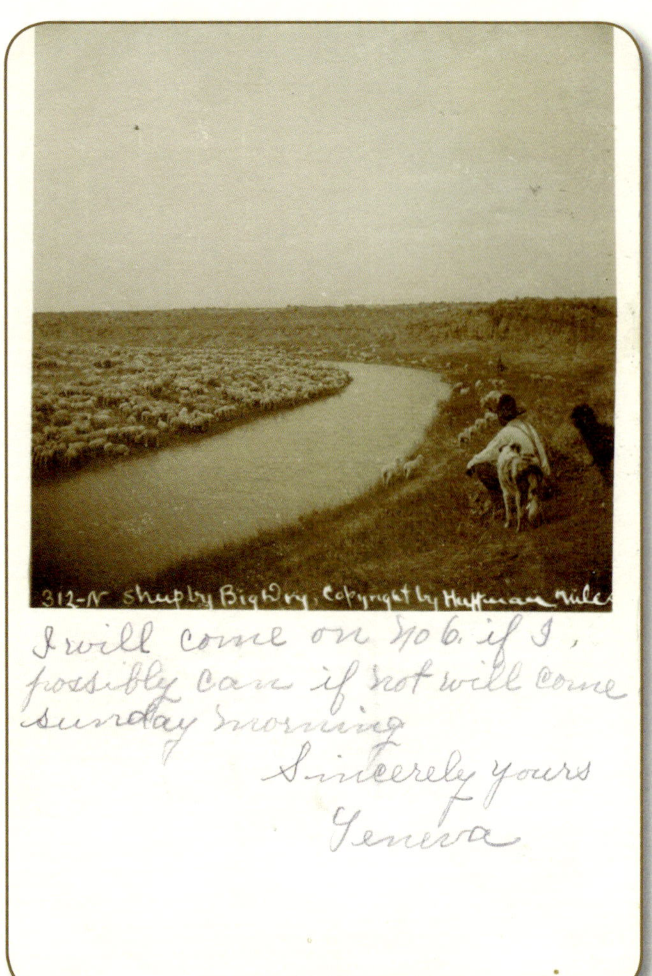

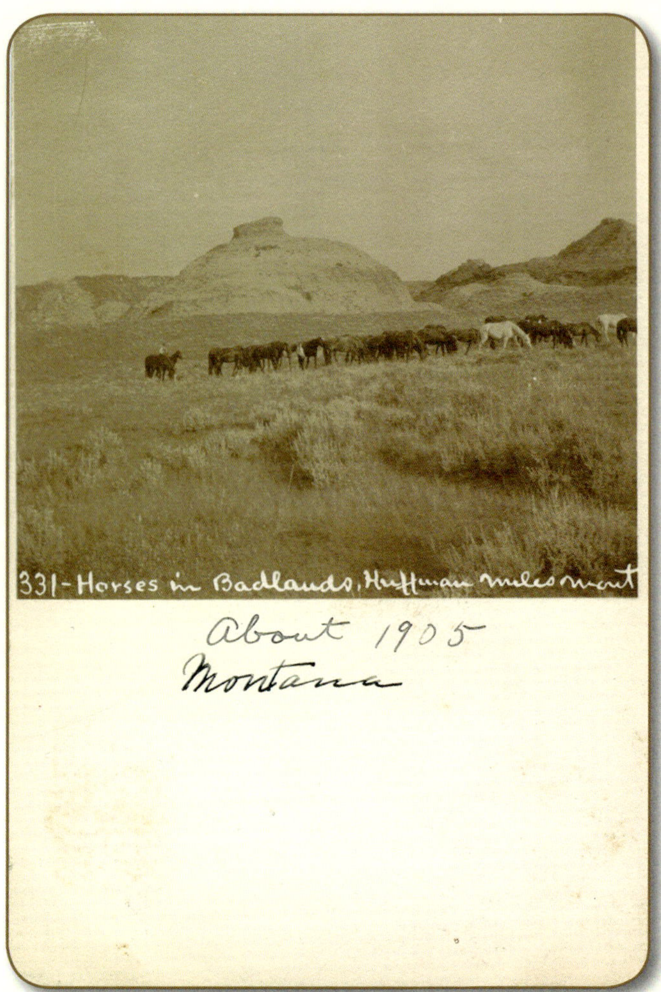

ABOVE LEFT: *312N Sheep by Big Dry*

ABOVE RIGHT: *331 Horses in Badlands*

BELOW: *392 A Wolfer and Outfit*

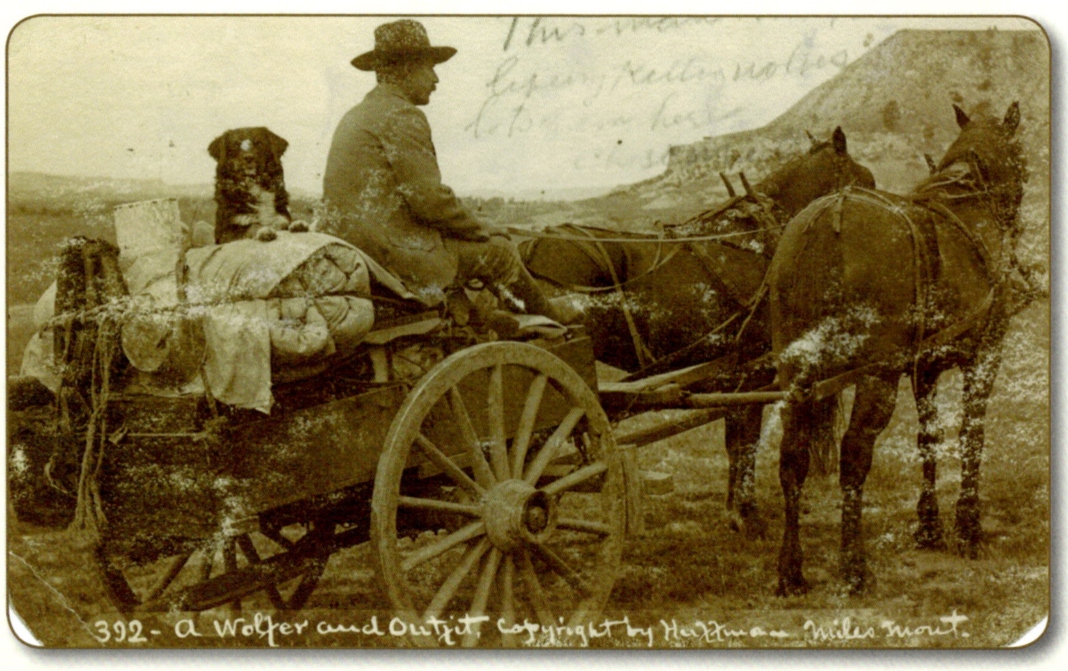

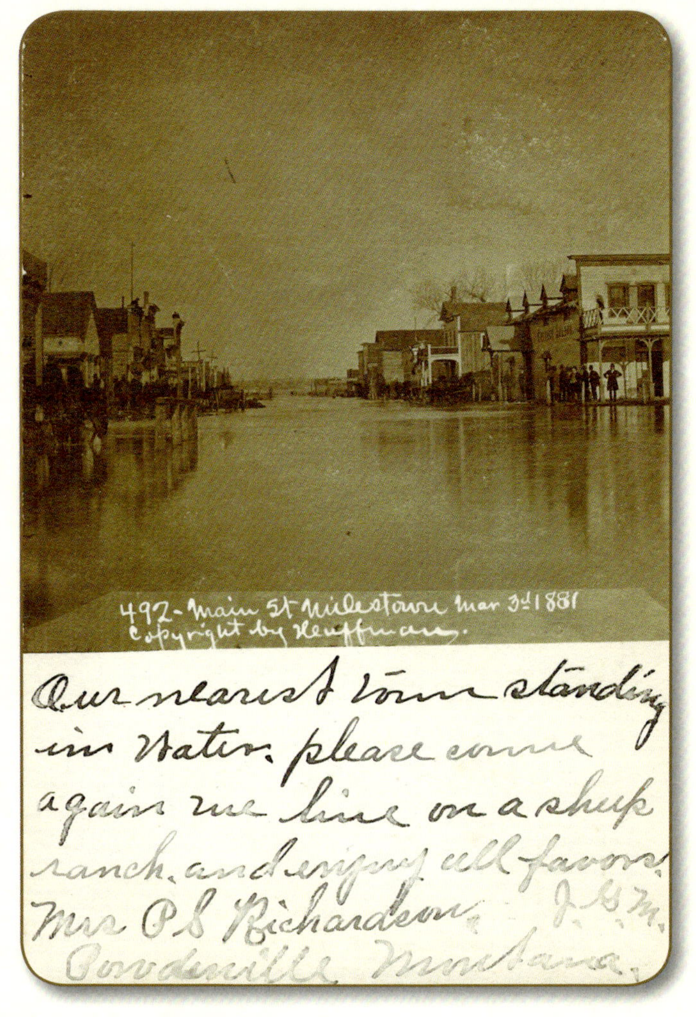

ABOVE: *492 Main St. Milestown Mar. 3rd 1881*

BELOW: *565 Drifter Sheep Wagon and Band on Winter Bed Grounds*

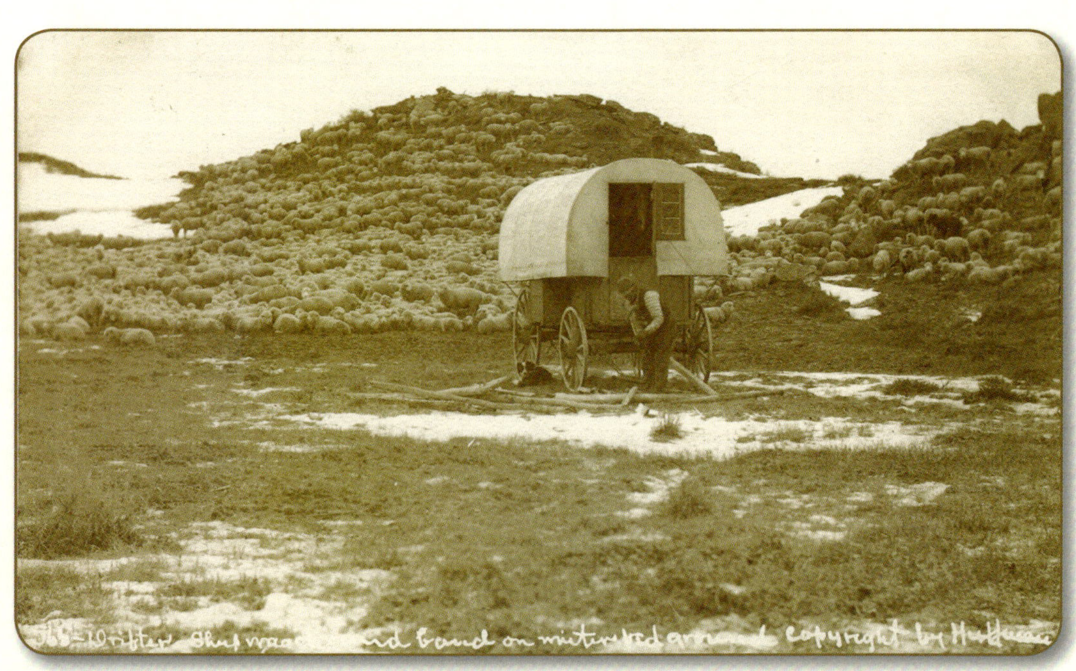

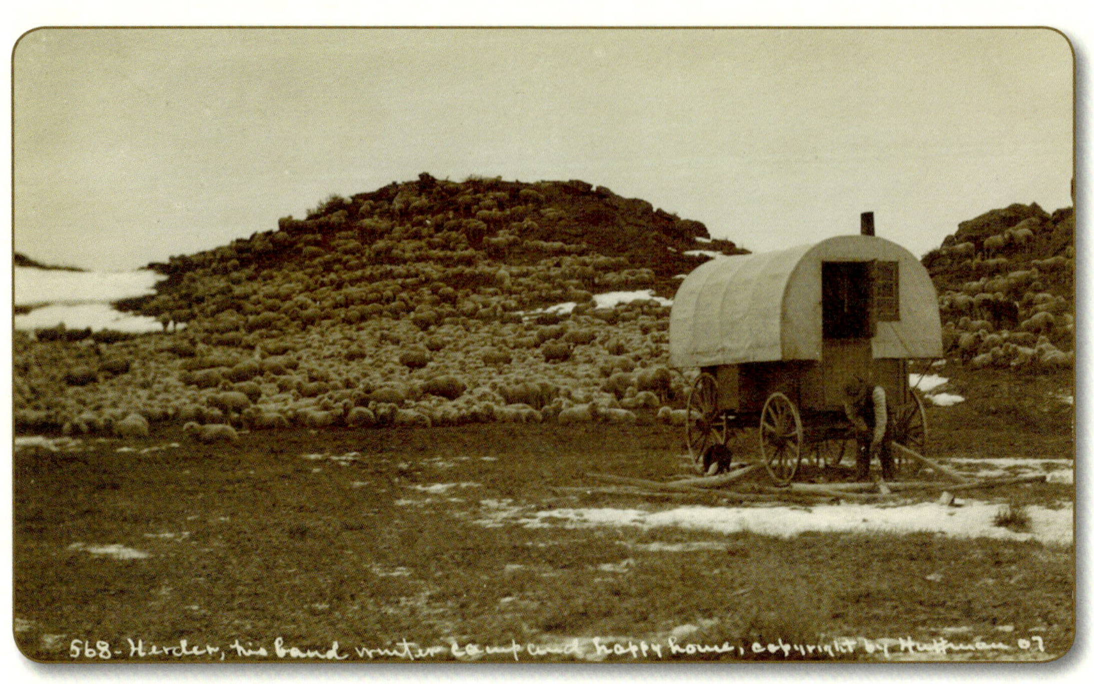

ABOVE: *568 Herder, His Band Winter Camp and Happy Home*

BELOW: *569 Pushing Them from Bed Cold Morning*

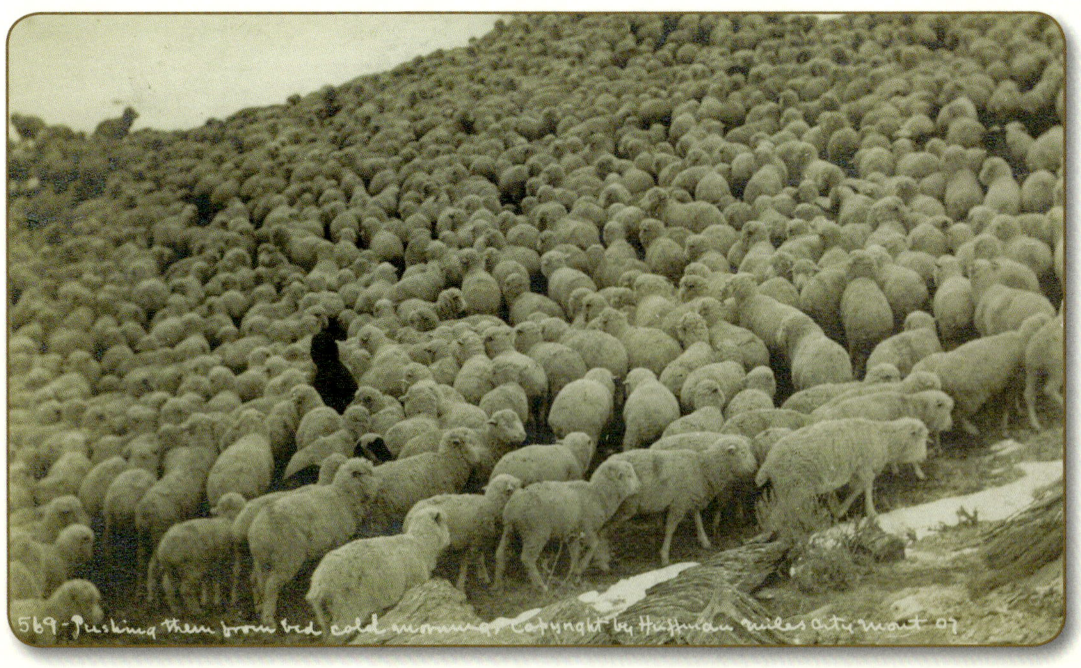

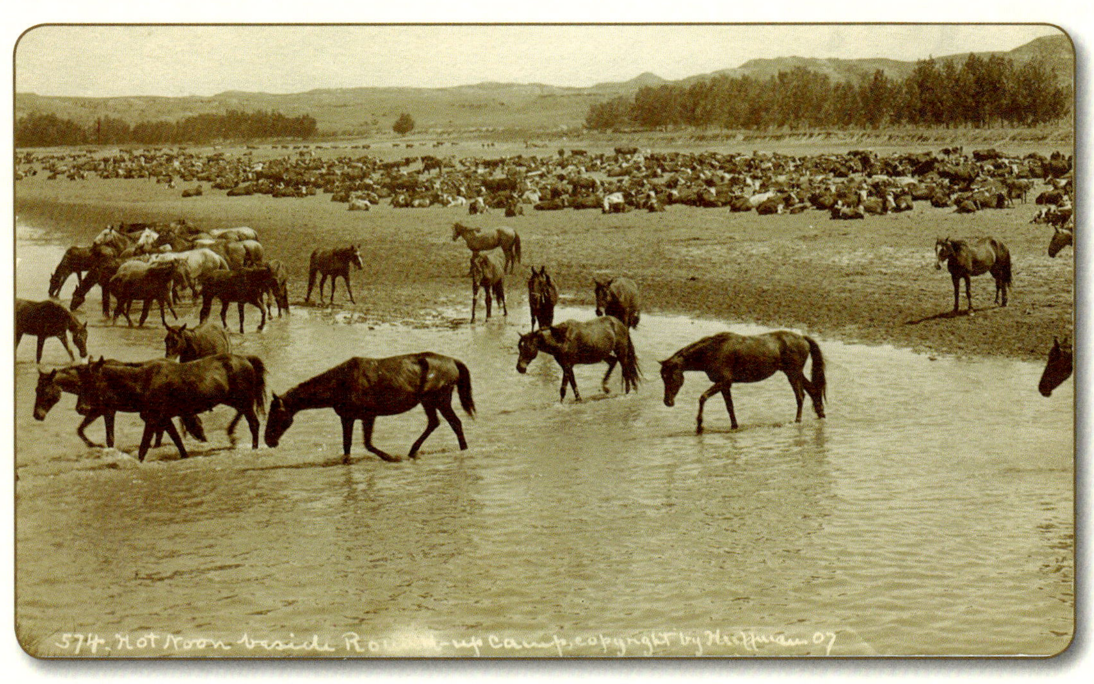

ABOVE: *574 Hot Noon Beside Round-up Camp*

BELOW: *580 Bender's Ranch, A Relic of the Seventies*

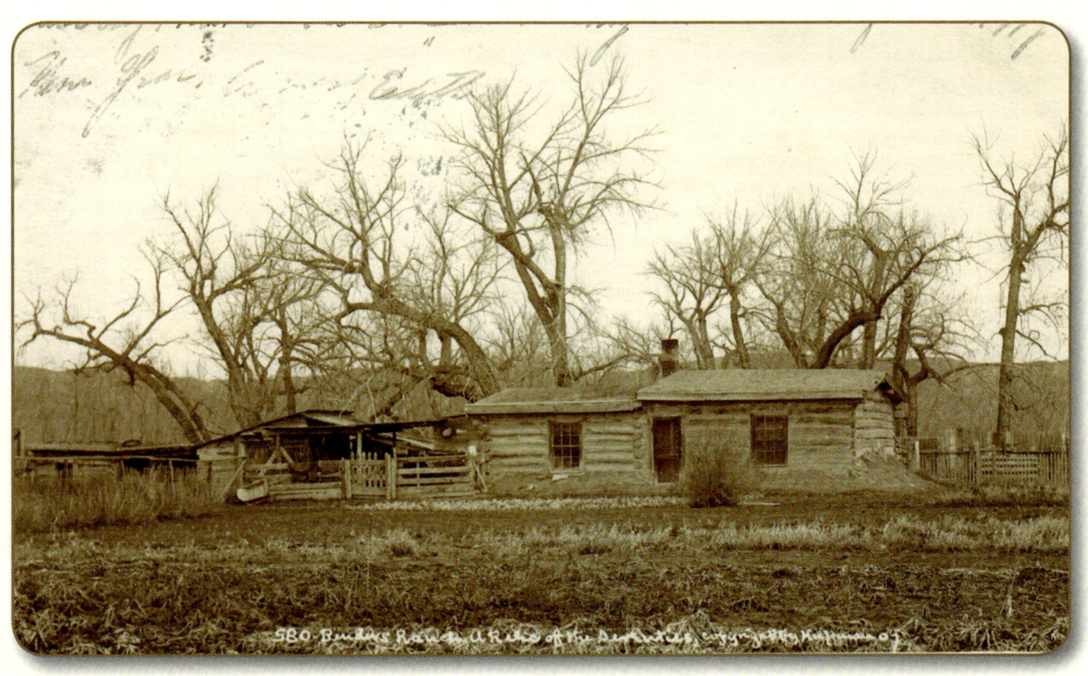

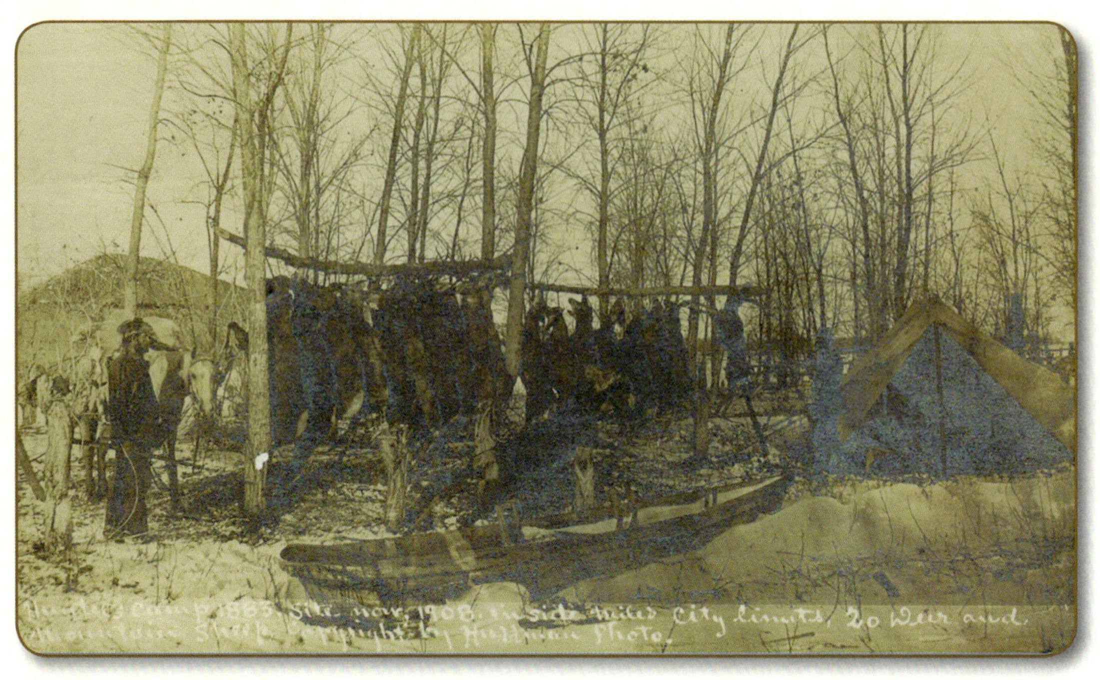

ABOVE: *Hunter's Camp 1883*

BELOW: *Roped, Heeled & Stretched*

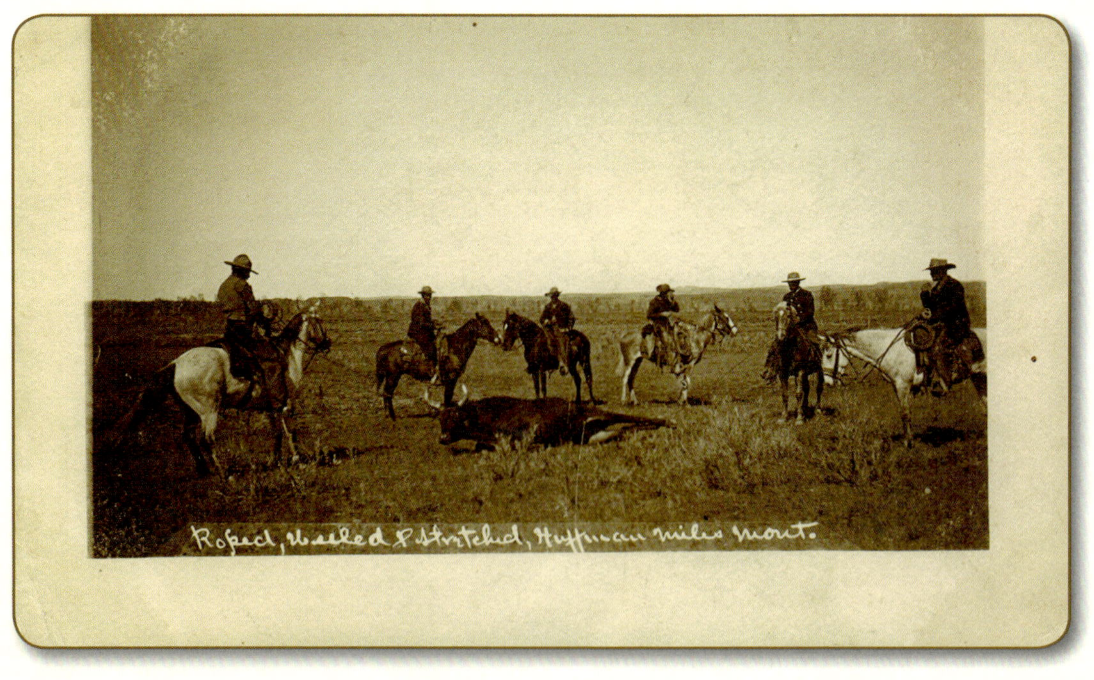

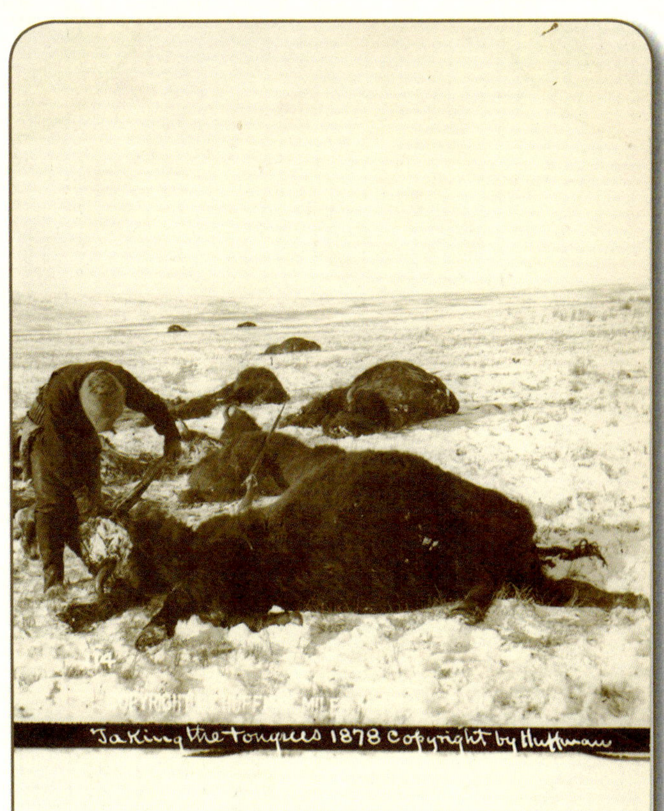

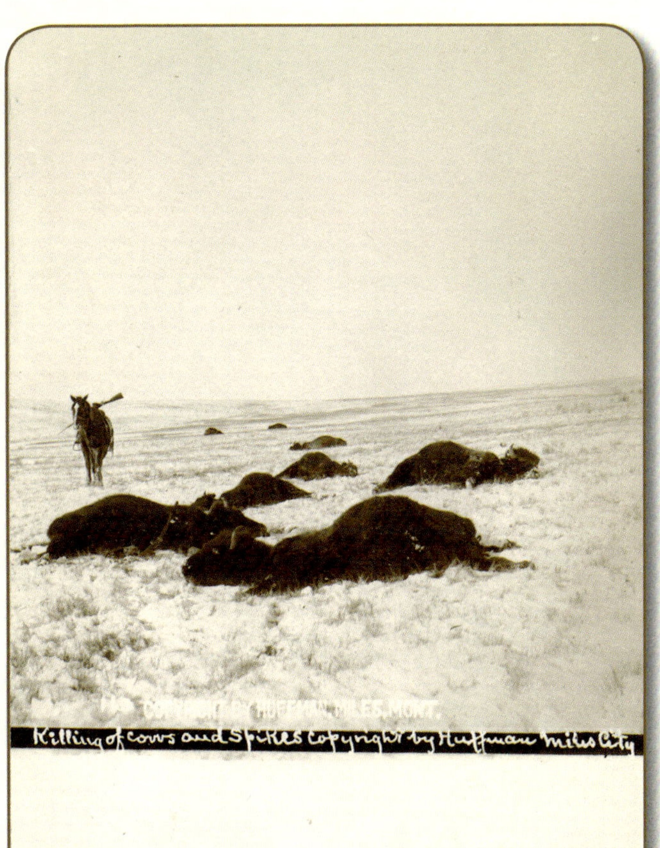

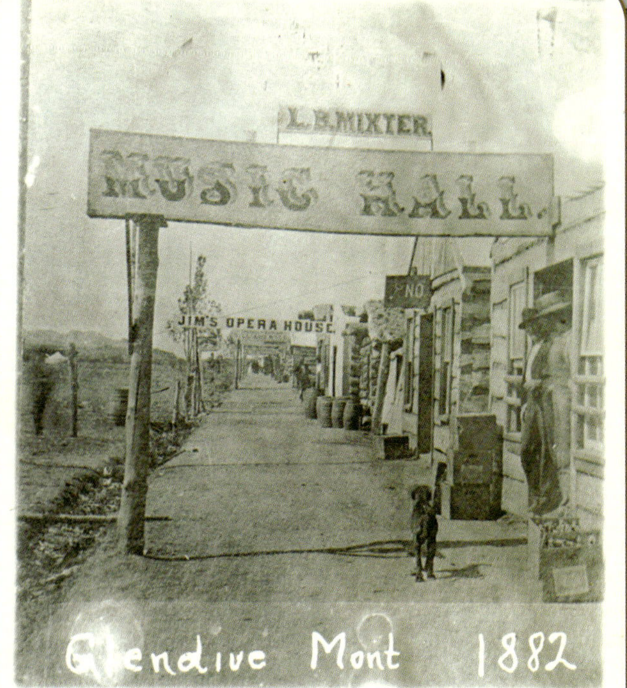

ABOVE: *Taking The Tongues 1878*

ABOVE RIGHT: *Killing of Cows and Spikes*

RIGHT: *Glendive Mont 1882*

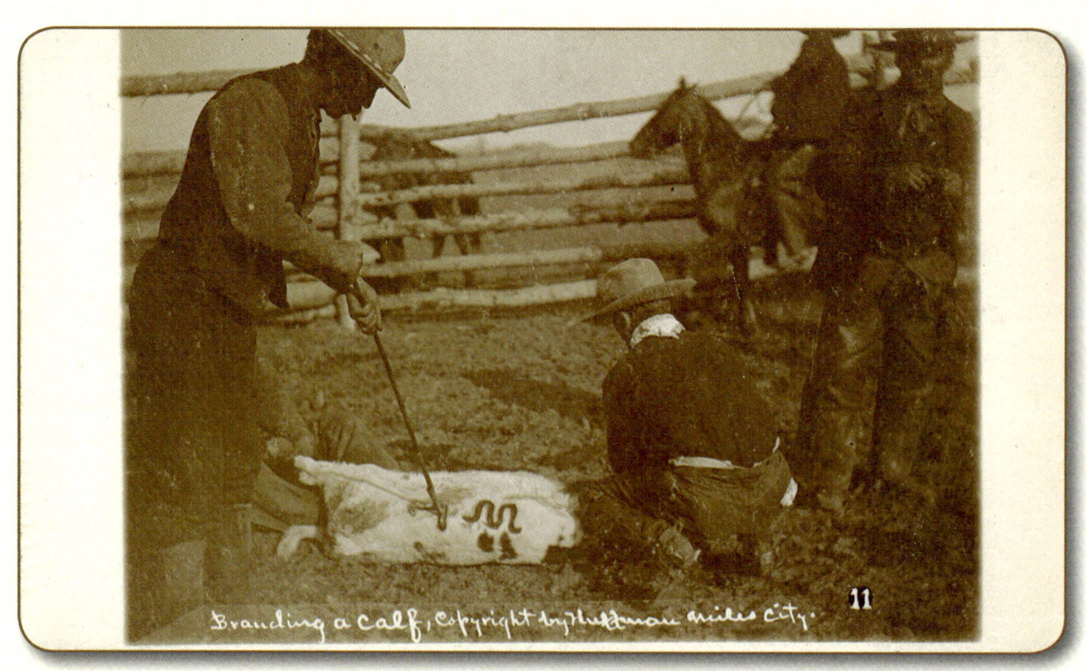

ABOVE: *Branding a Calf*

BELOW: *Blasting Yellowstone Bluffs*

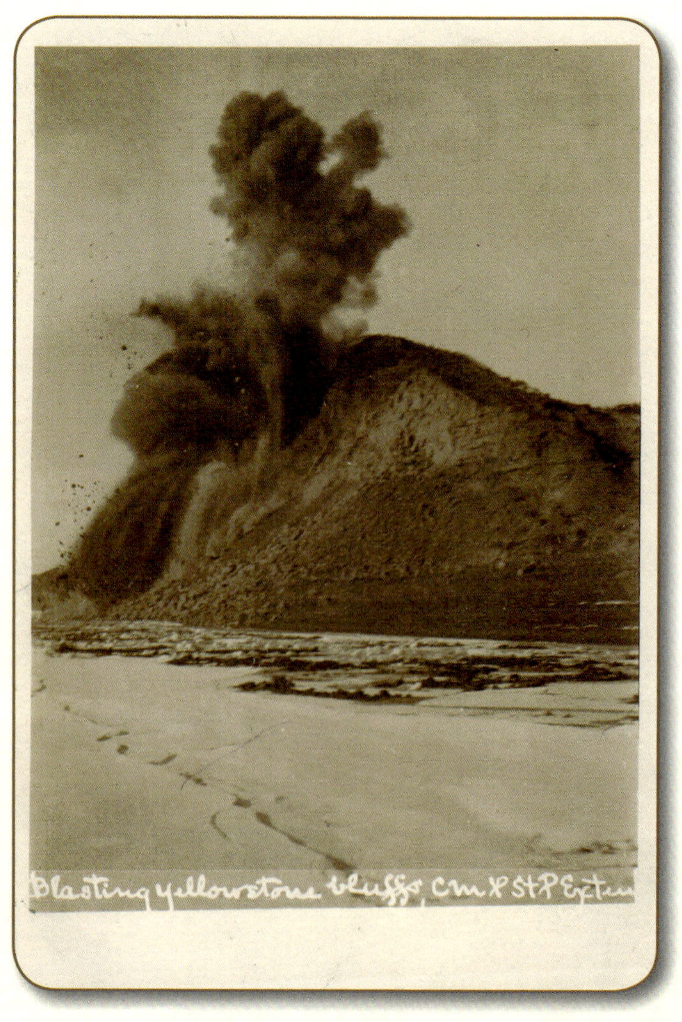

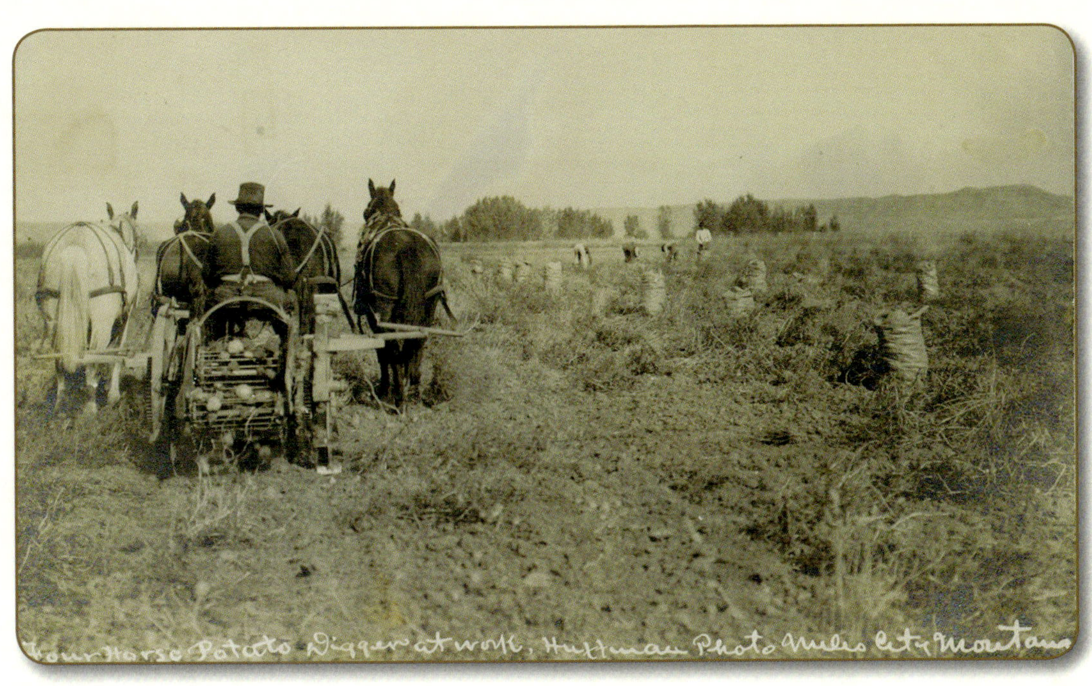

ABOVE: *Four Horse Potato Digger at Work*

BELOW: *Hardware Dept. Hamilton Merc. Stacey, Mont.*

COURTESY OF MONTANA HISTORICAL SOCIETY RESEARCH CENTER PHOTO ARCHIVES, PAC 2013-50

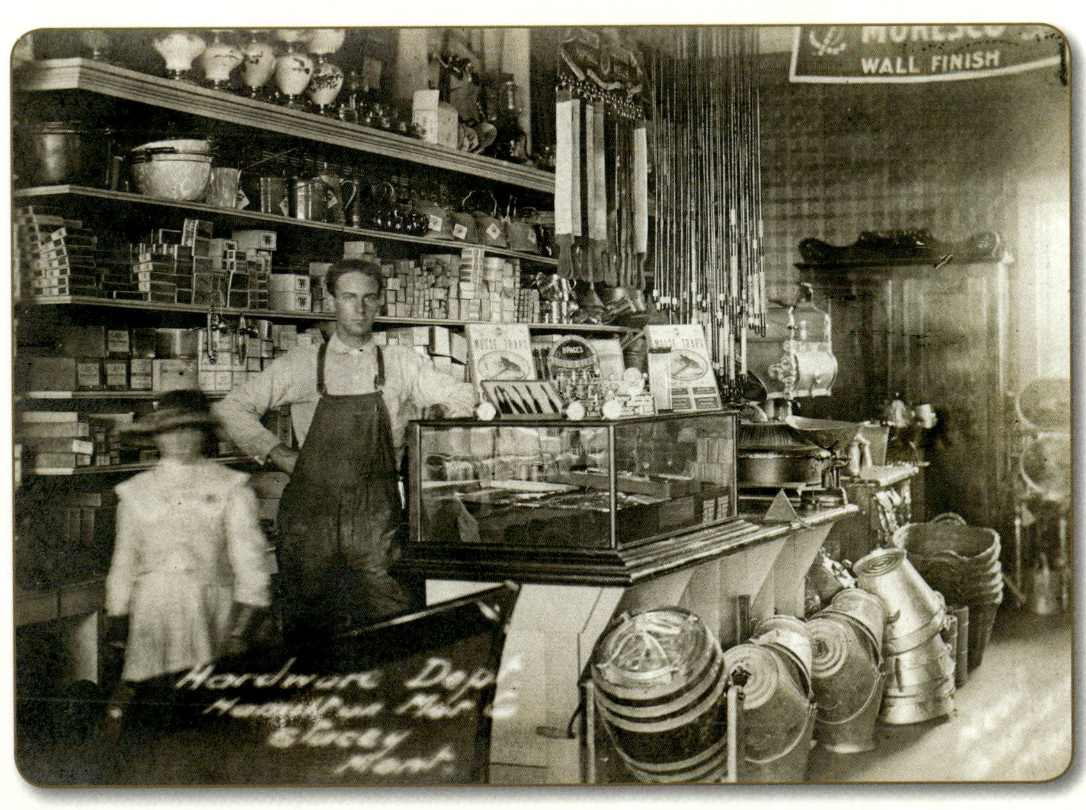

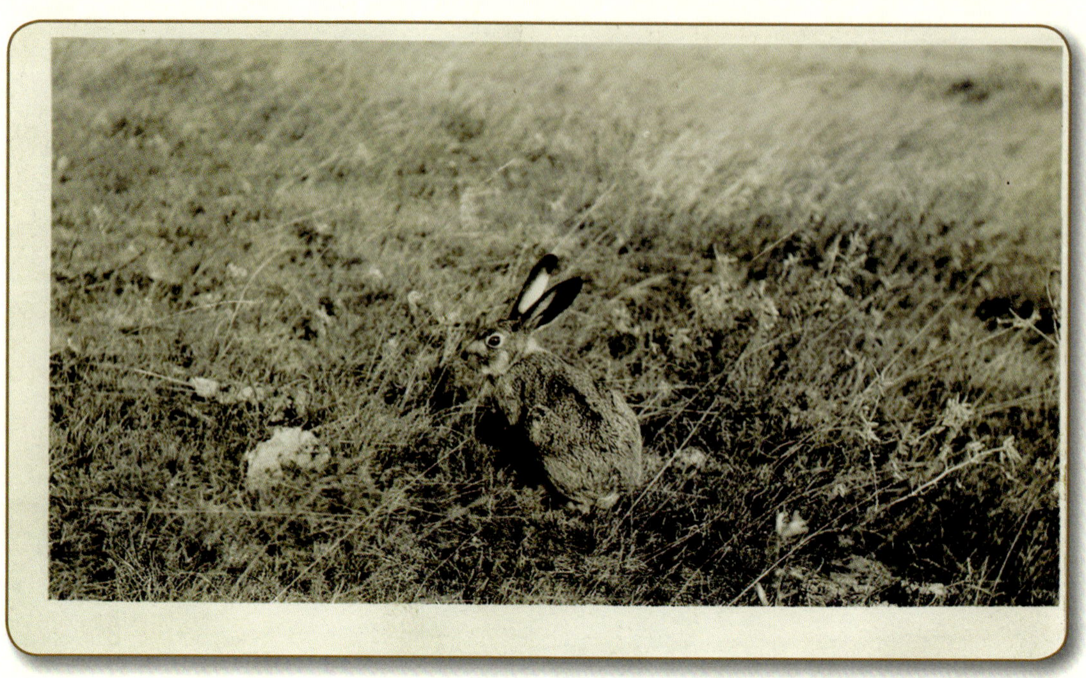

ABOVE: *A John Rabbit*

BELOW: *Round-up Scene*

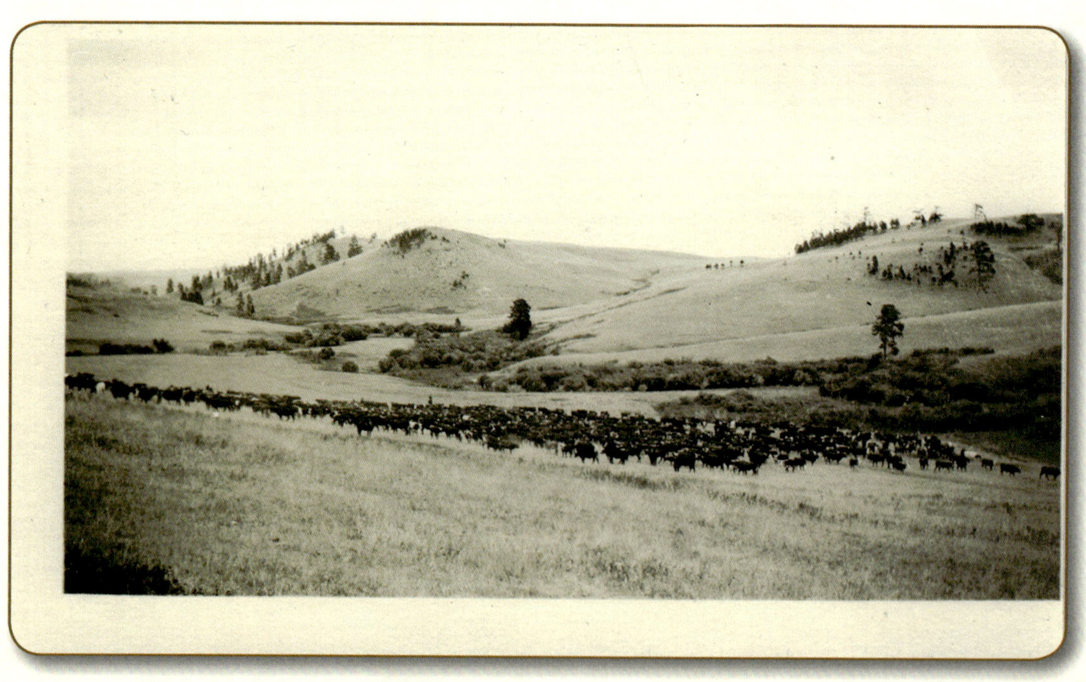

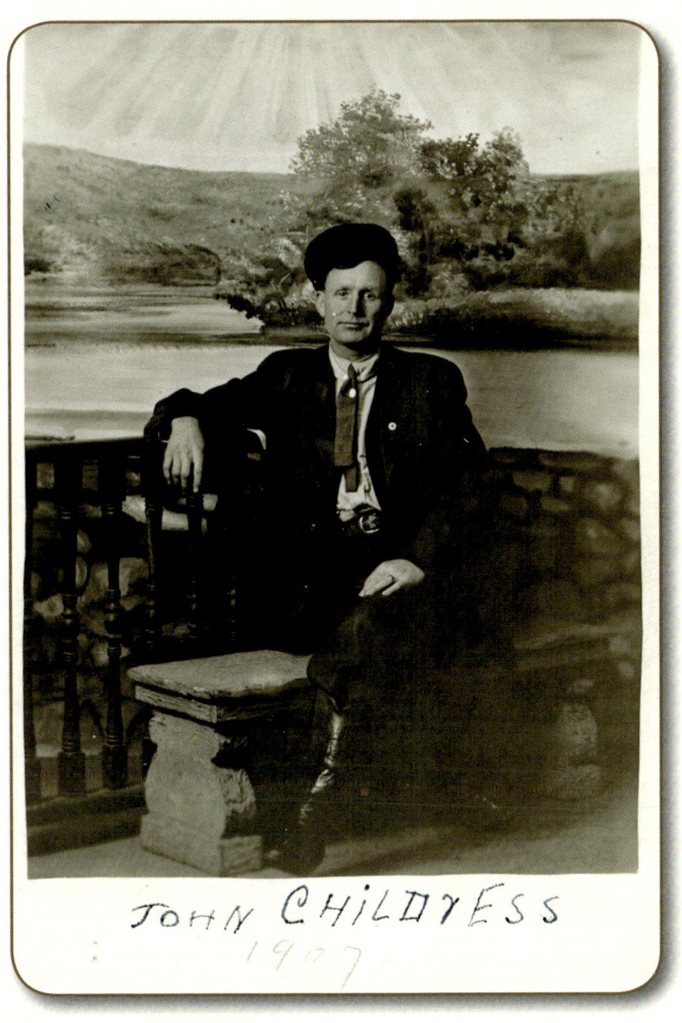

ABOVE: *John Childress*

BELOW: *Women in Hats, Miles City*

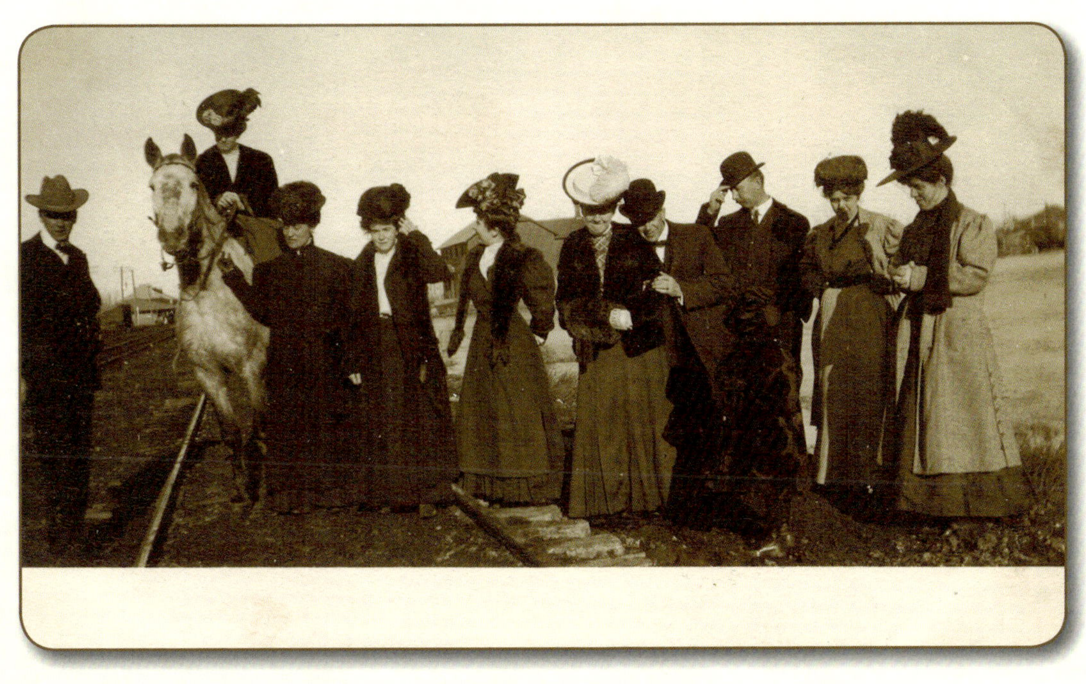

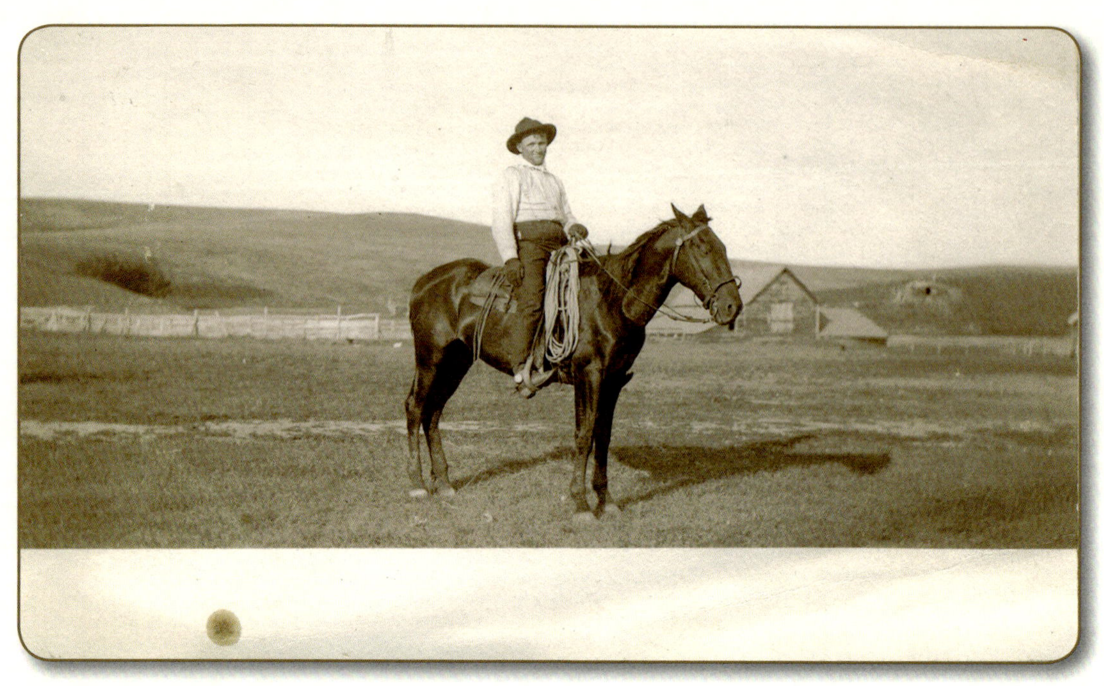

ABOVE: *Cowboy on Horse*

BELOW: *673 Cattle & 5 Herders*

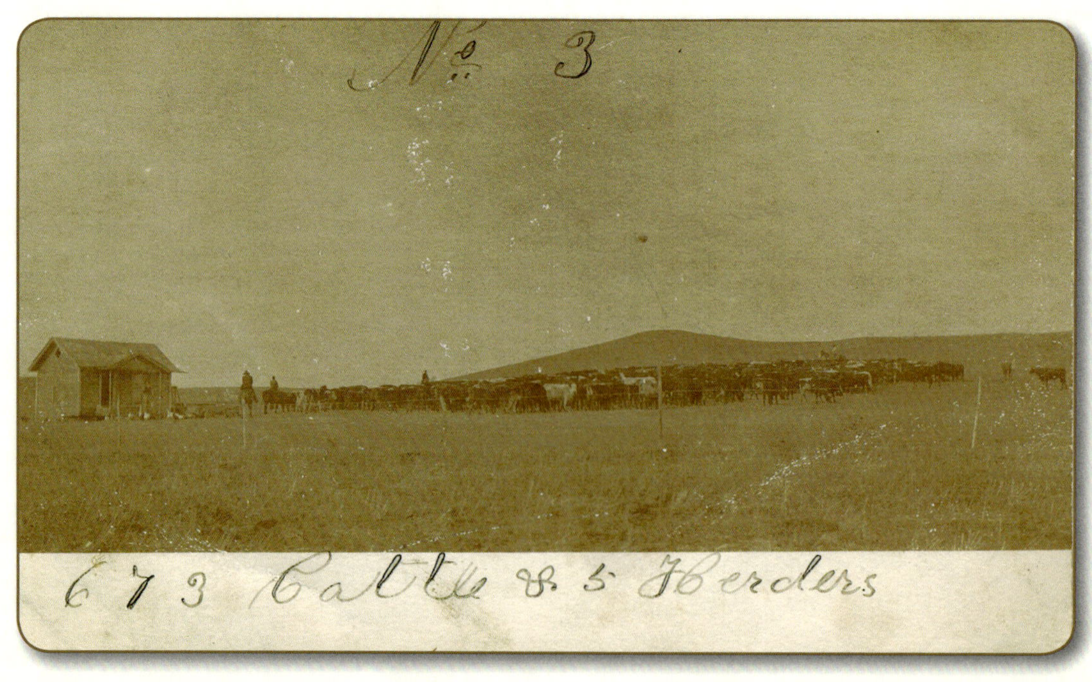

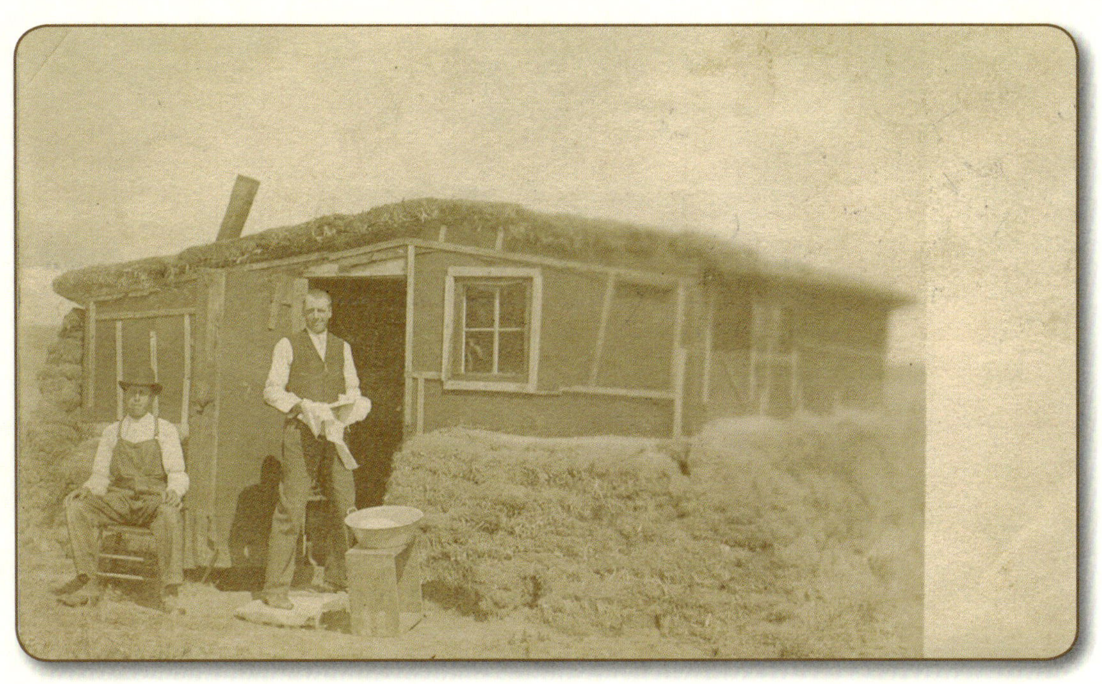

ABOVE: *Two Men in Front of Sod Roof Shack*

BELOW: *Working a Little Bunch in the Hills*

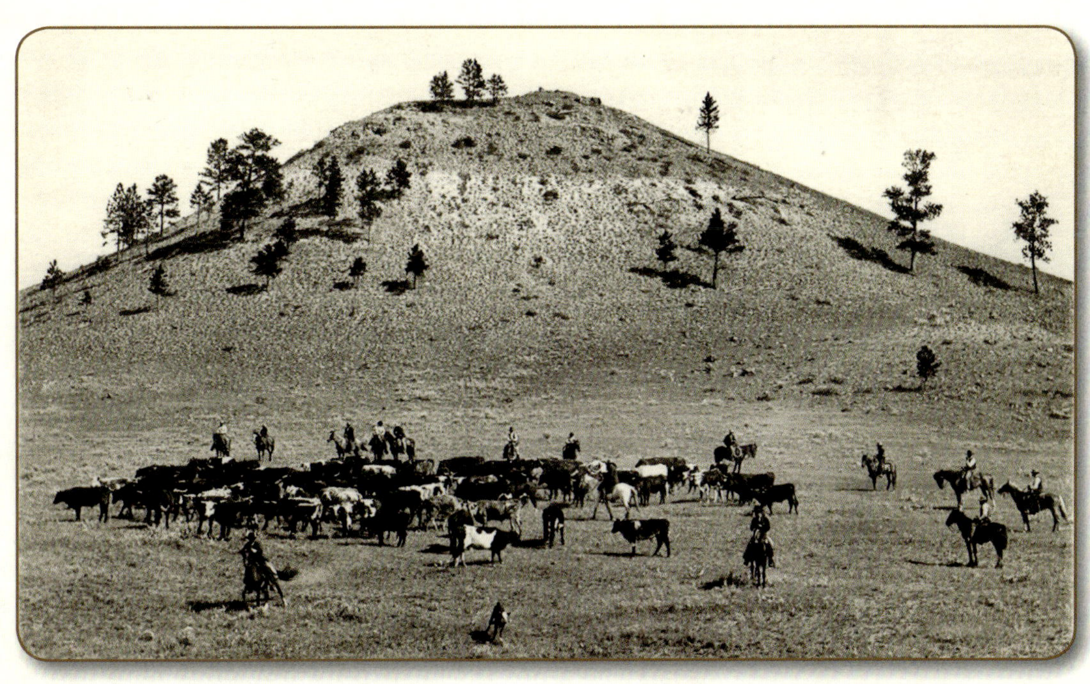

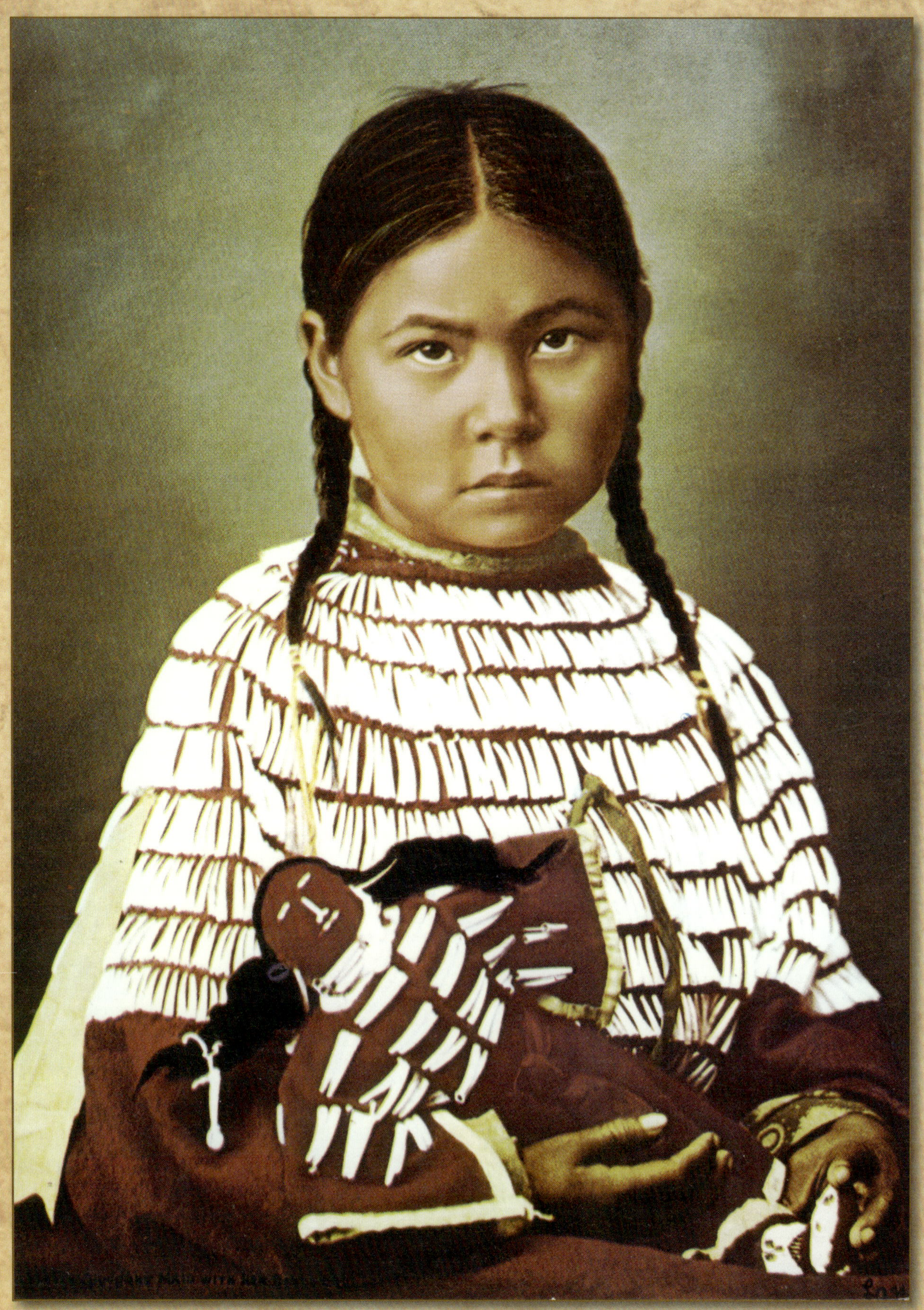

ABOVE: *Cheyenne Maid with Her Doll*

Coffrin's Old West Gallery

PRINTED COLOR POSTCARDS

During the 1960s and 1970s Jack Coffrin produced a series of Continental size (4 x 6 inch) printed color postcards. Although we don't know the exact number of individual images, we can speculate. In 1975 he published a 28 page, 9 x 6½ inch colored booklet with 23 plates.

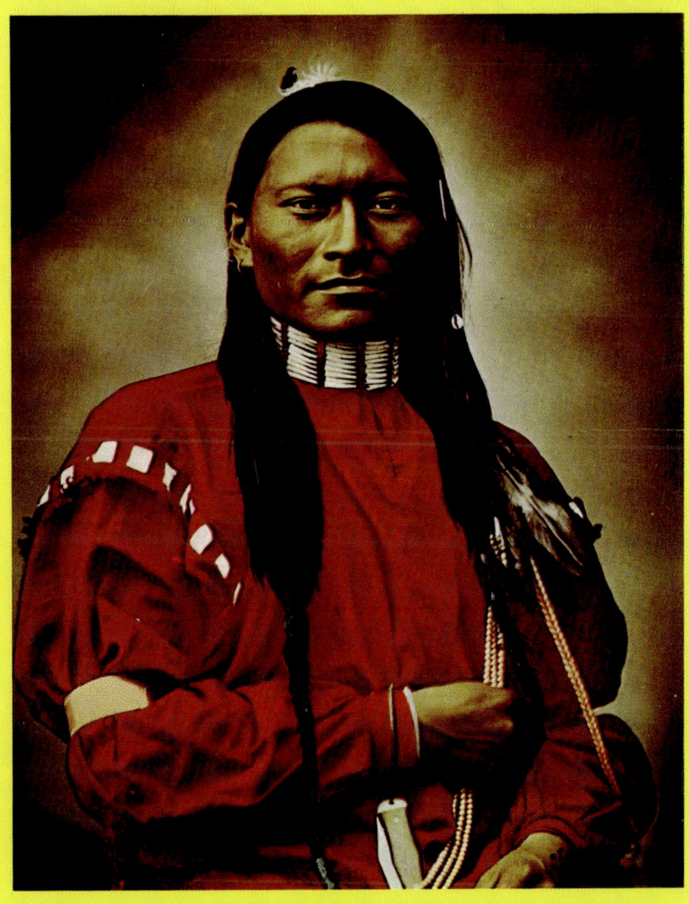
The Huffman Pictures

Photographs of the Old West

Indian Portraits and Scenes — Buffalo — Bull Train and Jerkline — Calamity Jane — Roundups and Ranches — Sheepherder & Wagon — and the Hon-yocker. All in color.

ABOVE: 1975 booklet with 23 images.

Inside the back cover he states, “From the Huffman collection of more than a thousand negatives this book presents 23 of his best. To produce these color illustrations from the black and white negatives, enlargements are made on which the color artist applies the oil colors carefully to represent the landscape just as it is now and was in Huffman’s time. . . From those hand-colored enlargements the color printing plates were made for this book.” We believe postcards were probably made from all 23 images. We have 17 individual cards and a 12-view souvenir folder from 1975—a total of 19 different images, all of which appear in the 1975 booklet.

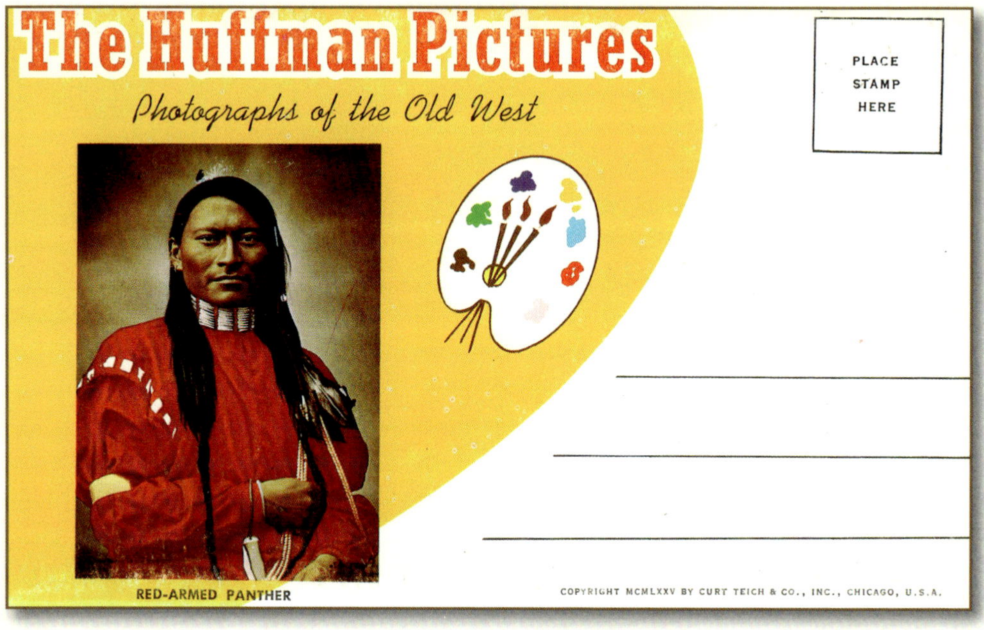

Following are the 19 images in our collection and the additional four “probables” from Coffrin’s 1975 booklet. We also have one card not in the 1975 booklet—*Spotted Eagle’s Sioux Village*. It is also the only card we have that was printed in 1973.

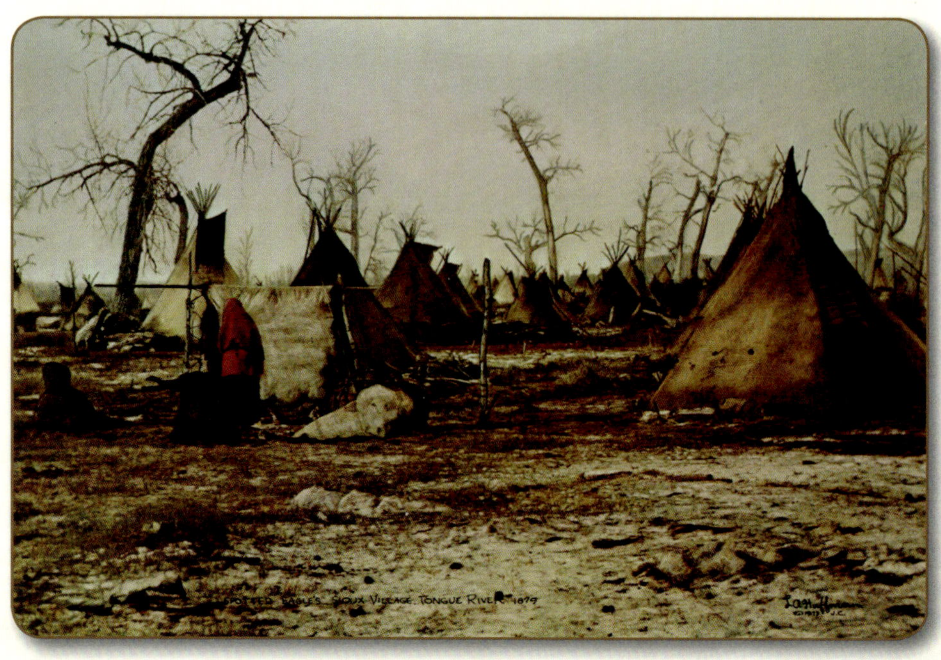

Of our total of 18 individual cards, 16 are by Curt Teich Color. Also printed on the back is a brief description of the image with the statement "the hand colored photograph from which this picture was made is on display at Coffrin's Old West Gallery in Miles City, Montana." Fifteen of our cards were published in 1968, two (plus the souvenir folder) in 1975 and one in 1973. All of them state "Jack Coffrin" and "The Huffman Pictures" on the back.

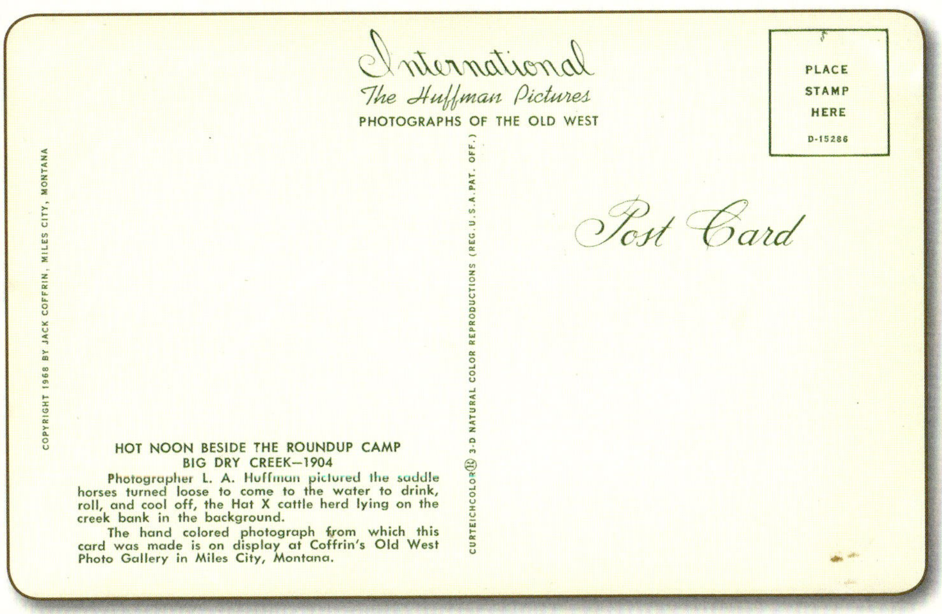

ABOVE: The back of all but three of the cards.

FACING PAGE, TOP: 1975 Souvenir folder with 12 images.

FACING PAGE, BOTTOM: *Spotted Eagle's Sioux Village, 1880.*

To Summarize:

- Jack Coffrin probably produced at least 24 postcards, possibly a few more;
- Most cards were produced in 1968 with the same card design;
- Cards from this series are relatively common and are readily available on the collector's market.

Following are 23 additional color images from Coffrin's 1975 booklet, all of which were likely used on postcards.

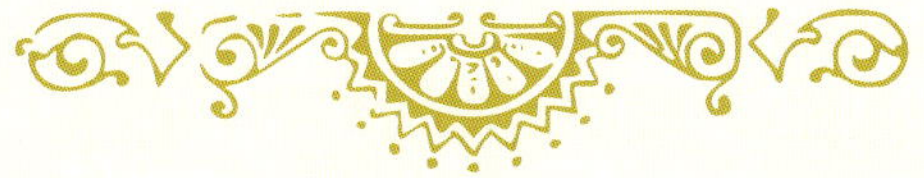

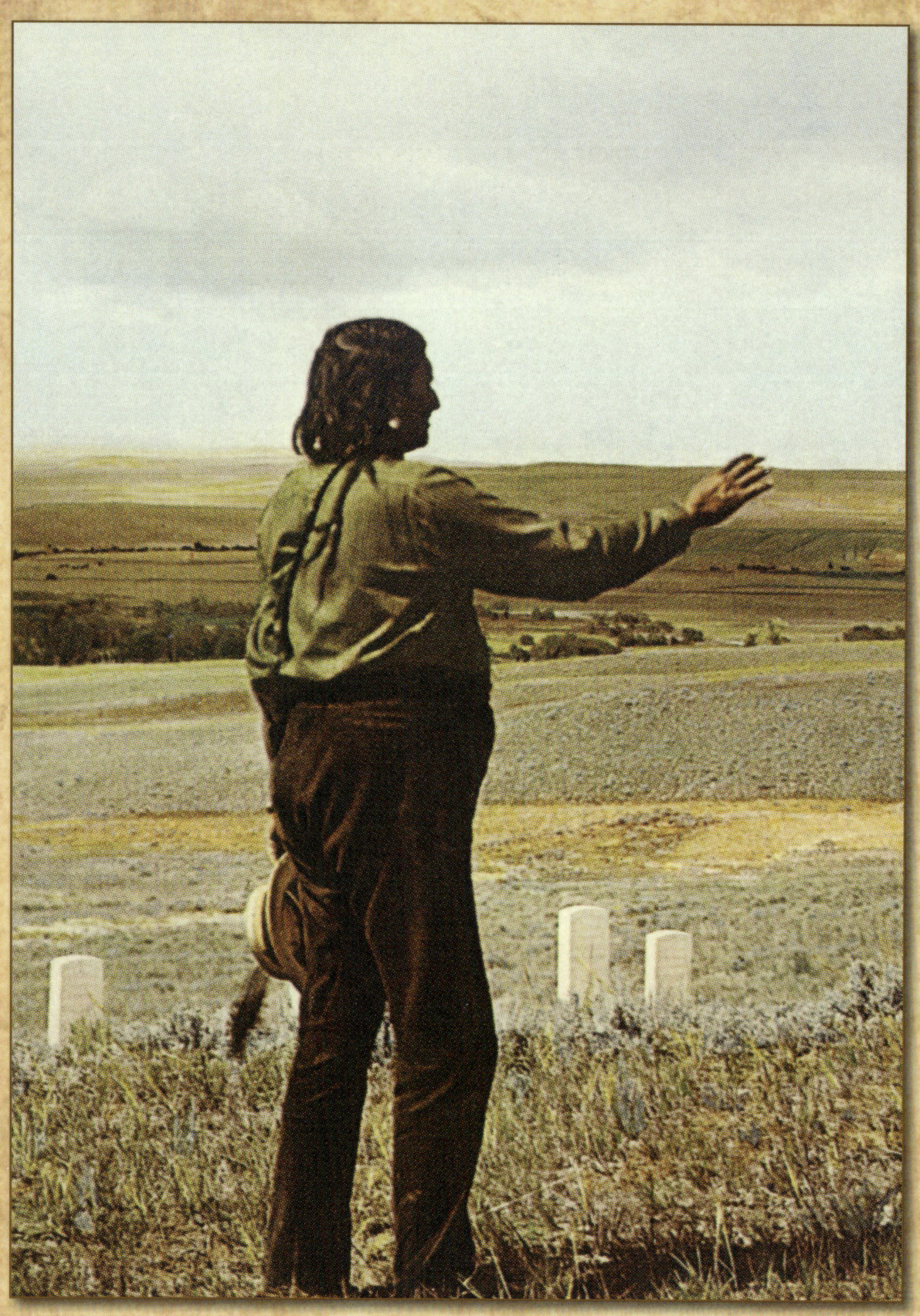

ABOVE: *Old Cheyenne "Two Moon" at Custer Battlefield*

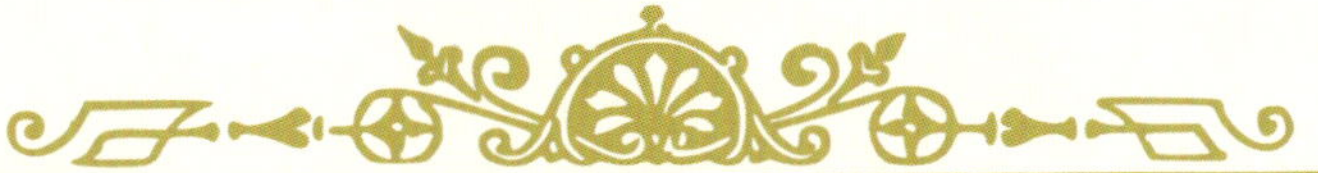

Coffrin's Printed Color Cards

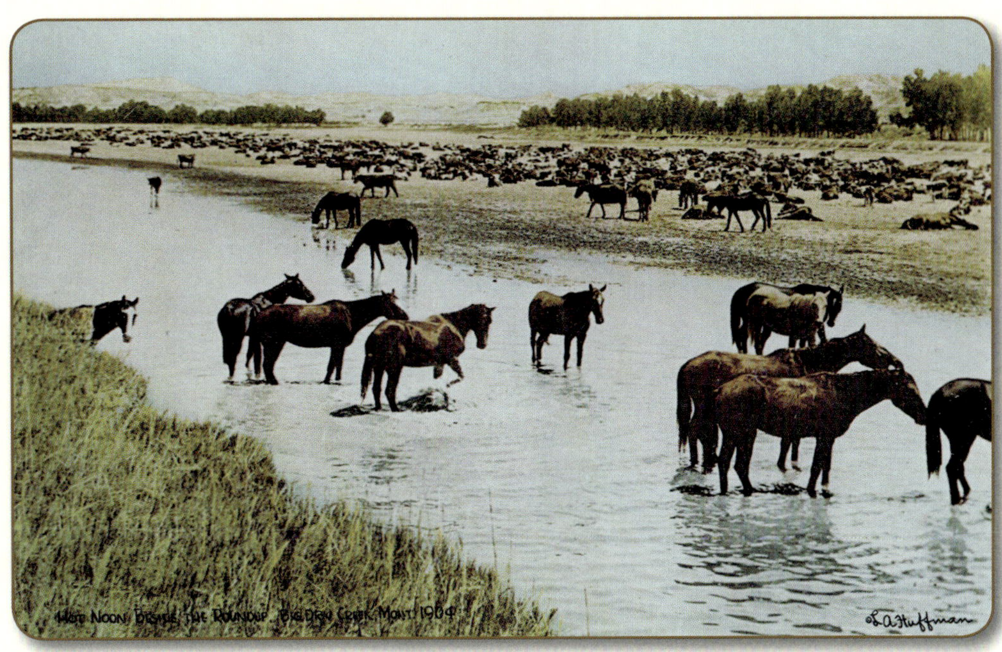

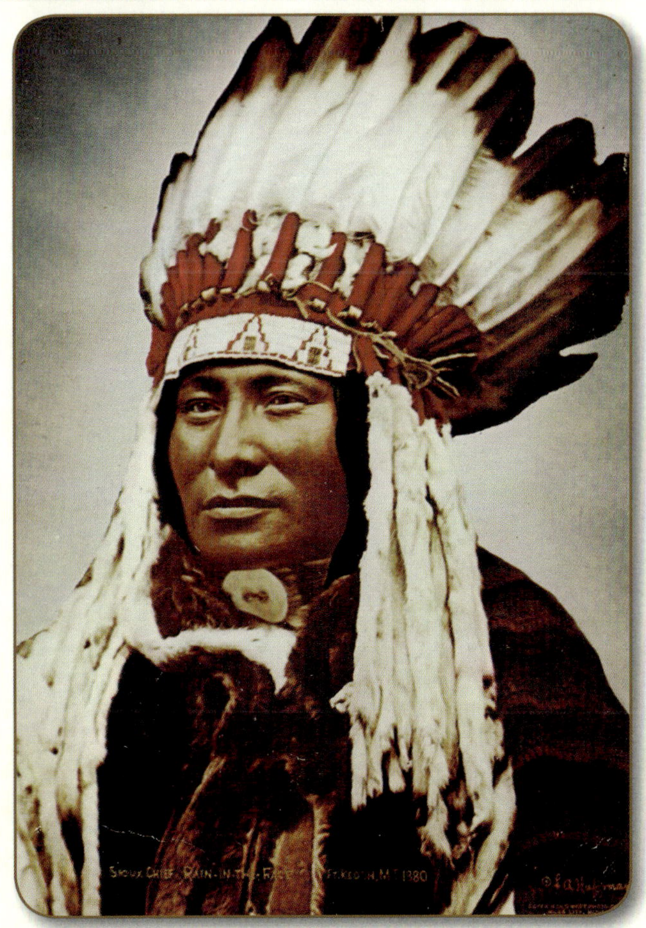

ABOVE: *Hot Noon Beside the Round-up Camp*

RIGHT: Sioux Chief—Rain-in-the-Face

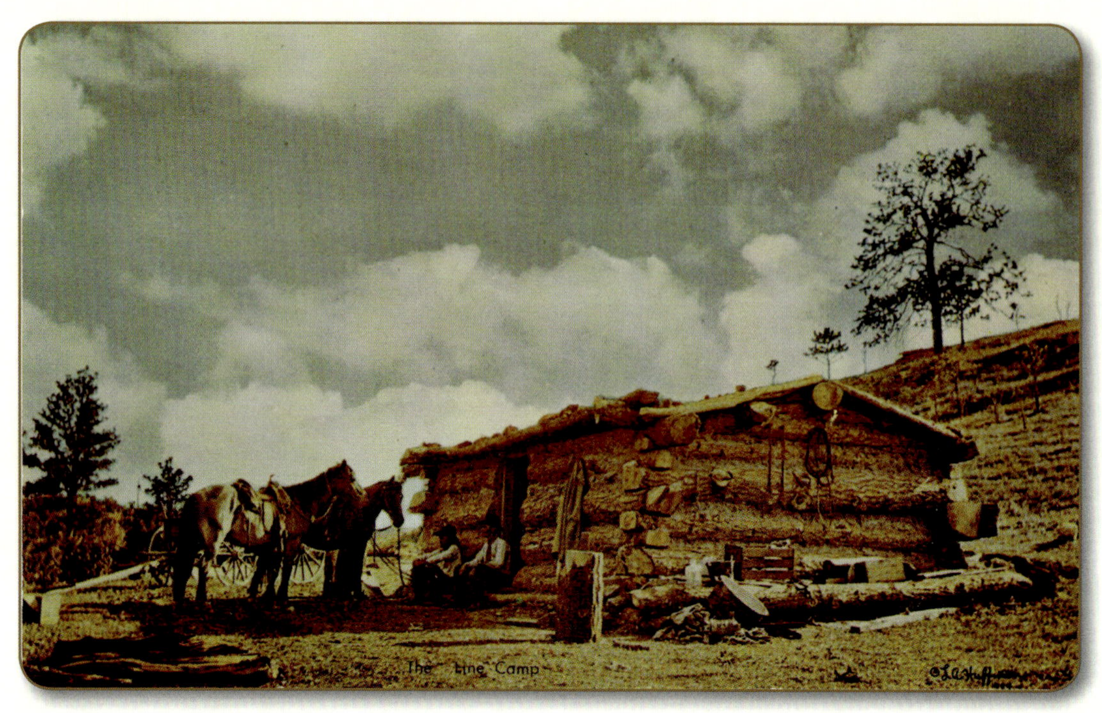

ABOVE: *The Line Camp*

BELOW: *Drifter Sheep Wagon and Band*

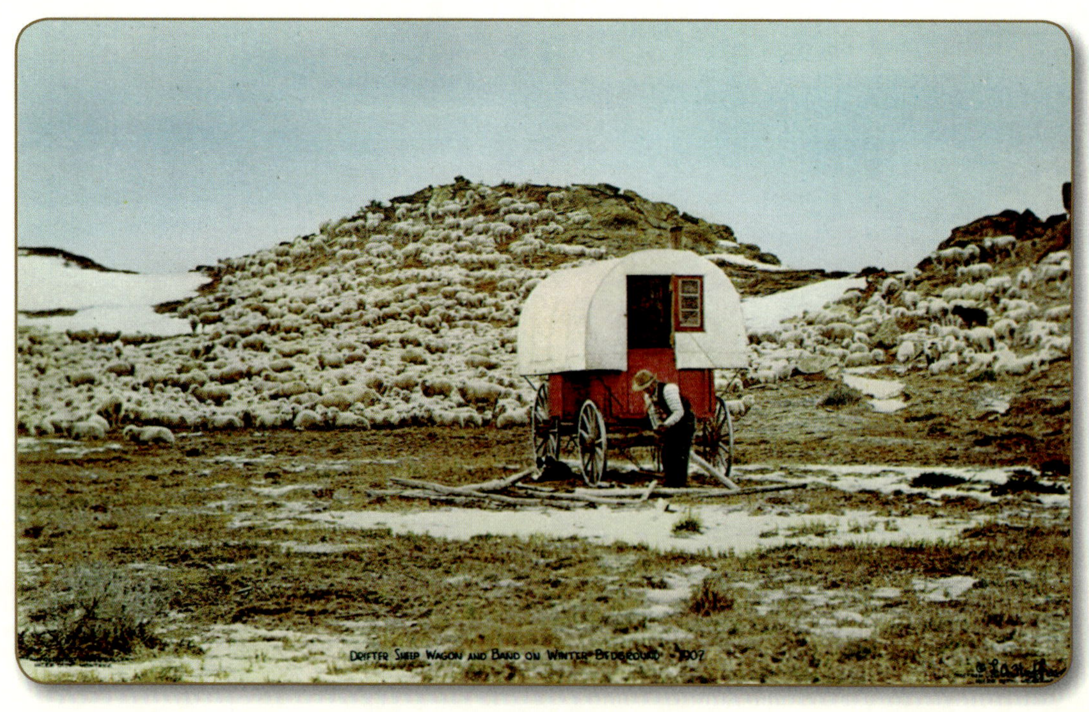

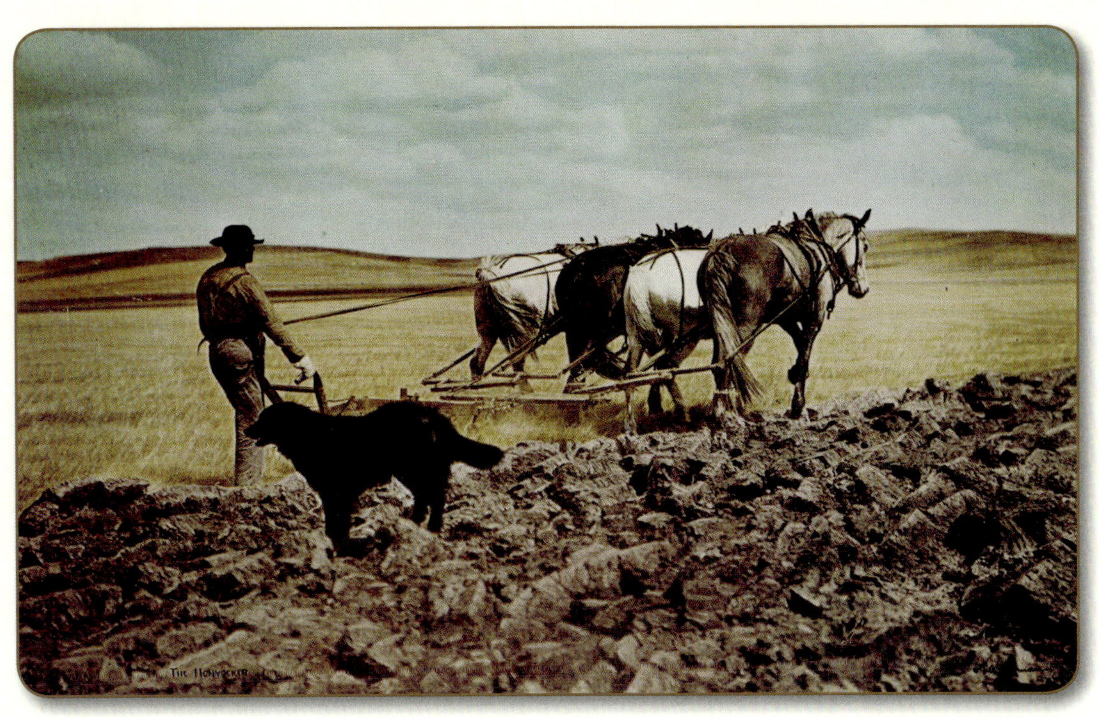

ABOVE: *The Honyocker*

BELOW: *Waiting for the Irons to Heat*

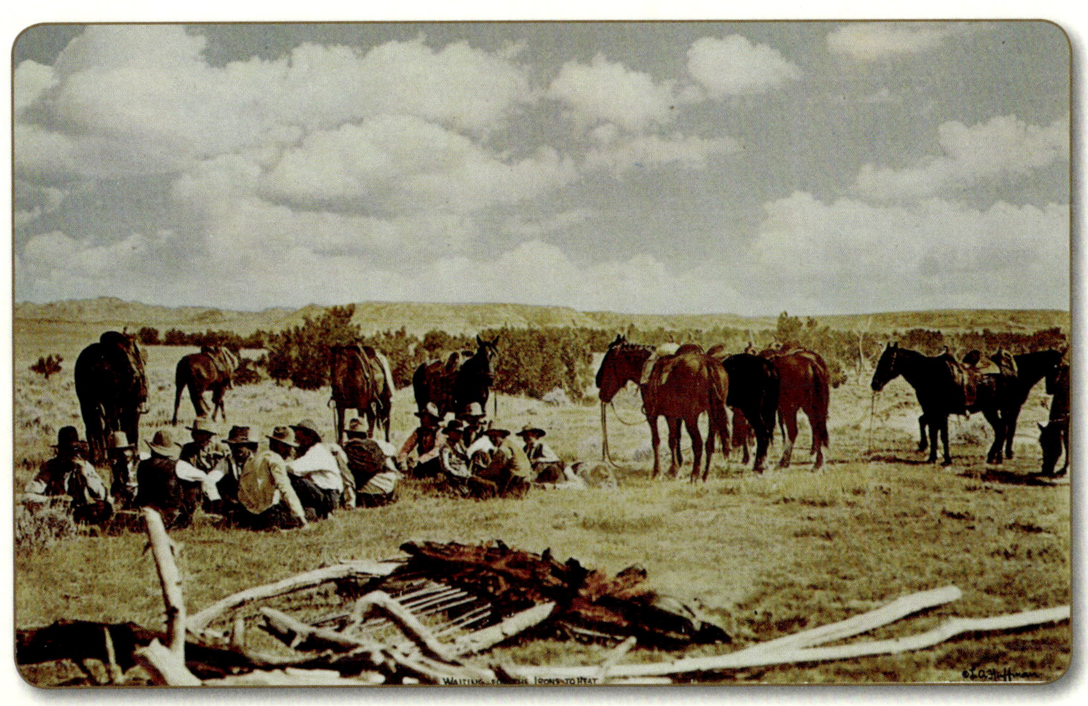

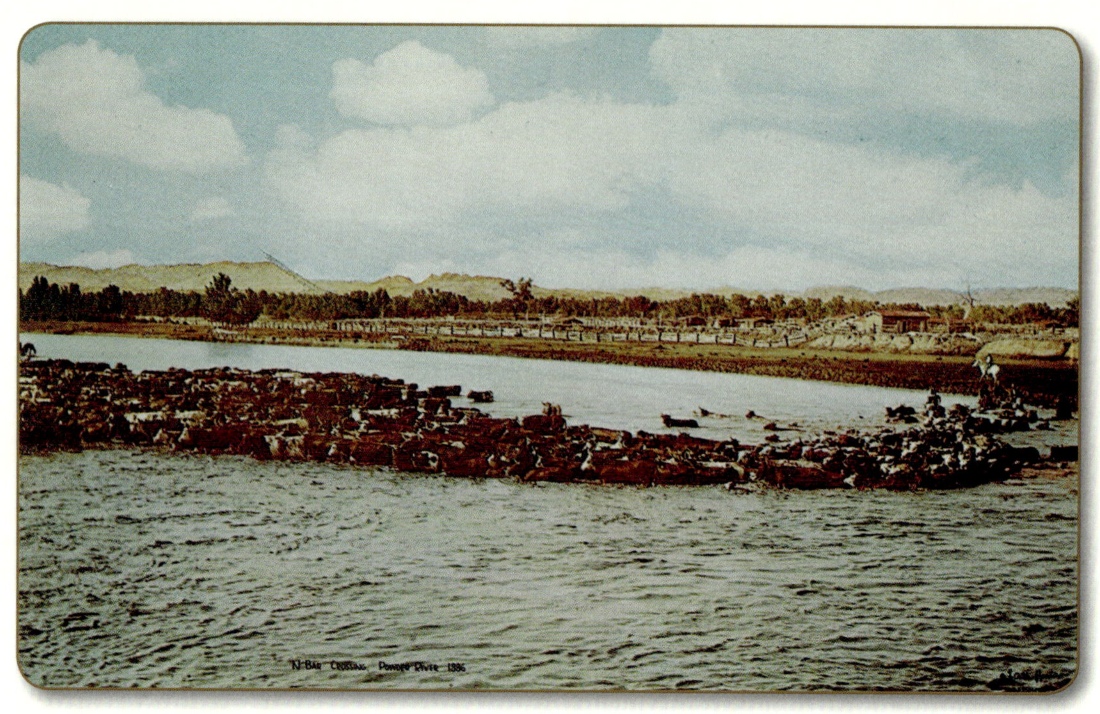

ABOVE: *N Bar Crossing*

BELOW: *Buffalo Grazing the Big Open*

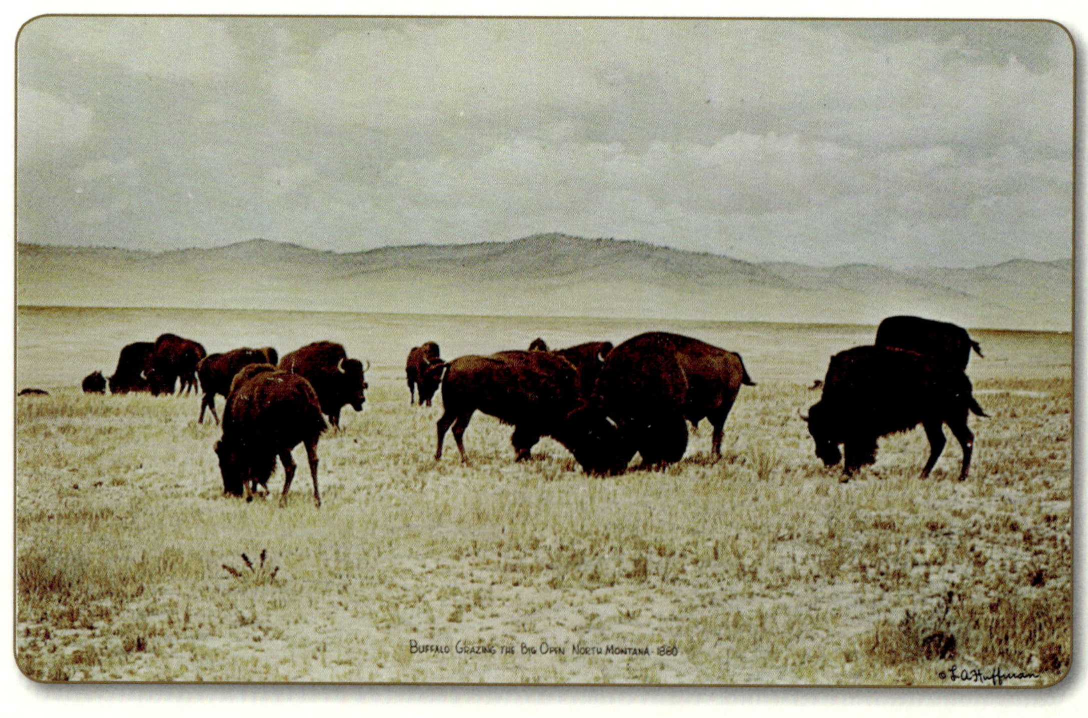

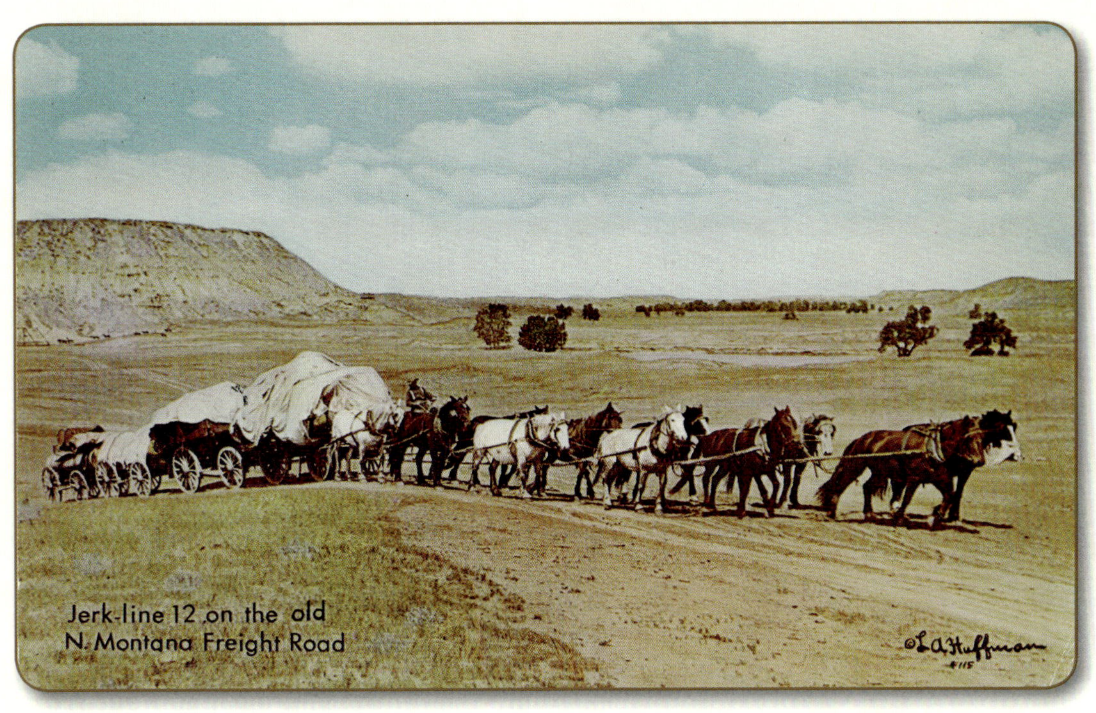

ABOVE: *Jerk-line 12 on the old N. Montana Freight Road*

BELOW: *Diamond R Bull Train*

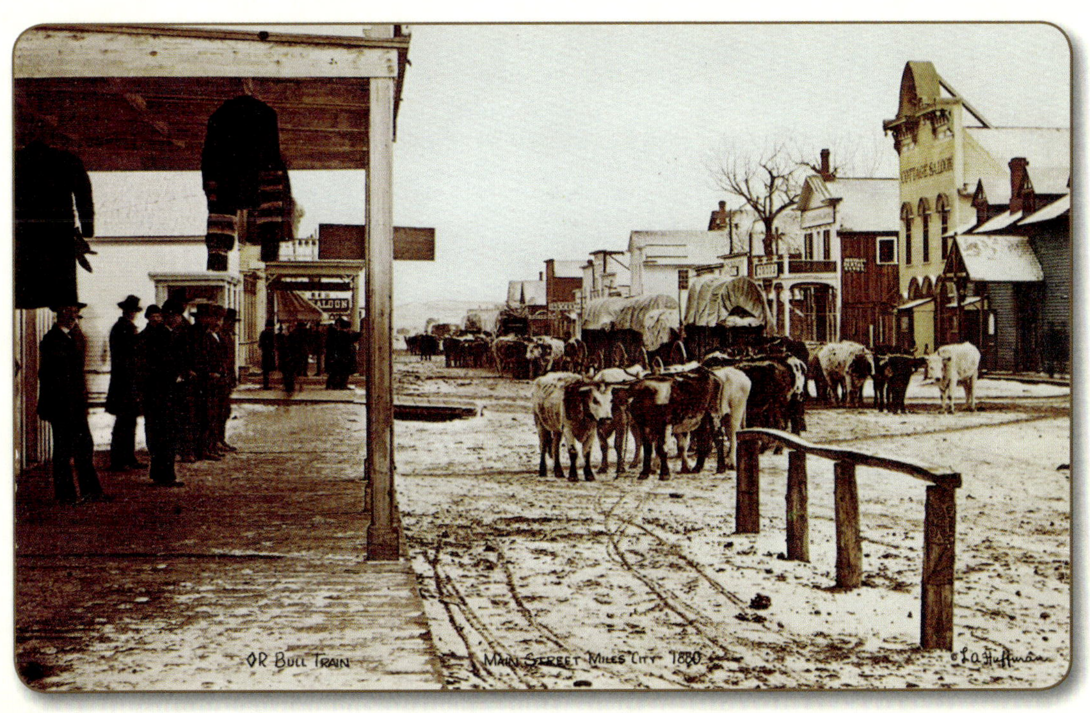

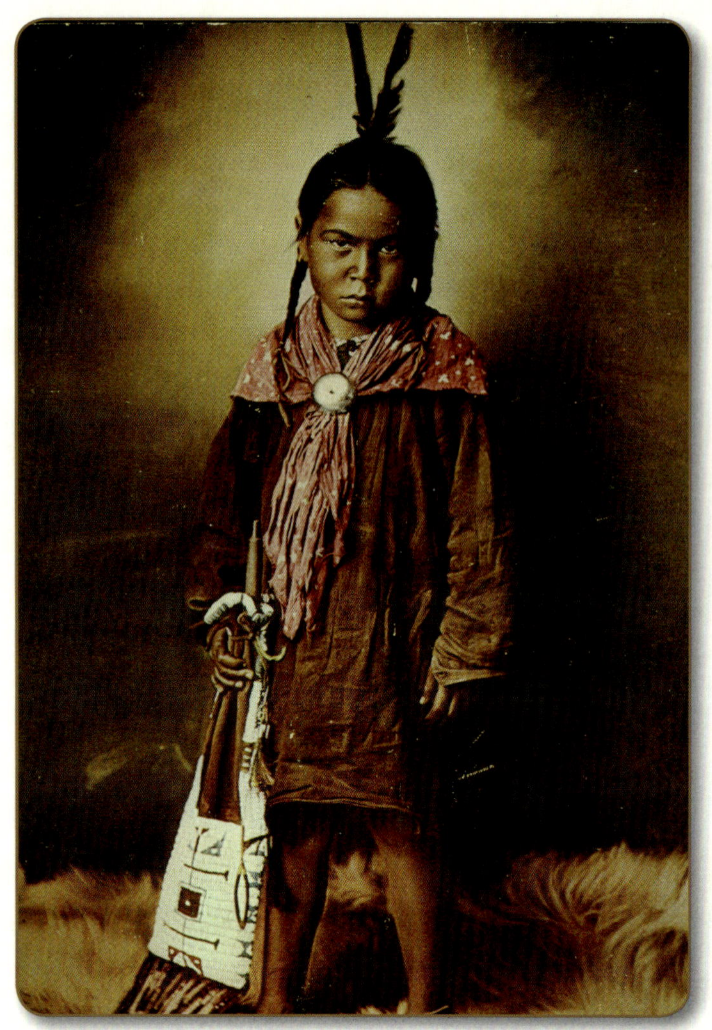

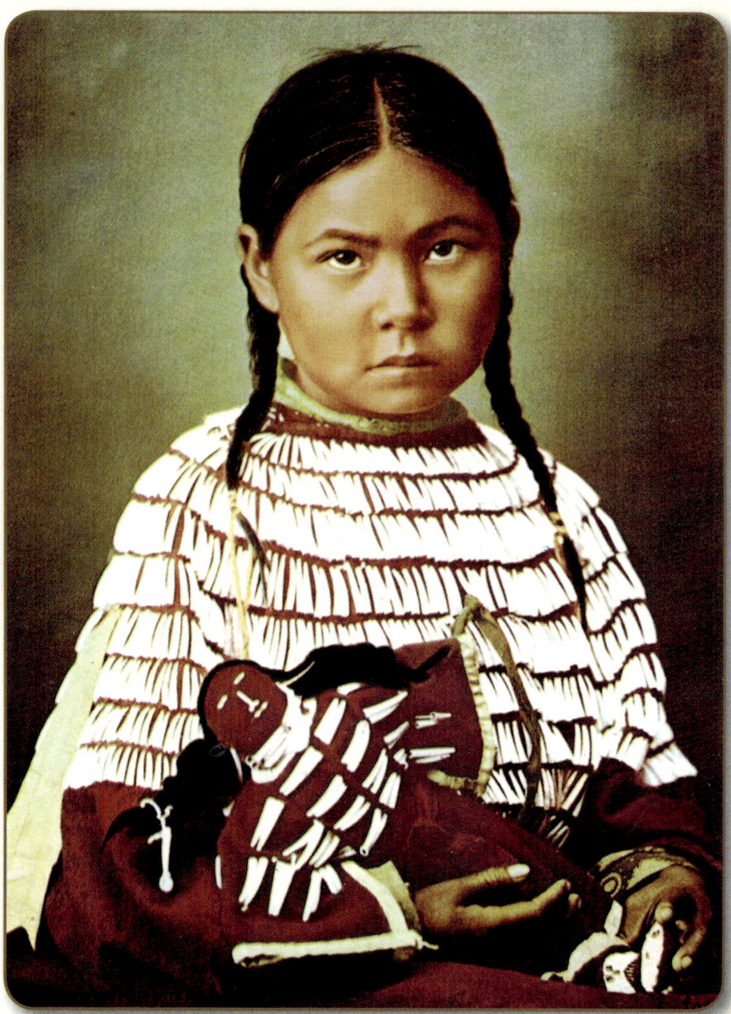

ABOVE: *Young Cheyenne Bearing Pipe*

ABOVE RIGHT: *Cheyenne Maid with Her Doll*

RIGHT: *First Pull at the Latigo*

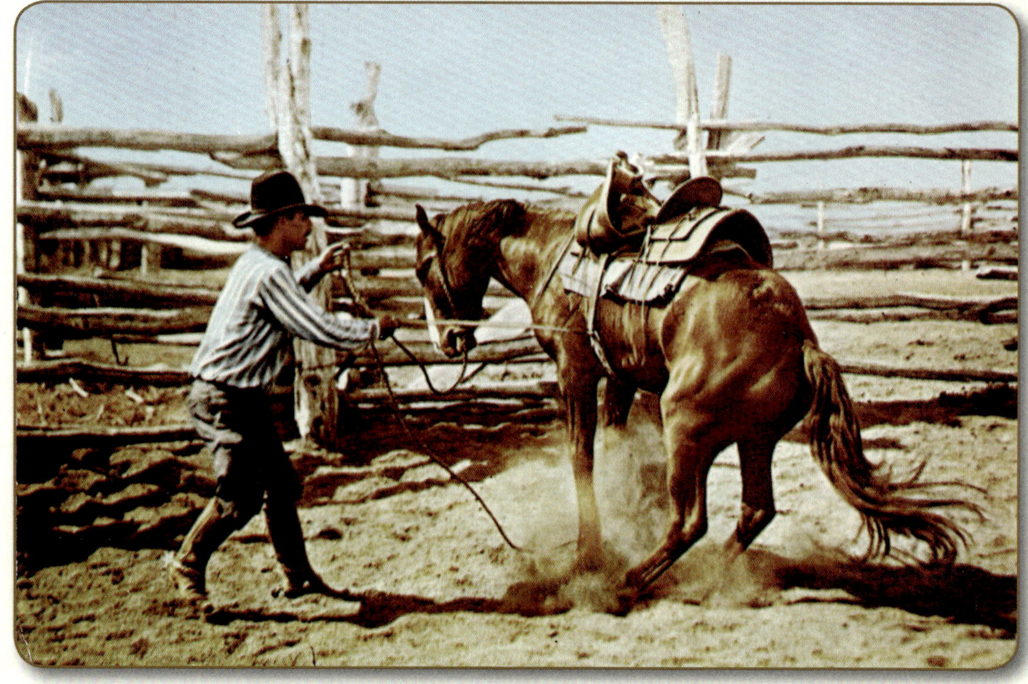

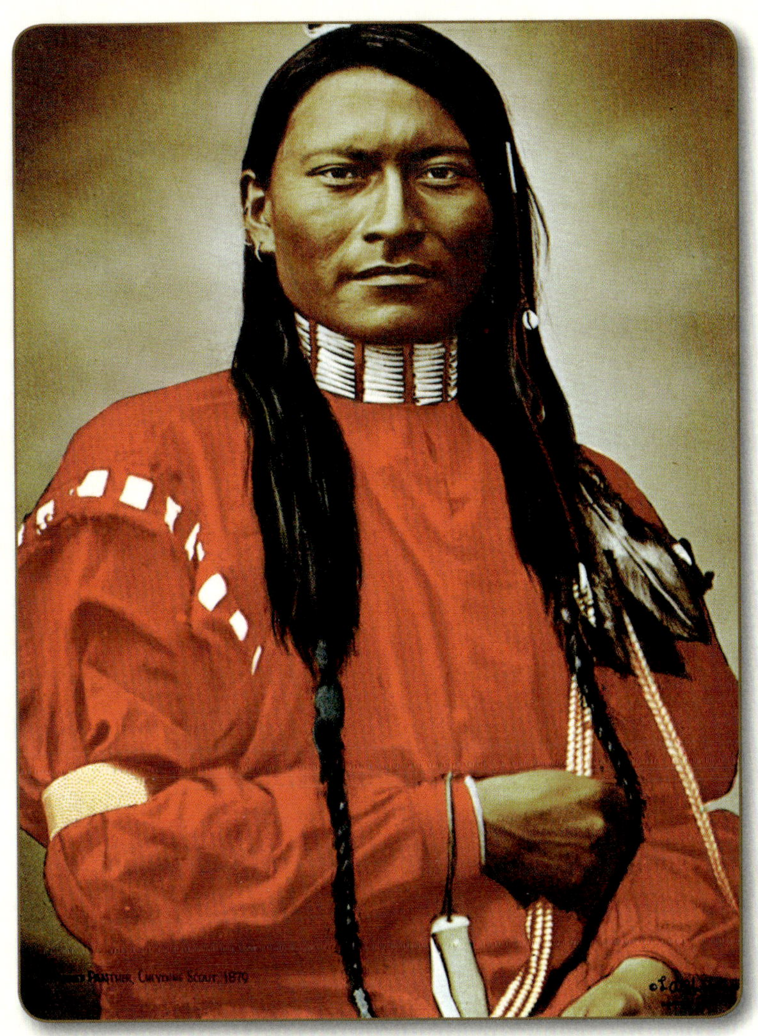

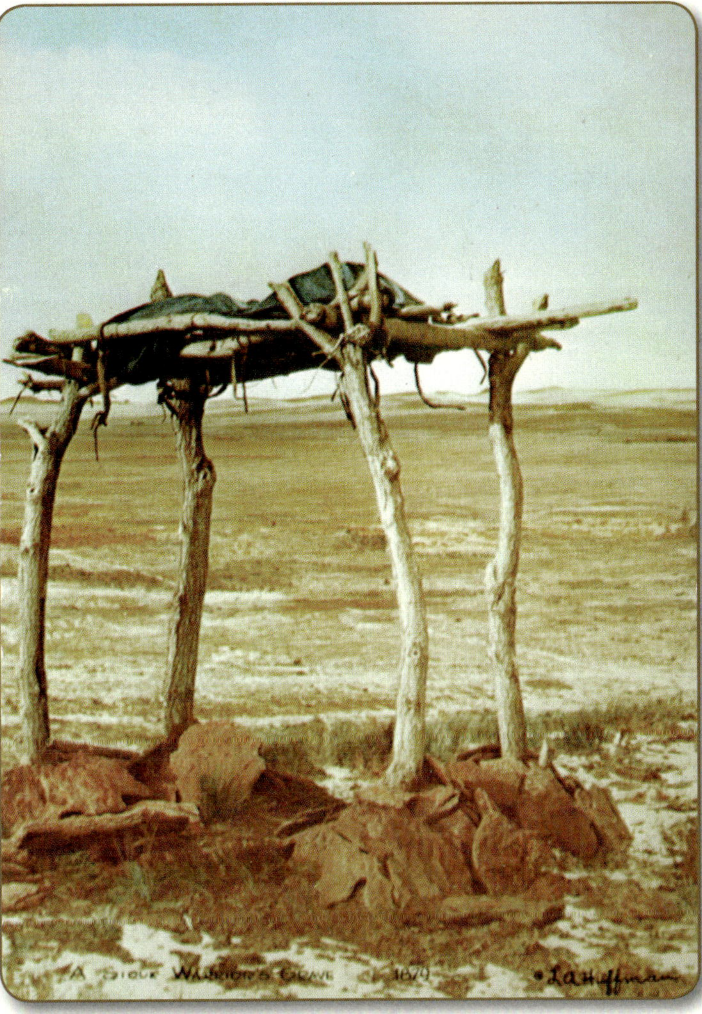

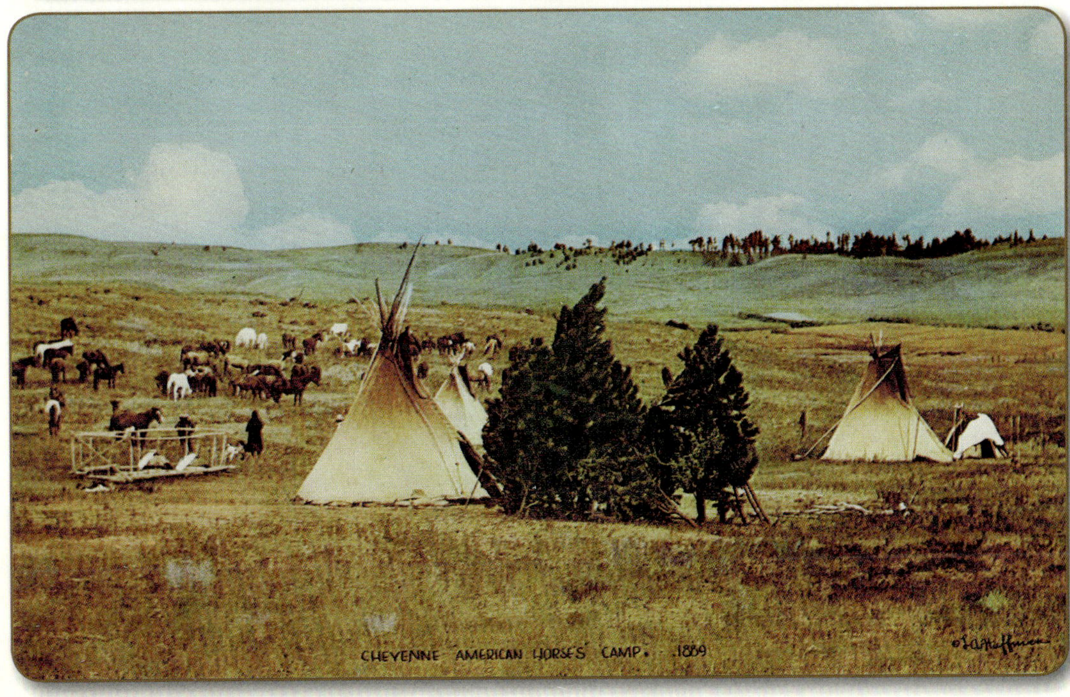

ABOVE: *A Sioux Warrior's Grave*

ABOVE LEFT: *Red-Armed Panther*

LEFT: *Cheyenne American Horse's Camp*

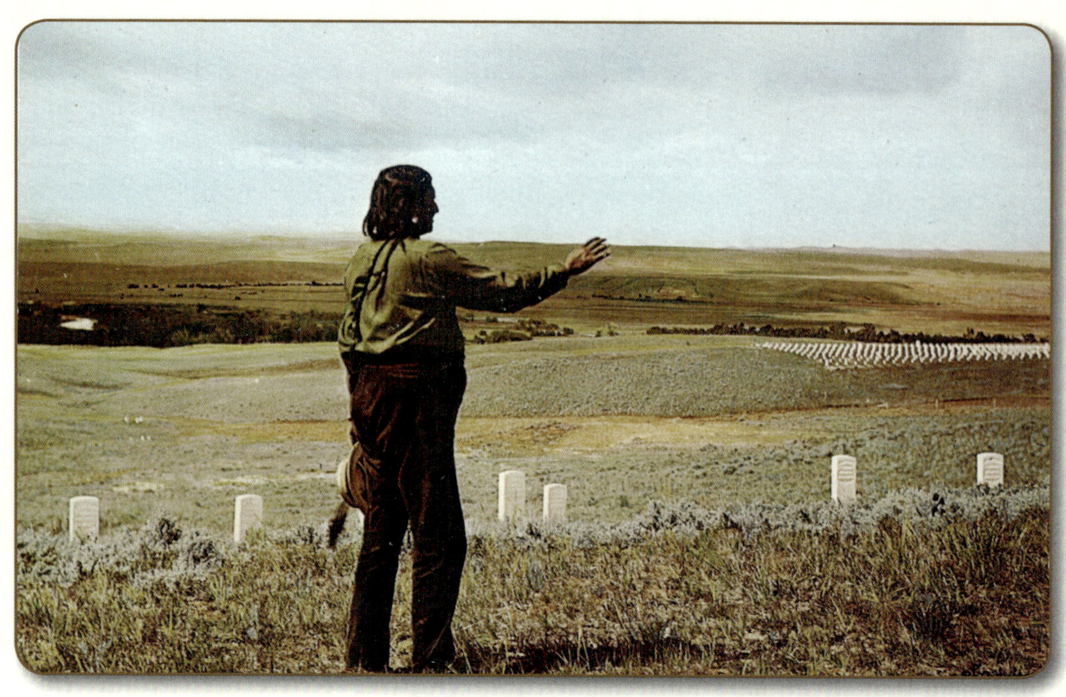

ABOVE: *Old Cheyenne "Two Moon" at Custer Battlefield*

RIGHT: *Young Cheyenne Mother and Child*

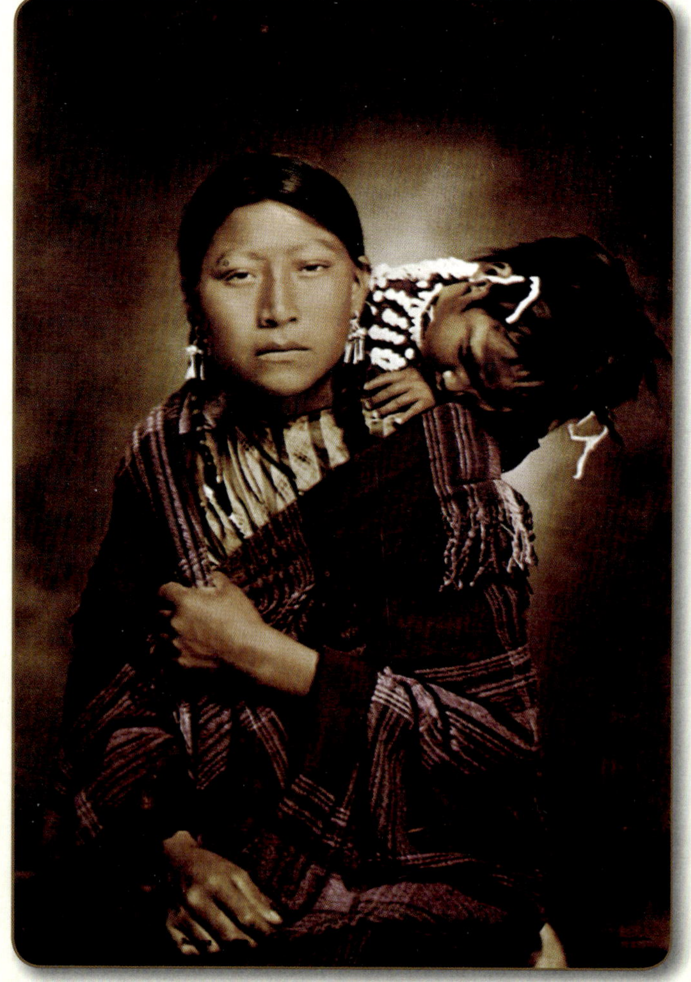

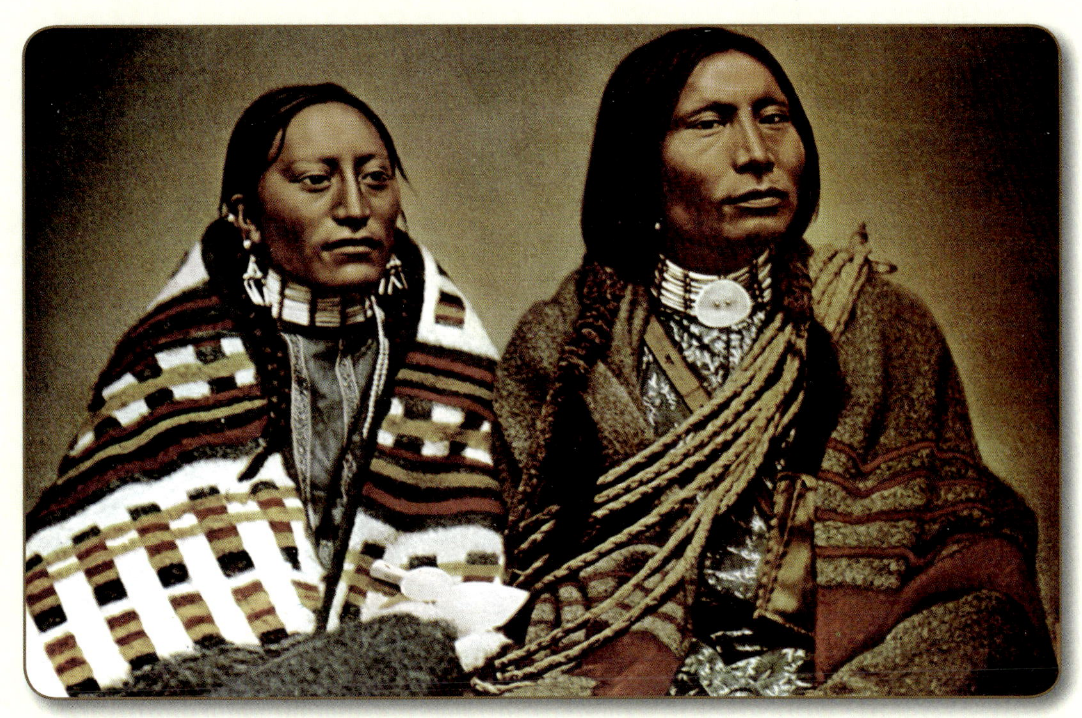

ABOVE: *Man-on-the-Hill and Wife*

RIGHT: *Brave Wolf and Wife*

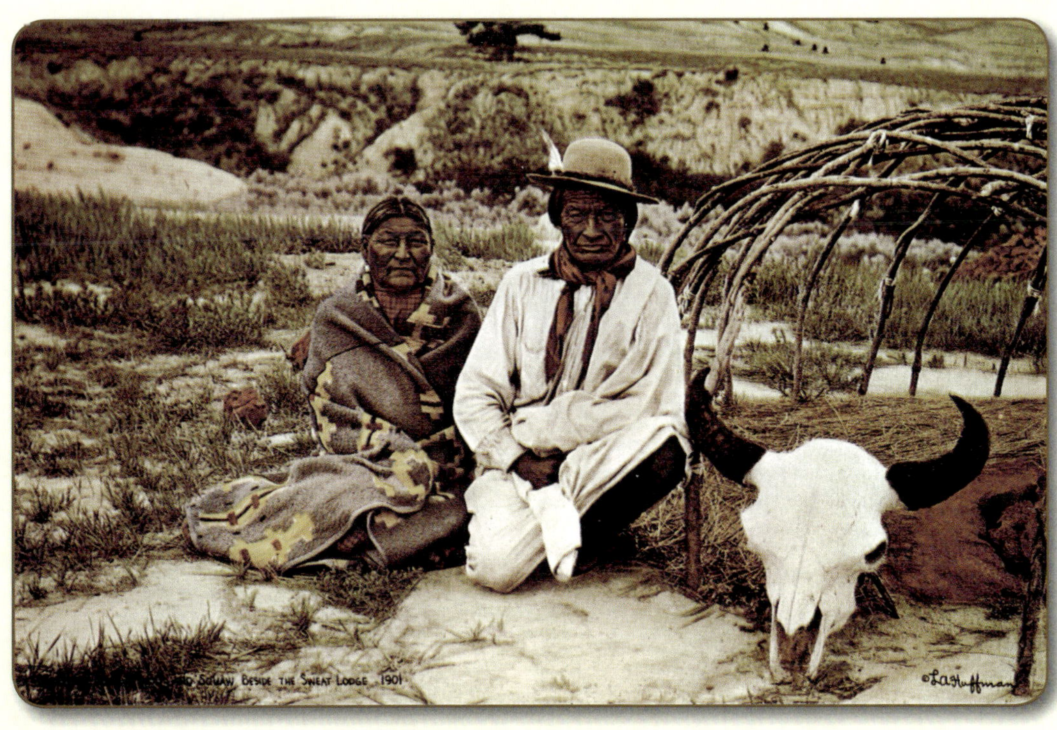

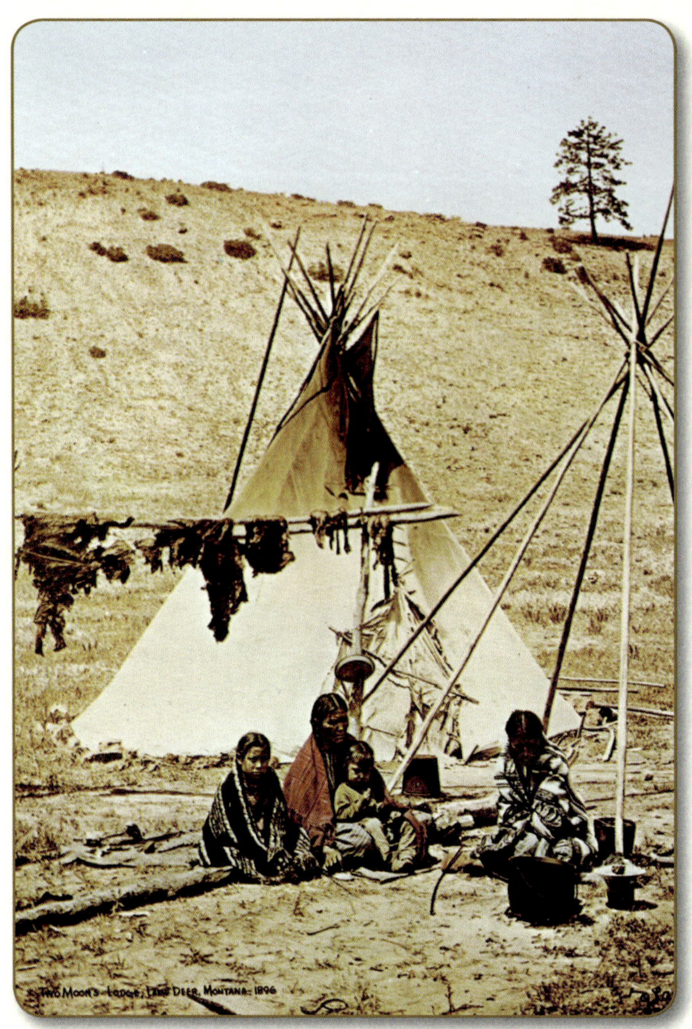

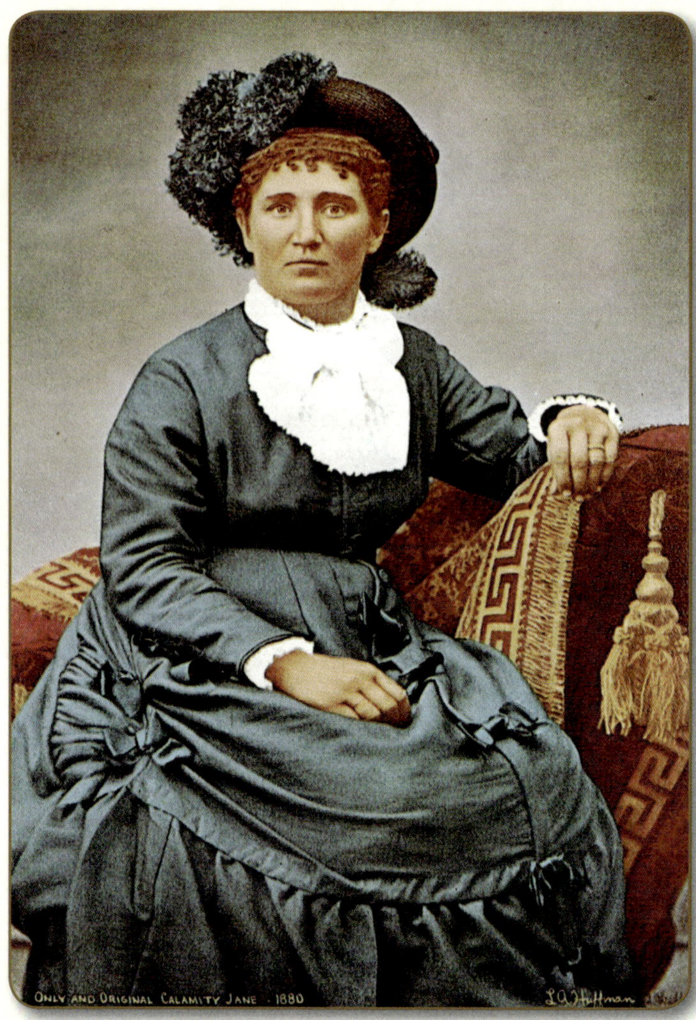

ABOVE: *Two Moon's Lodge*

ABOVE RIGHT: *Only and Original Calamity Jane*

RIGHT: *Interior of an Old Time Ranch, Powder River*

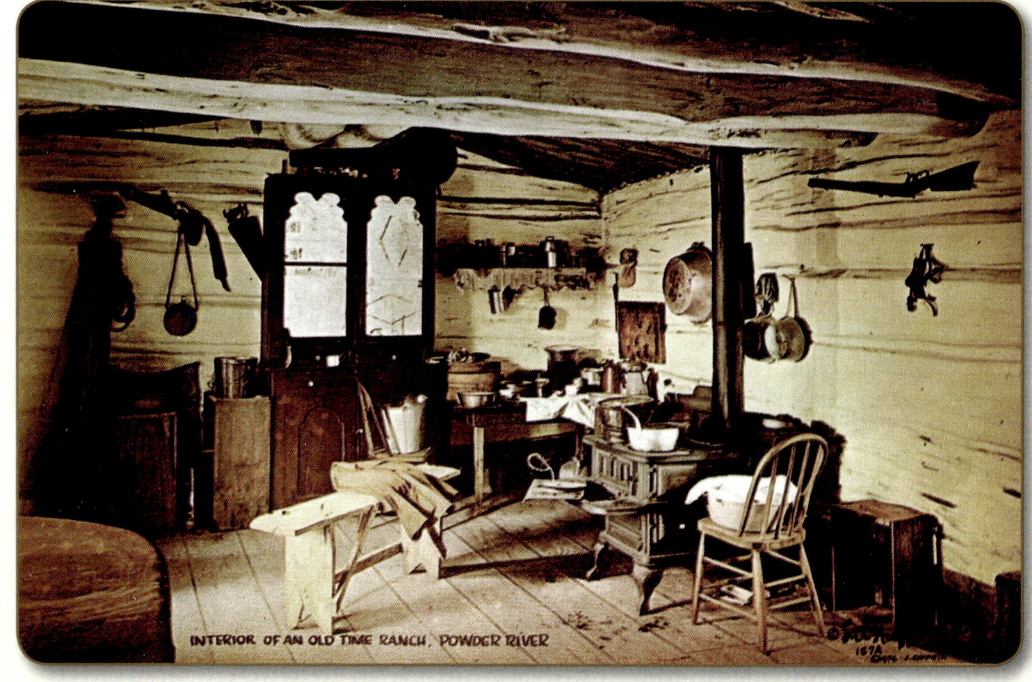

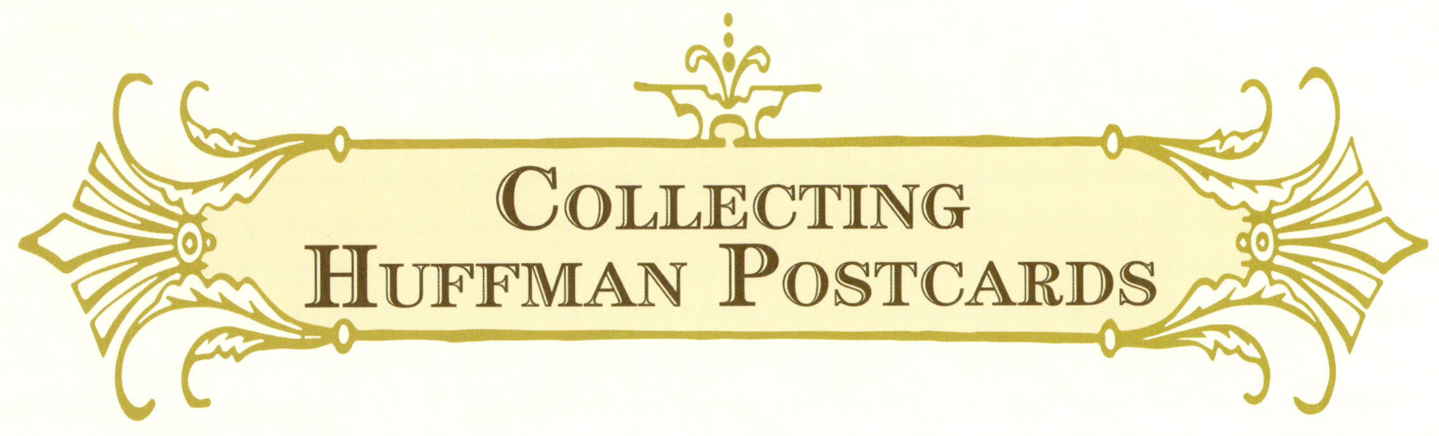

Collecting Huffman Postcards

We have been encouraged to include a brief discussion concerning the collecting of Huffman's postcards. While a true price guide is beyond the scope and intent of this book, some general observations may be both interesting and useful. Although not at the same high level as during the aforementioned Golden Age of Postcards time period, Deltiology (the collecting of postcards) is still a popular pastime today.

Collecting postcards is subject to the same basic tenets of the supply/demand equation as most other collectibles. The premise being: the higher the demand and the shorter the supply, the greater the value of the object. While there are special circumstances that affect both sides of the equation, that's generally how it works. With one major exception, the places collectors look for postcards haven't changed much over the years. They still frequent garage and estate sales, visit antique shops and shows, trade with other collectors and sometimes travel to regional antique, photographic or paper fairs or to antique and collectible auctions. The exception is the Internet; it arrived 20 plus years ago and, as Huffman said when the railroad arrived in Miles City in 1881, "it changed everything." Ebay and other collectibles websites have created new venues and opportunities for existing collectors to add to their collections and have also generated interest that can create new collectors. It has made a literal world of difference in the general field of collecting.

As is often the case with advances in technology, it can bring both good and bad news. For collectors, the good news is greatly expanded exposure and nearly effortless worldwide access to opportunities to add to their collections. The bad news is the dramatic increase in competition for those occasional rare and "one of a kind" items that may become available. Increased competition usually translates to higher cost. Ebay has become the venue of choice for many dealers, especially for scarce or unusual examples, and has resulted in fewer buying opportunities at the local level. Many local auctions are no longer local as live internet bidding has often been added to the event. At Antiquarian Book Fairs we notice many people "comparison shopping" as they wander around; it's as easy and close as the screen on their smart phones.

Condition is the third major factor, after scarcity and desirability, that affects value. Generally speaking, the better the condition, the higher the value. Premium condition often brings a premium price. For most collectors, something less than perfect is usually acceptable. On the scale of poor, good, very good and fine, very good or better is often where collectors draw the line. A grade of very good may include some minor blemishes but would have no serious defects. For scarce or rare items, most collectors are more forgiving of condition until they find a better example. Items of average scarcity in poor condition usually have little value.

With regard to a postcard collector's preference between a postally used or an unused postcard, it's a tossup. Some collectors prefer postally used cards because the postmark date and location can add historical context, and the card may contain an interesting message. Other collectors prefer the unused examples, mainly because of the "clean condition" factor. Postally used postcards are not considered a drawback from a value standpoint, as long as the card is in collectible condition. In fact, if the card bears a message that is pertinent to the image, the value of the card would be enhanced for most collectors.

Postcards and other collectibles are not fair-traded items; prices can vary and cause confusion. We are often asked "How can I determine what is a fair price?" Our answer is usually the commonly accepted definition of fair market value—the amount agreed upon between a willing buyer and willing seller where both parties are knowledgeable about all of the factors that affect value, both positively and negatively, and where neither party is under any pressure to buy or sell. The most important part of that definition is the word knowledge. Collectors occasionally have the good fortune to buy a rare item for a fraction of its worth. The opposite is also true. Most of us have experienced the frustration of paying more than something is worth. Lack of knowledge has contributed to both examples, one by the seller, the other by the buyer.

Auction prices can be useful but also misleading. High prices are sometimes the result of two spirited bidders getting carried away. It may be a new record but it may not be a price that can be duplicated in the general marketplace. An unusually low price can result when there is low interest among bidders because no serious collectors of that item were present. Before drawing conclusions you have to know who was in the audience.

Sellers can ask whatever they want, and it is not unusual to find a range of asking prices for what appears to be very similar items. This is especially obvious on many of the Internet sites. While these sites can be useful for gaining knowledge, they are hazardous to use as a price guide. It is important to remember that asking prices are not the same as selling prices, and Internet prices are asking prices. When dealers are trying to convince us that their prices are reasonable, they sometimes refer us to an Internet listing where someone is asking perhaps twice as much for the same thing. Our response is usually the caveat, "Yes, and the whole world (literally) has looked at it and decided not to buy it at that price because it's still available!" It is still buyer beware.

Most serious collectors spend a lot of time researching and learning as much as they can regarding their chosen field. It is interesting and can help focus collecting effort. The new knowledge also makes for a better informed and discriminating buyer. This book is about the supply side of the equation and provides new information about Huffman's postcards.

There is an old saying that price guides are obsolete as soon as they are printed. Things change, sometimes quickly. The loss or addition of just one or two serious collectors of a specialized collectible can significantly affect demand. There are always exceptions for individual items. The Great Recession of 2008 negatively impacted nearly all fields of collecting; average items in most have still not recovered to pre 2008 levels. With that warning in mind, following is information about Huffman's printed and real photo postcards, including a range of values based on observations in the marketplace. The values are for postcards in good collectible condition, offered in the open market by a knowledgeable seller.

Huffman Postcard Values

1907 Series—25 Printed Cards

- All numbers except 5 and 27, 3,000 printed .... $20 - $45
  - * *Four buffalo images, numbers 8, 9, 25, 26 and 10,* Saddling the Wild Horse *are much harder to find than the others and would be at the upper end of the range.*
- Numbers 5 and 27, probably 6,000 printed .... $10 - $15
- Hand-colored, estimated less than 25 examples for each card. .... $50 - $100
  - * *Some numbers may not exist in hand-colored format*

1926 Series—15 Printed Cards

* *Sold as a set and issued in a printed envelope; 1,000 sets were printed.*

- Full set, no envelope .... $125 - $150
- Full set in original unlined envelope (see text on page 54) .... $150 - $200
- Full set in original lined envelope.. $150 - $175
- Individual cards .... $10 - $20
  - * *Three landscapes, numbers 7, 8 and 9, at the lower end of the range*
- Original envelopes (see text on page 54), unknown number printed, but probably fewer than 100 total
  - Unlined .... $25 - $50
  - Lined .... $15 - $25

1928 Series—5 Printed Cards

- First printing (two-cent stamp block), 5,000 of each printed .... $15 - $25
- Second printing (one-cent stamp block) unknown printing, estimated more than 5,000.. $12 - $20

1968 - 1975 Coffrin Published Chrome Cards

- Estimated printing unknown, but common .... $1 - $4

1906 - 1912 Real Photo Postcards

* *All Huffman real photo postcards are rare; probably no more than 10 or 12 were made of any card. Value largely depends on subject matter and image quality (toning and clarity). Prices for even low interest subjects probably start at $175 - $200. Values below are for cards in collectible condition with good image quality.*

- Scenic views and low interest subjects .... $175 - $300
- Close-up or exceptional cowboy images .... $500 - $800
- General roundup, sheepherder, animal images .... $200 - $500
- Buffalo images .... $400 - $800
- Native American theme images. . ... $500 - $1000
  - * *Close-up or exceptional views at the upper end of the range*
- Miscellaneous views .... $250 - $750
  - * *Value depending on image*

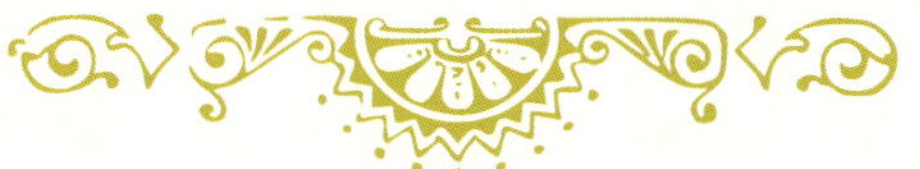

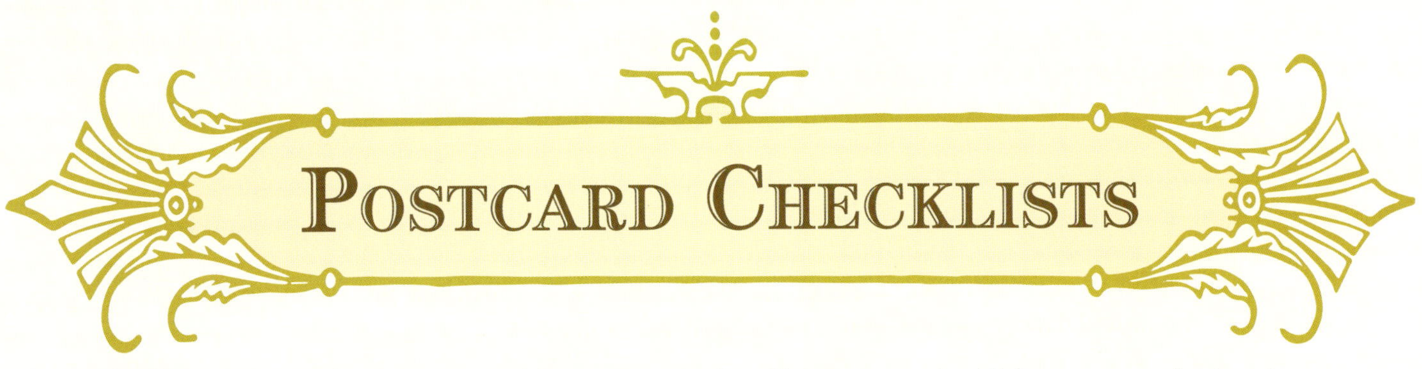

Postcard Checklists

Following is a list of the five different groups of Huffman postcards. All four groups of printed cards are on divided back stock; real photo cards appear on both undivided and divided backs.

1907 Series—25 Numbered, Printed Cards

1. *Sioux Warrior's Grave* (HC)
3. *Rain-in-the-Face*
(4) *A Killing of Elk 1875*
5. *A Killing of Cows & Spikes*
6. *A Cut Horse at Work*
7. *Old Catholic Mission, Tongue River Montana*
8. *After the Chase*
9. *Killing of Cows and Spikes*
10. *Saddleing a Wild Horse* (HC)
11. *A Wolfer's Roost* (HC)
12. *The Deserted Camp* (HC)
13. *A Crow Hunter—Winter Dress* (HC)
14. *Mrs. Bad Gun* (HC)
16. *Fierce Old Crow Buck* (HC)
17. *A Cheyenne Mother* (HC)
18. *Mrs. White Elk* (HC)
19. *Montana Manhunters of the Seventies* (HC)
20. *A Hansome Young Cheyenne*
21. *Bringing a Calf to the Branding Fire* (HC)
22. *A Buffalo Family*
23. *An Old Time Tail holt*
24. *A Relic of the Seventies* (HC)
25. *Herd of Wild Buffaloes*
26. *15 Wild Buffaloes Grazing* (HC)
27. *A Hot Noon at the Round up* (HC)

1907 Series Notes

1. Hand-colored examples exist for several, perhaps all of the images; observed colored cards are designated by (HC).
2. The numeral 4 does not appear on card number 4.
3. During the 1960s—1970s an advertisement (in red) was added to the backs of many of the cards by the Coffrin Studio. It is unknown how many images may carry this overprint (see text on page 30).
4. 3,000 cards were printed for all numbers except 5 and 27 which probably had 6,000 each.

1926 Series—15 Numbered, Printed Cards

1. *Where Custer Fell*
2. *The First Monument on Custer's Hill*
3. *Rain-in-the-Face*
4. *Buffalo Grazing the Big Open*
5. *L. A. H. and a Young Bull*
6. *Old Two Moon*
7. *Rosebud, Montana Lies Behind Trees*
8. *The First Camp on the Rosebud*
9. *Site of the Second Camp*
10. *Gen'l Godfrey, Mr. Camp, and Mr. Bird Grinnell*
11. *Gen'l Godfrey and a Bunch of Old Timers*
12. *Monument and Graves Custer's Hill 1916*
13. *Gen'l Godfrey and the Late W. M. Camp 1916*
14. *Gen'l Godfrey and W. M. Camp Searching for Cartridge Shells 1916*
15. *The Home of the Huffman Pictures*
   Issued envelope—unlined (see text on page 54)
   Issued envelope—lined (see text on page 54)

1926 Series Notes

1. Sold as a set, 1,000 sets produced.
2. Issued in a printed manila envelope (see text on page 54).
3. At least a small number of hand-colored cards exist.

1928 Series—5 Colored, Printed Cards, in alphabetical order

First Printing—Two-Cent Stamp Block

1. *A Familiar Picture in Northern Pacific Country*
2. *Buffalo Grazing the Big Open*
3. *Evening at the Round-up*
4. *Jerk-line Twelve on the Old Freight Road*
5. *Sits Down Spotted, a Crow Hunter*

Second Printing—One-Cent Stamp Block

6. *A Familiar Picture in Northern Pacific Country*
7. *Buffalo Grazing the Big Open*
8. *Evening at the Round-up*
9. *Jerk-line Twelve on the Old Freight Road*
10. *Sits Down Spotted, a Crow Hunter*

1928 Series Notes

1. 5,000 of each card were made in the first printing; an unknown number, but probably more than the first, were made in the second printing.

Real Photo Postcards—117 Known Images in Four Groups

1. Numbered and titled, in numerical order
2. Titled with no numbers, in alphabetical order
3. Known Huffman images, no numbers or titles
4. "Probables" based on card type and image
   * Type of card back designated by undivided (u), divided (d), both (b), unknown (-)

Group 1: Real Photo Postcards—Numbered and Titled, in Numerical Order

	Huffman Number	*Title*
1.	1	*Plenty Bird in Sweat Lodge* (u)
2.	5-B	*Rangers in the Badlands* (u)
3.	6-B	*Snubbing a Wild Mare* (u)
4.	7-B	*Putting on a Hackamore* (u)
5.	8	*Cheyenne Agency, Lame Deer* (u)
6.	8	*Gravel Pit Calabar* (d)
7.	11	*Gravel Pit Calabar* (d)
8.	12	*Gravel Pit Calabar* (d)
9.	15	*Gravel Pit Paragon* (d)
10.	21	*Indians Racing, Lame Deer* (u)
11.	N-22	*OC Ranch, Otter Creek, Mont.* (d)
12.	23	*Sunday Morning at the Mission* (-)
13.	25	*American Horse's Camp* (u)
14.	28	*Cheyenne Indian Police* (u)
15.	N-35	*Elks Parade Miles City, Mont 1909* (d)
16.	37.	*Old Mission Tongue River, Mont.* (u)
17.	40	*Indian Earth Lodge* (u)
18.	41	*Squaw Fleshing Hide* (u)
19.	55	*Spotted Elk* (-)
20.	78	*Cheyenne Indians Dancing Lame Deer, Mont* (u)
21.	85	*Young Cheyenne Squaw & Papoose* (u)
22.	94g	*Sioux Grave* (u)
23.	99	*Crows* (u)
24.	115	*A Killing of Buffaloes Near Miles City, 1878* (u)
25.	116	*A Monster Buffalo Bull* (u)
26.	118	*Glendive* (d)
27.	151	*Hunter's Horse Ranch* (u)
28.	176	*Roundup Breaking Camp* (u)
29.	179	*Catching Fresh Horses in Rope Corral* (-)
30.	182	*The Bow Gun Boys at Dinner* (u)
31.	183	*Camp of Big CK Box Creek* (u)
32.	185	*C. Horse Camp* (u)
33.	186	*Wood's Sheep Ranch, Big Powder* (u)
34.	190	*Skinning Buffalo Jan 82* (u)
35.	194	*Round-up Cutting* (u)
36.	203	*Branding Calves in Corrall* (u)
37.	229	*N Bar Crossing Big Powder* (u)
38.	231	*SH Outfit on Trail* (u)
39.	233	*Roundup YT, Little Pumpkin* (u)
40.	237	*Roundup at Work, Powder River* (u)
41.	243	*Cattle Drifting on Open Range* (u)
42.	247	*Cook & Pie Biter at Work* (-)
43.	249	*Telling Off the Riders For The Circle* (u)
44.	256	*Red Nut* (u)
45.	257	*Night Hawk in His Nest* (b)
46.	259	*Roundup on the Move* (u)
47.	260	*MacQueen House* (u)
48.	261	*Saddling a Wild Horse* (-)
49.	274	*Riding a Bronco* (d)
50.	279	*Horse Play, Tailing a Broncho* (u)
51.	292	*Ash Point, Custer Battlefield* (-)
52.	295	*The Old Stockade, Main St. 1878* (u)
53.	298	*Miles From North* (d)
54.	301	*Sheep at Water, Powder River* (u)
55.	305	*Sheep on Benchland of Yellowstone* (u)
56.	310	*Wool Teams and Warehouse, Miles City* (u)
57.	312N	*Sheep By Big Dry* (u)
58.	331	*Horses in Badlands* (u)
59.	392	*A Wolfer and Outfit* (u)
60.	487	*Bull Train Main St. Miles 1880*—near (u)
61.	487	*Diamond R Bull Train, Main St. Miles City 1880*—far (u)
62.	492	*Main St. Milestown Mar. 3rd 1881* (u)
63.	497	*Logan's Rustic Bridge, Old Ferry, Corrall and Store Miles City 1880* (u)
64.	501	*Hot Time in Old Milestown That Night 1881* (u)
65.	539	*Sheep on the Range, Montana* (d)
66.	559	*Sparrow Hawk, Cheyenne* (u)
67.	561	*Rangers on Winter Range, Breaks of Yellowstone* (u)
68.	563	*Sheep on Winter Range* (u)
69.	564	*Sheep on Winter Range, Yellowstone Breaks* (d)
70.	565	*Drifter Sheep Wagon & Band on Winter Bed Grounds* (u)
71.	566	*Drifter, Sheep Wagon and Band with Camp* (u)
72.	567	*Sheep, Winter Range, Breaks of Yellowstone Mont.* (u)
73.	568	*Herder, His Band, Winter Camp and Happy Home* (u)

74. 569 *Pushing Them From Bed, Cold Morning* (b)
75. 573 *A Killing In Velvet 1875* (u)
76. 574 *Hot Noon Beside Roundup Camp* (u)
77. 580 *Benders Ranch, a Relic of the Seventies*—near (u)
78. 580 *Benders Ranch, a Relic of the Seventies*—far (u)
79. 581 *Main St., Miles City, West of 8th*—down (u)
80. 581 *Main St. Miles City, W of 8th*—across (u)

Group 2: Real Photo Postcards—Titled with No Number, in Alphabetical Order

81. *Blasting Yellowstone Bluffs* (u)
82. *Branding a Calf* (u)
83. *Cutting Out the Cows & Calves* (u)
84. *Four Horse Potato Digger at Work* (d)
85. *Glendive, Mont.* 1882 (d)
86. *Hardware Dept., Hamilton Merc., Stacey, Mont.* (d)
87. *Hunter's Camp 1883* (d)
88. *Killing of Cows & Spikes* (u)
89. *Roped* (u)
90. *Roped, Heeled & Stretched* (u)
91. *Roping a Maverick* (d)
92. *Rounded Up* (u)
93. *Roundup Outfit Breaking Camp* (-)
94. *Sheep By the Water* (d)
95. *Taking The Tongues* (u)
96. *The Roundup on Big Pumpkin '07* (d)
97. *"They're Off" Custer Co. Fair Miles City, Mont* (d)
98. *Where Custer Fell* (u)

Group 3: Real Photo Postcards—Known Huffman Images, No Number or Title

99. *St. Labre School*—boys (-)
100. *St. Labre School*—girls (-)
101. *Heard Something Drop* (from 1885 Series) (-)
102. *John Rabbit* (d)
103. *Working a Little Bunch in the Hills*—1 (d)
104. *Working a Little Bunch in the Hills*—2 (d)
105. *Roundup Scene*—1 (d)
106. *Roundup Scene*—2 (d)
107. *Sheep on Benchland* (d)
108. *Branding a Calf* (d)
109. *Corbin's Ranch* (d)

Group 4: Real Photo Postcards—"Probables" Based on Card Type and Image

110. *Two Women and a Dog* (d)
111. *John Childress* (d)
112. *Running Horses* (d)
113. *Women in Hats—Miles City* (d)
114. *Cowboy on Horse*—1 (u)
115. *Cowboy on Horse*—2 (u)
116. *673 Cattle and 5 Herders* (u)
117. *Two Men in Front of Sod Roof Shack* (u)

Real Photo Postcards Notes

6. This number 8 may mean it is the 8th of 15 images taken at this site in 1913 (see Nos. 7, 8 & 9).
9. Location is probably Calabar, not Paragon.
26. The same image appears with no number (see No. 85)
63. Another with the same number and image but different title—*Rustic Bridge & Ferry, Main St. 1880.*

Coffrin's Old West Gallery—24 Colored, Printed Cards in Alphabetical Order

1. *A Sioux Warrior's Grave*
2. *Brave Wolf and Wife Beside the Sweat Lodge*
3. *Buffalo Grazing the Big Open*
4. *Cheyenne American Horse's Camp*
5. *Drifter Sheep Wagon and Band*
6. *First Pull at the Latigo*
7. *Hot Noon Beside the Roundup*
8. *Interior of an Old Time Ranch*
9. *Jerk-line 12 on the Old N. Montana Freight Road*
10. *Little Cheyenne Bearing Pipe*
11. *Main Street Miles City 1880*
12. *Man-on-the-Hill and Wife*
13. *N Bar Crossing*
14. *Old Cheyenne Two Moon at Custer Battlefield 1901*
15. *Only and Original Calamity Jane*
16. *Red Armed Panther*
17. *Shy Little Cheyenne Maid with Her Doll*
18. *Sioux Chief Rain-in-the-Face*
19. *Spotted Eagle's Sioux Village*
20. *The Honyocker*
21. *The Line Camp*
22. *Two Moon's Lodge, Lame Deer*
23. *Waiting for the Irons to Heat*
24. *Young Cheyenne Mother and Child*
25. Souvenir folder with 12 images

Coffrin's Old West Gallery Notes

1. Coffrin produced at least 24 postcards, possibly a few more.
2. Most cards were produced in 1968; at least one or more was produced in 1973 and 1975.
3. Printing quantity unknown, but relatively common.

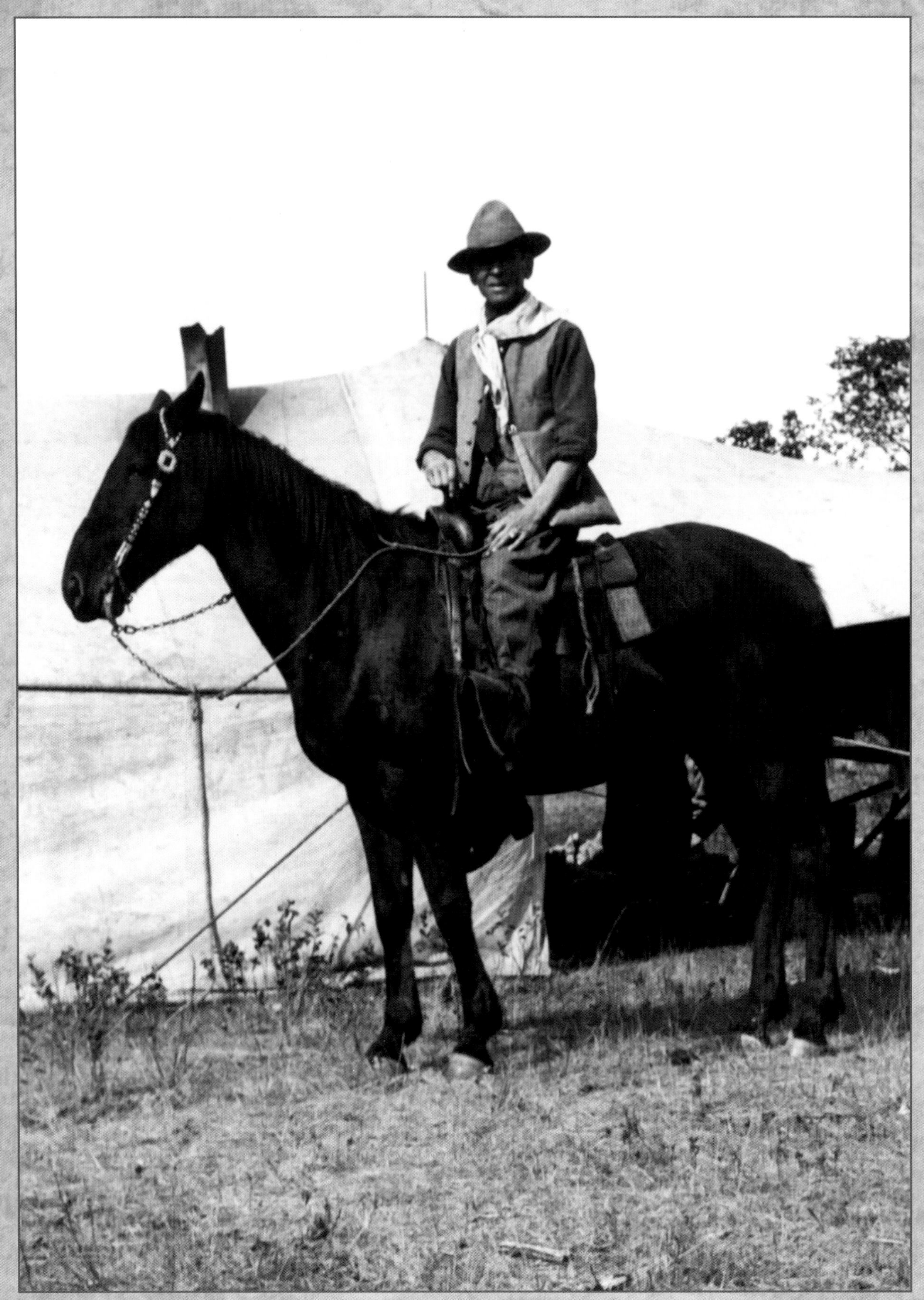

ABOVE: Huffman on his "4 legged tripod."

Acknowledgments

Our thoughts of the possibility of a Huffman postcard book began about 15 years ago, shortly after the acquisition of a large Huffman collection and the 2003 publication of *L. A. Huffman, Photographer of the American West* by Larry Len Peterson. Through the years we have had hundreds of conversations with people about some aspect of Huffman's work. Postcards were frequently a part of the discussion and often started with a question. They always appreciated the information we gave them, and many suggested that we make it more generally available.

Many of those past conversations were with Tom Mulvaney, longtime friend and serious postcard collector/dealer. Tom suggested we do a book on Huffman's postcards at least 10 years ago and has encouraged us ever since. He read the manuscript several times and always had valuable insight and suggestions from the perspective of a postcard collector. He furnished us with a few illustrations we didn't have and provided the value information for the "Collecting" chapter. Without his help this book would have been substantially different. We are grateful for the years of friendship and the encouragement and sharing of his knowledge along the way. Many thanks!

Special thanks to our friend and neighbor, Julie Saylor. She was not only the first reader of the manuscript, but also the middle and last reader. She was our go to person for questions of grammar and punctuation. She was also our "sounding board" for terminology and making sure we were including enough information for the general reader. We greatly appreciate all the time she spent and the suggestions she made.

Thanks to the following for collectively providing the necessary information for the chapter on real photo postcards: Richard Dreger, Bob Evans, Andrew Finch, Ken Hamlin, Paul Harbaugh, Jay Lyndes, Tom Mulvaney, the Montana Historical Society and the WaterWorks Art Museum, Miles City.

We frequently visited the Montana Historical Society Research Center in Helena and always appreciated the expert assistance of Lory Morrow, Jeff Malcomson, and other staff at the Photo Archives and Library. Thanks to Mary Robinson and the staff at the McCracken Research Library at the Buffalo Bill Center of the West in Cody, Wyoming. Special thanks to our son, Bob, of Bob Allen Images, Bozeman, for providing some last minute, high resolution copy photos and to brother Bill who continues to come to our rescue with answers to computer questions.

Thanks to Montana Huffman collectors John Fox, Jay Lyndes and Thomas Minckler for continued friendship and the occasional visits about Huffman and his work. Others who answered our calls are: Mark Browning, former director of the Custer County Art Center in Miles City; Steve Jackson at the Museum of the Rockies in Bozeman; Mike Jetty, Office of Public Instruction, Helena; and Dave Shors, Helena—thanks to all.

We would especially like to thank Kathy Springmeyer, Shirley Machonis, Steph Lehmann and other staff at Farcountry Press and Sweetgrass Books in Helena. We very much appreciated their friendly and professional help during the final stages of this project.

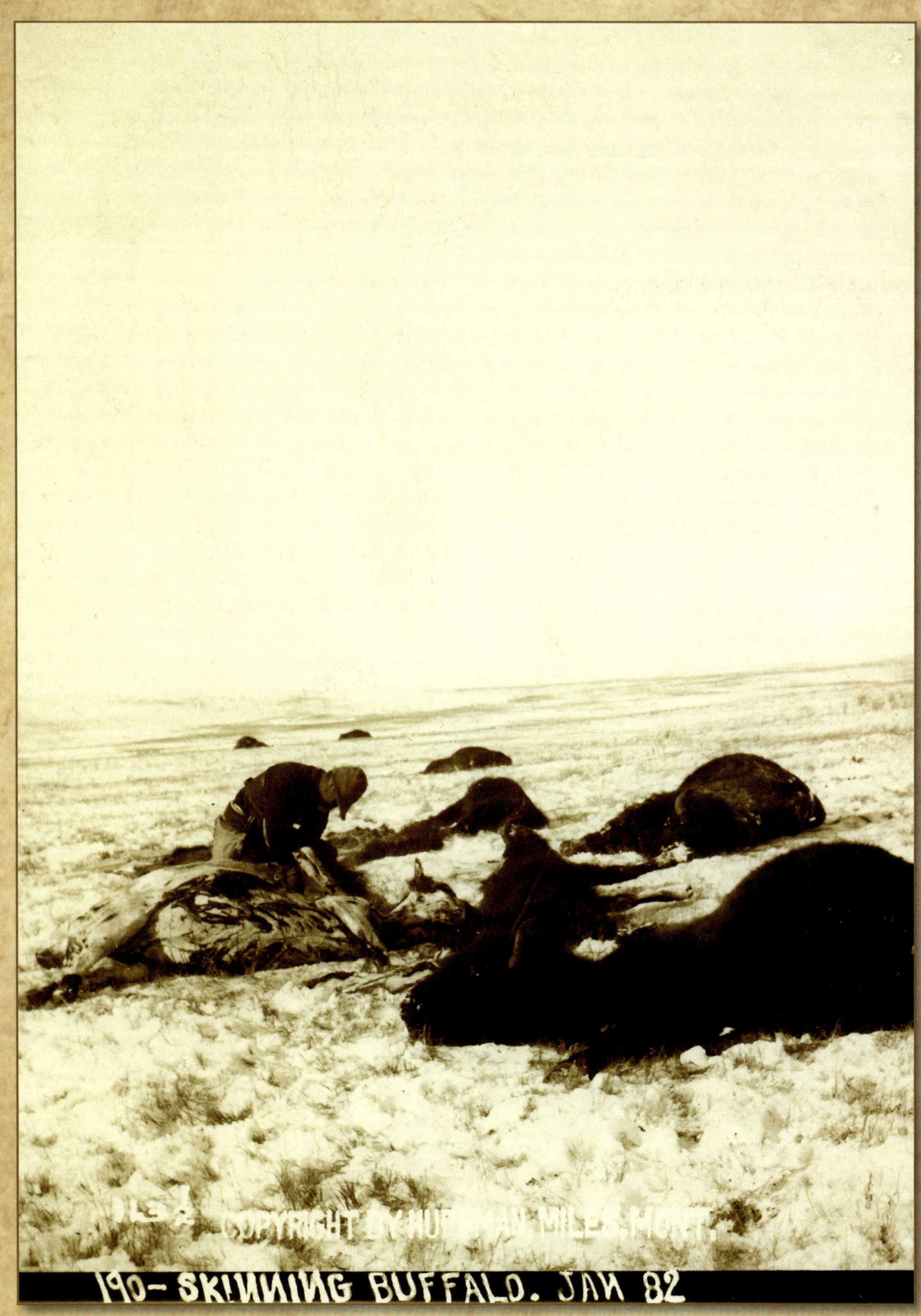
COPYRIGHT BY HUF MAN MILES, MONT.
190- SKINNING BUFFALO. JAN 82

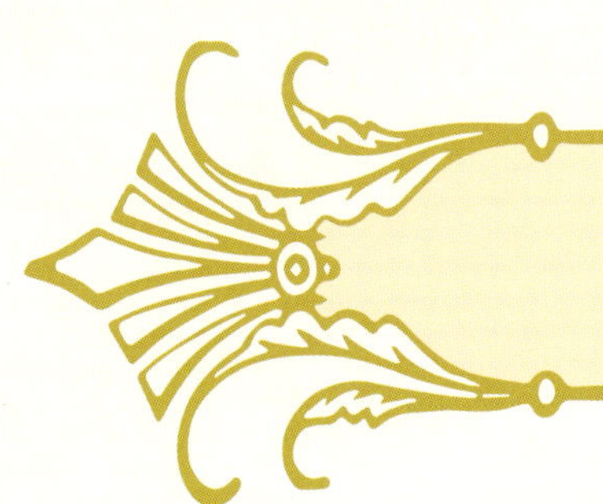

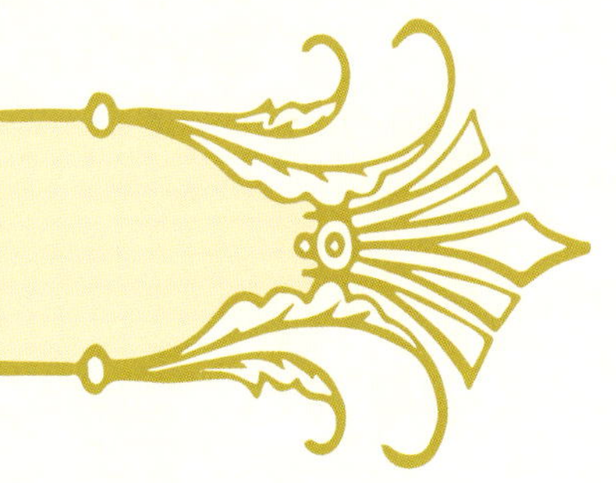

INDEX

Bold indicates a photo.